Observing the Observer

Observing the Observer

Understanding Our Selves in Field Research

SHULAMIT REINHARZ

New York   Oxford

OXFORD UNIVERSITY PRESS

2011

Oxford University Press, Inc., publishes works that further Oxford University's
objective of excellence in research, scholarship, and education.

Oxford New York
Auckland Cape Town Dar es Salaam Hong Kong Karachi
Kuala Lumpur Madrid Melbourne Mexico City Nairobi
New Delhi Shanghai Taipei Toronto

With offices in
Argentina Austria Brazil Chile Czech Republic France Greece
Guatemala Hungary Italy Japan Poland Portugal Singapore
South Korea Switzerland Thailand Turkey Ukraine Vietnam

Copyright © 2011 by Oxford University Press

Published by Oxford University Press, Inc.
198 Madison Avenue, New York, New York 10016
www.oup.com

Oxford is a registered trademark of Oxford University Press

ISBN 978-0-19-539780-2 (pbk)
     978-0-19-539781-9 (hbk)

Printing number: 9 8 7 6 5 4 3 2 1

Printed in the United States of America
on acid-free paper

To my daughter, Yael (Yali),
who delighted everyone on the kibbutz with her warm,
adventurous personality
and who provided me with lots of love every day.

ACKNOWLEDGMENTS

The late Dr. Arthur Mandel of the University of Michigan history department introduced me to the individual who later became my sponsor for this project. The sponsor himself and his wife deserve thanks for the many forms of assistance they gave me. The kibbutz managers (*mazkirim*) and committee chairs could not have been more helpful. Words cannot describe my gratitude to the kibbutz members themselves—those who were my interviewees, those who took care of my daughter, those who found archival documents for me, those who were my neighbors, and those who became my friends. They were always willing to teach me and explain things so that I would understand.

I would like to thank my daughter Yael for allowing me to quote extensively from field notes about her. She not only adjusted to a very unusual set of circumstances but also gave me a window into the lives of young kibbutz children. Our loving closeness helped me understand the significance of family as a retreat/relief from intense community.

My dear friend Ruth Gruschka has consulted with me on every research project I have undertaken in Israel. She visited me frequently on the kibbutz, boosting my spirits when I was low. Fellow sociologists Terry Arendell, Rosanna Hertz, and Marjorie DeVault read this book in its earlier manuscript stage and gave me useful feedback and encouragement. Jessica Parlon, my assistant; Beth Bowman, a Brandeis University student; and Abby Rosenberg, librarian of the Brandeis University Women's Studies Research Center prepared the bibliography and worked with me to dot the *i*'s and cross the *t*'s as the book was being prepared by my editor, Sherith Pankratz at Oxford. One member of the kibbutz obtained permission from the kibbutz members to use their photographs to illustrate this book. Thanks to all of you.

Without my husband's constant help during weekly visits to the kibbutz, I could not have carried out much of this study. And without his constant reminder to "finish the book," it would still be in my drawer. I am indebted to him for his confidence in my work and for his enthusiasm at its completion.

Oxford University Press and the author wish to thank the following reviewers who made comments on pre-publication drafts of this manuscript:

Melani Cammett, Harvard University
Linda Grant, University of Georgia
Cynthia Miller-Idriss, New York University
David Schweingruber, Iowa State University

CONTENTS

INTRODUCTION

Observing the Observer is a book about and for social researchers who do field-work. At the same time, it tries to engage some of the debates and conversations about fieldwork that have arisen in the literature, particularly the feminist literature. Finally, *Observing the Observer* is designed for students who are in the process of learning how to do fieldwork themselves. A fieldworker—usually a sociologist or anthropologist—is a person who goes into a social setting (e.g., a fishing village, a medical clinic, a street corner) in order to study certain phenomena that occur there and then report what she/he has found, connecting the findings to the work of other researchers and to theory. Field research of this type—also called "ethnography" and "participant observation research"—has been going on since the early nineteenth century and is one of the accepted ways of understanding social life. Frequently fieldworkers utilize interviews and analysis of existing materials as additional sources of information.

Early practitioners of fieldwork, such as the British sociologist Harriet Martineau, traveled to the United States from England in the mid-1830s to explore American democratic institutions. On the ship voyage to her research destination, she wrote *How to Observe Morals and Manners*,[1] and on her return, she wrote the first draft of *Society in America*.[2] At approximately the same time, Alexis deTocqueville also traveled to the United States to study the country and its people, a trip that led to the publication of *Democracy in America*.[3] The difference between the two observers' books is instructive. Where Martineau saw slavery and the exclusion of women from public electoral life, deTocqueville saw a well-functioning constitution and flourishing voluntary societies. Why? In the introduction to his book, deTocqueville wrote:

> Among the novel objects that attracted my attention during my stay in the United
> States, nothing struck me more forcibly than the general equality of condition

---

[1] Harriet Martineau, *How to Observe Morals and Manners* (New Brunswick, NJ: Transaction Books, 1838/1989).

[2] Harriet Martineau, *Society in America* (Garden City, NY: Anchor Books, 1961).

[3] Alexis deTocqueville, *Democracy in America* (New York: Vintage, 1954).

1

among the people. I readily discovered the prodigious influence that this primary fact exercises on the whole course of society; it gives a peculiar direction to public opinion and a peculiar tenor to the laws; it imparts new maxims to the governing authorities and peculiar habits to the governed.

I soon perceived that the influence of this fact extends far beyond the political character and the laws of the country, and that it has no less effect on civil society than on the government; it creates opinions, gives birth to new sentiments, founds novel customs, and modifies whatever it does not produce. The more I advanced in the study of American society, the more I perceived that this equality of condition is the fundamental fact from which all others seem to be derived and the central point at which all my observations constantly terminated.

By contrast, Harriet Martineau began her book with words that reflect the skepticism of a researcher with regard to her findings and the necessity of letting the reader know who she is and what she did:

> In seeking for methods by which I might communicate what I have observed in my travels ... two expedients occurred to me; both of which I have adopted. One is, to compare the existing state of society in America with the principles on which it is *professedly* founded [. . .] The other method . . . is to enable my readers to judge for themselves . . . what my testimony is worth. For this purpose, I offer a brief account of my travels, with dates in full; and a report of the principal means I enjoyed of obtaining knowledge of the country.[4]

Her approach prompted her to explore how being a woman, deaf, a Britisher, and other factors affected her conclusions. More than 170 years ago, she had already adopted what has come to be called a "reflexive stance" toward fieldwork.

The contrasts in the perceptions of these two travelers were not related to the sites they visited because archival information exists that show that their travel routes were very similar.[5] Rather, their differing views most likely stemmed from the gendered and class perspectives of the researchers and the kinds of people with whom they spoke.[6] Martineau became deeply engaged in the society she studied and at one point seriously considered purchasing a young girl who was being sold as a slave, in order to free and then employ her. At another point, during her stay in Boston, she was run out of town for her abolitionist sentiments.[7] In her book about how she planned to observe in the United States, she did not mention becoming politically engaged during her research trip. But something happened to her. Something emerged in the field.

---

[4] Harriet Martineau, *Society in America*, pp. 48–49 (Garden City, NY: Anchor Books, 1962).

[5] Michael R. Hill, "The Methodological Framework of Harriet Martineau's Feminist Analyses of American Society," American Studies Association, November 2, 1990, New Orleans, Louisiana.

[6] See Michael R. Hill, "A Methodological Comparison of Harriet Martineau's *Society in America* (1837) and Alexis deTocqueville's *Democracy in America* (1835–1840)," in Michael R. Hill and Susan Hoecker-Drysdale (eds.), *Harriet Martineau: Theoretical & Methodological Perspectives*, pp. 59–74 (New York: Routledge, 2001). See also Seymour Martin Lipset, "Harriet Martineau's America," in Harriet Martineau (ed.), *Society in America* (Garden City, NY: Anchor Books, 1962).

[7] See also Patricia Madoo Lengermann and Gillian Niebrugge (eds.), *The Women Founders: Sociology and Social Theory, 1830–1930: A Text/Reader* (Long Grove, IL: Waveland Press, 1998/2007).

Many years later something analogous happened to Polish anthropologist Bronislaw Malinowski (1884–1942). In 1914 he left Europe for Papua (later named "Papua New Guinea") and the Trobriand Islands to conduct field research. The outbreak of World War I, however, prevented him from returning home, and he was stranded in the middle of the Pacific Ocean. At first he tried to stay aloof from the Trobrianders, following the tradition of his ethnographic predecessors who felt superior to the natives and had no need to interact with them other than for the purpose of obtaining information. As the title of a documentary about his work (*Off the Verandah*) indicates, only gradually did Malinowski abandon the idea of conducting research interviews on his own turf, that is, his verandah, where he felt safe and in control.[8] Slowly he became part of the natives' community, observing them in their interaction *with one another,* not just with him. This is not the place to discuss Malinowski's conclusions, which have generated both respect and controversy over the years. Nor do we need to examine his diaries, which shed light on his personality. Rather, my point is that in both cases—Martineau and Malinowski—the researchers changed in the field because of what they brought to it and what happened to them when they were there.

I contend that deep immersion in another social world compels the researcher to reexamine himself/herself and perhaps to change.[9] Deep immersion may be most characteristic of field research that entails moving far from one's home (as is true of the two cases cited), living there day and night, speaking a foreign language, and spending an extended period of time in the field away from one's social circle. These are the characteristics of the study on which I will report in this book, a year-long stay in a kibbutz[10] in Israel in 1979–1980.[11] By contrast, field research that allows the researcher to live at home has other interesting challenges, such as learning how to negotiate two worlds on a frequent basis. This book, *Observing the Observer,* offers a framework for understanding the researcher in the fieldwork setting that builds on the notion of change and emergence discussed earlier.

---

[8] Videotape directed by Andre Singer, 1985. A segment of the series Strangers Abroad. Written and presented by Bruce Dakowski. Interviews of professor Sir Edmund Leach (King's College, Cambridge), Helena Wayne (Malinowski's daughter), professor Sir Raymond Firth (emeritus professor, London University), and professor Lucy Mair (emeritus professor, London University).

[9] See Elena Sztokman's unpublished manuscript, *Stand Up and Be Counted,* for an example of a researcher leaving her religious orientation and community as a consequence of interviewing and doing fieldwork.

[10] A kibbutz is a physical place in Israel as well as the group of people whose members inhabit that place, analogous to the way the phrase *research center* is used. One can be on, in, or at the kibbutz. The word is Hebrew and means "collectivity."

[11] The kibbutz as a social organization has changed enormously since the time of my study, a theme discussed continuously in the Israeli and world press. See "Kibbutz Movement Facing Lean Times," *New York Times,* p. A3, December 3, 1989; Yossi Melman, "Struggling to Survive, Kibbutzim Lose Identity," *Los Angeles Times,* January 6, 1991; Henry Kamm, "Even in the Kibbutz, Socialism Is under Challenge," *New York Times International,* p. A4, September 10, 1991; Karby Leggett, "Pay-as-You-Go Kibbutzim," *Wall Street Journal,* p. B1, May 26, 2005; Isabel Kershner, "The Kibbutz Sheds Socialism and Gains Popularity," August 27, 2007; Arik Mirovsky, "The Kibbutz Movement—Round Two," *Haaretz Weekly,* p. A7, March 28, 2008.

The way I came to write this book in the first place is actually relevant to the final product and illustrates the significance of using empirical data to generate conclusions.[12] Specifically, I spent 327 days in the field, and on each day I took field notes that recorded what I had observed and experienced. (I also have one hundred taped interviews and several boxes of documents collected in the field.)

The question then is, "What to do with all of this material?" Field notes can be analyzed in many ways. In some instances, researchers pose a hypothesis in advance of entering the field and look for evidence relating to it. In other cases, such as my own, I had a general topic—aging on a kibbutz—in which I was interested, but my orientation was to try to understand that topic within its context, not to explore a hypothesis. My questions were, "How does a kibbutz deal with its aging population? Who are the elderly on a kibbutz, and how do they experience their lives?" I was aware of the fact that the kibbutz as an institution received high marks for its ways of dealing with issues confronted by the elderly.[13]

When I left the field and returned home to the United States, I explored many themes embedded in my field notes. In other publications, I have written about the conclusions I reached that relate to my initial questions.[14] But as a person with a long-standing interest in research methods, I also decided to try something unusual. I decided to carry out an experiment:[15] I would examine references to *myself* in my field notes, in chronological order. In other words, I converted myself into an object of study. When I compiled this information, I realized that I did not refer to myself in a consistent manner throughout a year's worth of field notes, nor did I focus on the same perspective throughout. Rather, different aspects of myself were salient, both to others and myself, as time went on. At the end of my stay in the kibbutz, I had become somewhat aware of this process, but it was only from a review of my field notes that a pattern became clear. Here is an excerpt from my field notes that registers partial recognition of this phenomenon.

> 284:10: I bounce back and forth between inhabiting roles and perceiving through those roles: medically [being ill], consultant [writing a report], sociologist

---

[12] I am inspired to offer this narrative by Laurel Richardson, "The Collective Story: Postmodernism and the Writing of Sociology," *Sociological Focus* 21(3):199–208, 1988, and by Karen McCarthy Brown, "Writing about 'the Other," *Chronicle of Higher Education*, A56, April 15, 1992.

[13] See, for example, "Relief for the Elderly," *Jerusalem Post*, July 17, 1980: "A particularly fine example has been set by the kibbutzim, where older members are provided with opportunities, tailored to their individual capacities, for employment in light industry."

[14] "Aging on a Kibbutz: Some Ideas for American Community Psychology," *Division of Community Psychology Newsletter* 14(3):7, 1981; "Utopias for the Elderly: Kibbutzim, Social Planning and Historical Communes," in Yaacov Oved, Idit Paz, and Yosef Gorni (eds.), *Communal Life: An International Perspective*, pp. 517–530 (New Brunswick, NJ: Transaction, 1987); research report presented to the kibbutz at the end of my stay, "The Elderly Population in Kibbutz: Problems and Suggestions" (Hebrew and English), June 1980.

[15] See George E. Marcus and Michel M. J. Fisher, *Anthropology as Cultural Critique: An Experimental Moment in the Human Sciences* (Chicago: University of Chicago Press, 1986).

[detecting patterns], person [having/lacking wisdom], Zionist [feelings about kibbutz, Israel], me [private behavior].[16]

I began to see that a careful analysis of field notes could illuminate aspects of the self or "selves" in the community's culture. For example, one aspect of myself I discuss later is "being an academic." As it turns out, "being an academic" is a highly charged identity in the particular setting I studied. Thus, for each setting it is mandatory to understand *what aspects of the researcher are significant, what the meanings of those aspects of the self are, and how those meanings affect the way the researcher can carry out her/his fieldwork.*

By reading and coding my field notes in terms of who I was in the field, I could ask, "How did people label me? How was I labeling myself?[17] What kinds of problems did I encounter personally? What kinds of satisfactions? How might I have seen things the way I did, as a consequence of who I was?" By analyzing my field notes this way, I reached the empirical conclusion that with the passage of time, one can identify *an array of relevant and not arbitrary selves within the researcher rather than just one vague self.*

After reaching this general conclusion, I tried to categorize and make sense of this vast array. In doing so, I defined a three-part pattern that I believe can be applied to most field research experiences.[18] Although I realize that the pattern I am offering represents a broad generalization based on a single case study, I believe the logic underlying the pattern does not depend on the characteristics of this particular case.[19] Specifically, my field notes suggest that there is a tripartite division among selves in the field, which I label as **research selves, personal selves,** and **situational selves.** In other terms, these are selves that are concerned with doing the research (research selves), selves that one brings to the field (personal selves), and selves that are created in the field (situational selves). This book, *Observing the Observer,* follows this structure by presenting material in three sections, using the terms *research* (chapters1-3) *personal* (chapters 4-7) and *situational*

---

[16] I devised this notation system shown at the start of this quote to signify the TWO HUNDRED AND EIGHTY FOURTH day in the field, the TENTH page of field notes for that day. At the time of the study, personal computers had not yet become available. Thus, I typed or handwrote my field notes.

[17] See Buford H. Junker, *Field Work: An Introduction to the Social Sciences* (Chicago: University of Chicago Press, 1960), especially p. 139: "Three aspects of the question, 'Who am I, as a social science field worker?' may be briefly put as follows: 1) What are my social skills, given my intellectual, sensory, and other attributes, and my experience, for gathering information-in-society? 2) Who am I (and who might I become) in the eyes of the people in the situations(s) I want to study, and what effect does this have on my acting in roles in relations with them? 3) Who am I, again, given the best obtainable estimates of 1 and 2, and in my own judgment and in that of others, A) what can I do as a field worker to get what information I can out of the situation? B) Am I fully willing and ethical as I am able to do this work to get this information for the purposes of a social science?"

[18] Shulamit Reinharz, "Who Am I? The Need for a Variety of Selves in the Field," in Rosanna Hertz (ed.), *Reflexivity and Voice*, pp. 3–20 (Thousand Oaks, CA: Sage, 1997).

[19] See Bent Flyvbjerg, "Five Misunderstandings about Case-study Research," *Qualitative Inquiry* 12(2):219–245, for a cogent discussion of the necessity of producing case studies.

(chapters 8-10). Before plunging into this three-part pattern, however, I will tie these new ideas to previous writing on the topic, particularly ideas of researchers who have influenced my thinking.

To my mind, John Van Mannen, Peter Manning, and Marc Miller, authorities on qualitative research methods, made a major contribution when they asserted, "The self is the key fieldwork tool."[20] If the self is, indeed, the key fieldwork tool, then one would expect that much of the methodological literature on fieldwork would concern the self. Surprisingly, however, this is not the case. In the past, some anthropologists wanted to write about it but were embarrassed about what they might reveal. A case in point is anthropologist Laura Bohanan, who wrote the story of her fieldwork experience (*Return to Laughter: An Anthropological Novel,* 1964) under the pseudonym "Elenore Smith Bowen." Instead of discussing the self, the vast majority of research methods literature concerns how the researcher should present her/his research role in the field. There is, in fact, very little discussion about what the self is or, to put it another way, who the researcher is. An exception is Amanda Coffey, who focuses on the ways gender, class, sexuality, and race influence fieldwork.[21] In *Observing the Observer,* I delve into selves that are even more varied, more specific, and locally rooted. As mentioned earlier, my focus in this book is to analyze the key fieldwork tool—the self. To do this, I offer an in-depth analysis, a "thick description" in Clifford Geertz's words, of one fieldwork project.[22] Because I have included a lot of the field notes themselves in this book, a second way of understanding its structure is as two parallel accounts in dialogue with one another—the field notes taken on the day I experienced events and the analytic narrative written many years later.

The self of the fieldworker going into the field is not the only relevant self. There is also the self of the fieldworker during the study and afterward. The fieldworker herself/himself is likely not to be aware of all the selves that she/he will discover while in the field. In this sense, fieldwork is analogous to, but not identical with, psychological therapy. Things change. The setting that the researcher is studying does not stand still just because the researcher is studying it. As Patricia Adler wrote in *Wheeling and Dealing* (1985), "Over a six-year period, I thus observed the transformation of Southwest County from a major wholesale marijuana market into a distribution center for the cocaine trade" (p. 9).[23] In my own study of a kibbutz, unbeknownst to me in advance, the entire community was enmeshed in, and involved me in, an enormous upheaval concerning child-care policy, even though I had come to the field to study old age!

The researcher does not remain the same from the beginning to the end of the study, particularly if the study takes more than a short period. One of the assets of

---

[20] John Van Mannen, Peter Manning, and Marc Miller, "Editors' Introduction," in Jennifer C. Hunt, *Psychoanalytic Aspects of Fieldwork* (Qualitative Research Methods Series 18), p. 5, 1989.

[21] Amanda Coffey, *The Ethnographic Self: Fieldwork and the Representation of Identity* (London: Sage, 1999).

[22] Clifford Geertz, "Thick Description: Toward an Interpretive Theory of Culture," in *The Interpretation of Cultures: Selected Essays*, pp. 3–30. (New York: Basic Books, 1973).

[23] Patricia A. Adler, *Wheeling and Dealing: Ethnography of an Upper-level Drug Dealing and Smuggling Community* (New York: Columbia University Press, 1993).

fieldwork is that it is rooted in evolving time, in the unfolding of events. Fieldwork requires time—one has to enter, carry out the interviews, collect the observations, and leave. And time means change, both in the researcher and in the people being studied. Some settings change faster than others—and some changes are more significant than others.

We may wish that time stood still, but it doesn't. A snapshot tells us only so much. As organizational sociologist Rosabeth Kanter wrote in *Evolve!*[24], strategic planning builds on the assumption that the organization will stand still so the plan can be implemented down the road. That's why strategic planning is frequently disappointing. Things happen. Nothing stands still. In fact, one of the most important challenges to social science is to develop models of human life that are simultaneously dynamic and structural. One consequence of time spent in the field is that there is an opportunity for things to transform and for the researcher to witness and undergo these alterations.

Much methodological writing about how researchers do (and should do) participant observation studies deals with the contrast between natives and strangers, between subjectivity and objectivity, and between insiders and outsiders. These works address important questions: Should researchers function in a covert or overt way? Should the researcher participate actively while in the field? How should the researcher take notes? Should the researcher adopt the beliefs of the members? Recent writing has been taking up the question of how the researcher should deal with unacceptable behaviors—such as insults—in the field. For example, in her study of Japanese women's exodus from Japan to the West, Karen Kelsky, a white American feminist married to a Japanese man, faced the challenge of being insulted for being married to a Japanese man. As she wrote:

> During my fieldwork, I found that both my personal convictions as a feminist, which prevented me from simply accepting informants' claims about an egalitarian, liberating West, and my personal circumstances, which directly contradicted informants' foundational beliefs in the abjection and unacceptability of Japanese men, made rapport difficult, at times impossible, to achieve.[25]

How should we deal with such topics as sexual violence that becomes "too personal"?[26] Many women have written about the problem of dealing with sexual harassment in the field as well.[27] By contrast, feminist ethnographers have also produced illuminating works about the ways in which fieldwork is so compelling that the researcher does not know how to stop collecting data.[28]

---

[24] Rosabeth Moss Kanter, *Evolve!: Succeeding in the Digital Culture of Tomorrow* (Boston: Harvard Business School Press, 2001).

[25] Karen Kelsky, *Women on the Verge: Japanese Women, Western Dreams* (Durham, NC: Duke University Press, 2001).

[26] Jayne Howell, "Turning Out Good Ethnography, or Talking Out of Turn?" *Journal of Contemporary Ethnography* 33(3):323–352, 2004.

[27] Carol A. B. Warren, *Gender Issues in Field Research, Qualitative Research Methods Series 9, A Sage University Paper* (Newbury Park, CA: Sage, 1988).

[28] Beverly Skeggs, "Theorizing, Ethics and Representation in Feminist Ethnography," in Beverly Skeggs (ed.), *Feminist Cultural Theory: Process and Production* (New York: Manchester University

It is important to recognize that the self is both *brought to* the field and *created in* the field. In each case this self is a complex constellation with historical, psychological, and sociological dimensions. Psychoanalyst and sociologist Jennifer Hunt has written about the *psychological* self that is brought to the field and its impact on fieldwork.[29] My perspective augments hers by focusing on the *sociological* self, the self brought to and created in the field by virtue of socially defined roles and expectations. The norms of the social setting and interaction with the research "subjects" produce the self in the field. This perspective builds on the classic insight of Charles Horton Cooley (1902) that our selves are, in large part, formed by a looking glass. To become a socialized human being, a person learns to views himself/herself through others' perceptions and in turn gains identity. Throughout life we learn to see ourselves as reflected by others. The looking glass self begins at an early age and continues throughout a person's lifetime unless the person has no social interactions. For my purposes, the field research setting consists of multiple looking glasses and is a time when the self is particularly amenable to formation and modification.

It is important to recognize that being a "researcher" is only one aspect of the researcher's self while in the field. Although the researcher may consider this to be the most salient part, community members may not agree. Researchers *bring* a multitude of role relationships, demographic characteristics, attitudes, personal styles, linguistic abilities, and physical appearances to the field. Similarly, doing fieldwork *creates* a wide range of aspects of the self through interaction while in the field. All of these factors influence an individual's ability to do fieldwork just as many factors influence the quality and success of a survey questionnaire. For this reason, some researchers are suitable in some studies, and others are more suitable in others. Not everyone can study every setting, group, or community.

Feminist methodological theory draws our attention to the fact that we bring gender and race into the field and that every field setting has its own definition of gender. Marxist and politically oriented fieldwork literature alerts us to our class and power status in the field. On the basis of these literatures alone, we now recognize that in the field, the researcher means many things to people. These things include a researcher, a gendered individual, and a person whose race/class/nationality/education connotes a particular power relation with others. All of these aspects of the self can be tools for understanding rather than factors that get in the way of understanding.

Researchers bring numerous other self attributes to the field. And many additional components are created in the field, depending on the setting. These "brought" and "created" selves are relevant to fieldwork *if* they are relevant to the people in the particular setting being studied. When they are relevant, they shape the relationships that can or cannot be formed and thus the knowledge that can or cannot be obtained by the researcher. Another way of putting my point is to say that

---

Press, 1995); see also Diane L. Wolf (ed.), *Feminist Dilemmas in Fieldwork* (Boulder, CO: Westview Press, 1996).

[29] Jennifer C. Hunt, *Psychoanalytic Aspects of Fieldwork, Qualitative Research Methods Series 18, A Sage University Paper* Newbury Park, CA: Sage, 1989).

the following questions must always be asked in fieldwork: Who exactly is this researcher who comes to this field? Who did she/he become in the field because of what kinds of relationships? What is the range of ways in which others see him/her?

More dramatically, I would say that unless the reader knows what the researcher's attributes mean to the people being studied, the reader (and the researcher herself/himself) cannot understand the phenomenon being studied. In anthropologist Pat Caplan's words:

> [A] number of factors . . . determines the kinds of data we collect, and our inter-
> pretation of them. One of the most important of these is our positionality—who
> are we for them? Who are they for us? Such questions have to be considered not
> only in the light of anthropology's current paradigms, but also in terms of such
> factors as our gender, age and life experience, as well as our race and nationality.

In their excellent book, *Membership Roles in Field Research*, Patricia and Peter Adler analyze various field projects. These include their own study of drug dealing mentioned earlier, Jennifer Hunt's study of the police, and Ruth Horowitz's study of Chicana gangs. However, in their opening sentence, they state the following:

> In conducting field research, sociologists are often compelled to put aside their
> academic or other everyday life roles. In their place, researchers must assume
> social roles that fit into the worlds they are studying. Their perspectives on these
> worlds and the kinds of information they can learn about them are greatly influ-
> enced, however, by the character of the research roles they choose.[30]

I start my book from the opposite direction. I contend that "academic and every-day life roles" cannot be put aside. As I discovered, one does not even know what roles are relevant until they are elicited in the field. Aspects of the self may change during the course of fieldwork, and aspects of the self that were hidden from the researcher may be revealed, but they are never "put aside."

Researchers are not omniscient. They have their blind spots like anyone else. They do not always know what roles will be meaningful to the community. Many of the attributes of the researcher may actually be irrelevant in a particular setting. But what is meaningful will become the basis of how she/he is perceived. How she/he is perceived will affect how the researcher understands herself/himself. And this understanding will affect the way the study proceeds.

Documentation of these processes is essential in fieldwork studies and does not constitute an unwarranted, narcissistic display of the self. Quite the contrary, understanding the role of the self in fieldwork will get us out of the epistemological tension between unreflexive positivism on the one hand and unproductive navel-gazing on the other. An essential element of the fieldwork process is understanding the relevance of and creation of different researcher selves in the research setting. In this way, the self becomes the key fieldwork tool. Like Pat Caplan,

> I have become aware that being an ethnographer means studying the self as well
> as the other. In this way, the self becomes 'othered', an object of study, while at the

---

[30] Patricia A. Adler and Peter Adler, *Membership Roles in Field Research, Qualitative Research Methods Series 6, A Sage University Paper*, p. 8 (Newbury, CA: Sage, 1987).

same time, the other, because of familiarity, and a different approach to fieldwork, becomes part of the self.[31]

So, too, Dan Rose argues that it is important for anthropologists (and sociologists) to learn how they are perceived and to reverse roles. He suggests that we should focus on the unnamed space, where "our" study of "them" meets and clashes with "their" study of "us."[32] My purpose in this book is to document this process. If I am successful, it should help us report fieldwork in ways that integrate a full discussion of what the researcher *became* in the field with how the researcher *understood* the field.

The Adlers discuss Ruth Horowitz's awareness of the shifting salience of various aspects of her self, while she conducted her research.

> Identities are not fixed but are affirmed or changed continually. It was an advantage [for me] to be appraised as a lady and a reporter, as that identity allowed me to maintain a degree of distance and legitimacy as a woman among men. However, the longer I remained with the group, the more I became aware that some of the young men were attempting to redefine my identity as a potential girlfriend, making my sexual identity salient ... After fifteen months, their sexual teasing of me increased significantly and several stated that I knew too much about them ... I began to be perceived as a threat to the group.[33]

In other words, Ruth Horowitz was aware that she brought attributes to the field that were "salient" to the people with whom she interacted. To them she was a lady first, then a reporter, then a sex object, and then a dangerous outsider.[34] My intention in discussing this issue, then, is to highlight the salience of the researcher's attributes in forming or not forming relations in the field, recognizing that the relations that one forms provide the basis for gathering data in the field. My hope is to highlight the issues that may be resting in the shadows of other methodologists' writings.

The implication of my argument is to draw our attention to ourselves, not in a solipsistic way but rather in a way that promotes methodological honesty and clarity. Who are we, really, in the field? Attending to the creation of selves in this way enables us also to be consistent with regard to our theories of social interaction. It makes no sense to say, for example, that gender and race matter everywhere and then to avoid discussions of gender and race when reporting on field relationships. What else matters? And what matters where?

---

[31] Pat Caplan, "Learning Gender: Fieldwork in a Tanzanian Coastal Village, 1965–85," in Diane Bell, Pat Caplan, and Wazir Jahan Karim (eds.), *Gendered Fields: Women, Men & Ethnography*, pp. 168–181 (New York: Routledge, 1993).

[32] Dan Rose, *Living the Ethnographic Life, Qualitative Research Methods Series 23, A Sage University Paper* (Newbury, CA: Sage, 1990).

[33] Adler and Adler, pp. 42–43.

[34] As David M. Hayano writes in *Poker Faces: The Life and Work of Professional Card Players* (Berkeley, CA: University of California Press, 1982), "Appendix A: A Description of Fieldwork Methods," his role in the gambling parlors was continuously changing and his outside role was irrelevant to the players.

Field research monographs must strike a balance between self and other in their reporting. We cannot condone the brief preface, afterword, or appendix that gives us some information about the researcher. Nor is it sufficient to have the "telling anecdote" that sums up how the researcher was seen in the field. Rather, we have to find a way of reporting the process of change.

The remainder of this book documents the actual process of change in the evolution of a multitude of roles in the field. I begin with "before entry into the field." After I arrived, the next stage was "telling me warning stories," then "telling me what to do." Next I found some "symbols of acceptance" as I worked my way into a "relationship with my sponsor." I then had to become "independent of my sponsor," in part by "getting other allies." Ultimately, my research role in this community became one in which I was continuously tested for my level of understanding. Even if people disagreed with my conclusions, I seem to have passed the test of at least trying to understand, doing no harm, and devoting a lot of time and energy to the research project. Thus, people were willing to talk to me informally and to engage in formal audiotaped interviews. They allowed me to attend the *sichot kibbutz*,[35] to attend committee meetings, and to participate in club activities. It seemed, ultimately, that being "willing to be tested" was the key to passing the test and being accepted as a researcher on this kibbutz. In the remainder of this section, I describe these steps, from "before entry" to "being tested."

As mentioned earlier, *Observing the Observer* draws primarily on a year-long field study I undertook in 1979–1980, the purpose of which was to analyze the living conditions and attitudes of elderly members in a particular kibbutz. As is critical in such studies, I took extensive field notes on a daily basis, collected a vast amount of printed literature and ephemera available on the kibbutz, and conducted interviews with every elderly member and many other people on the kibbutz. In fieldwork literature, these data collection activities are relatively undifferentiated. Instead, I will comment on all three activities, particularly showing the *difference* between writing field notes and conducting interviews. Writing field notes can actually be understood as a strategy for getting away from people.[36] For example,

> 61:5: Sitting here in my room, re-thinking the kibbutz, recharging my batteries before plunging into the *chadar haochel* again for another fray with the people.

Interviews, on the other hand, are a form of engagement with the people in the field. Interviews give the field setting members an opportunity for more control over the situation. The interview approach I used might be labeled "holistic interviewing," in the sense that I was interested in learning about the "whole person," particularly when I interviewed one of the elderly members of the

---

[35] Weekly town hall meeting of kibbutz members. This is the plural form.

[36] Perhaps this "informant-contact fatigue" explains the unusual photograph on the cover of the paperback book, James Clifford and George E. Marcus (eds.), *Writing Culture: The Poetics and Politics of Ethnography* (Berkeley and Los Angeles: University of California Press, 1986), which shows a researcher writing notes with his back to the people he is studying.

kibbutz, as can be seen in the italicized part of the interview transcript that follows. A holistic interview represents what *the subject* has to say. That is why it is so important to have both field notes (what the researcher sees and experiences) and interview transcripts for triangulation of meaning. Here is an example of how I started one of my first interviews. In subsequent interviews, I never had to ask someone what his or her name was. All interviews were conducted in Hebrew.

> ME: I will preserve confidentiality.
> HE: Confidentiality?
> ME: Confidentiality. So what you tell me, I'm not going to go and tell everyone. It will just stay with me. And even though my sponsor is helping me with the research, he is not involved with this stage, with these conversations; he won't be listening to the tapes. But the kibbutz requested of me that if there is an interesting tape, I put it in the archive. So, we'll see. Every evening, or actually every few days, I conduct one of these interviews, and we'll see what comes of it. I just started now. I didn't bring questions. *I just want to get to know you and, if you are willing, perhaps you would be willing to tell me about your life. And I'll listen.*
> HE: Fine. So, I'll tell you a little about the time before I came to Palestine.[37]
> ME: Great. And if I don't understand, I'll ask you questions.[38]
> HE: I am from Poland.
> ME: Oh, I'm sorry. Can you start with stating your name. I know your family name but not your first name.
> HE: SY, but they call me Ci. I am from a religious family, but a flexible one. As a child, I started to study in the *cheder*,[39] and like all children, I studied Bible, but it was a *cheder*, it wasn't a progressive school. And by the way, we lived in the city, the city of . . ., and we lived among Gentiles.

Interviewing people in their rooms in the evenings was one of my favorite activities on the kibbutz. The quiet and intimacy of the exchange, as we got to know one another and could explore ideas together, brought us into each other's lives in a way that I always sensed was good for both of us. I approached these interviews as if everything the person said was fascinating, listening with my heart and mind and what C. Wright Mills might call "the sociological imagination"[40] in which I was continuously trying to grasp the pattern that could link the individual's experiences with social institutions and his or her place in history. Hypotheses emerged as we spoke; some were reinforced, whereas others were dropped. And as the number of interviews I conducted in this way mounted, all the ideas and experiences that people shared with me began to mesh into a large whole.

---

[37] This was the most common way that the kibbutz elderly whom I interviewed began their story—the beauties and horrors of life before they came to Palestine.

[38] I wanted to make sure it could be a conversation and not a speech.

[39] A religious school for young children where teaching was done by rote. This is a significant detail because the kibbutz was founded with a radically secular, not religious, orientation.

[40] C. Wright Mills, *The Sociological Imagination* (New York: Oxford University Press, 1959/2000).

My interviews of some kibbutz members were not holistic but rather pointed as I tried to find the answers to specific questions about which the individual had expertise or special experience.[41]

In addition to the study of my interview transcripts, field notes, and written materials I gathered in the field, there were two other sources for the analysis in this book. First is feminist and poststructuralist theory, in particular its sensitivity to issues of gendered meanings, power relations, and hidden voices and identities. For example, it is only now, after reading these literatures, that I understand that identity in the field must be understood not only as what one brings to the field and how one is constructed in the field but also as **who one is not** in the field. Thus, I do not remember acknowledging in the field that I was not an Arab, not a Sephardic Jew, not a lesbian,[42] not a single woman, not a single mother, or not a married woman without a child, but I understand the salience of these nonidentities now. It is difficult to analyze the salience of what one is not, except to acknowledge that any of these nonidentities in the field may have been problematic in establishing trust and relationships or at least would have led to other kinds of relationships.

The second source of retrospective understanding stems from other academics who have written about their experiences and their interpretations of those experiences. Thus, Oonagh O'Brien's comment in her essay about fieldwork in North Catalonia that "housing is of vital importance in fieldwork," as are "choices about which part of the village to stay in," seemed familiar to me. But when she went on to write, "whether to stay with a family or not," I realized I had not asked myself that significant question.

The remaining chapters of this book deal with the selves that I *brought to the field* and *those that were created in the field* as I conducted this study of aging on a kibbutz. Each of these selves became a window into the community, a point of attachment to the setting, and a vehicle through which I could study my topic. Assignment of selves into the categories of research-related, personal, and situational is somewhat arbitrary. For example, I will discuss "being a worker" as a situational self because I understood that in order to understand this community (for research purposes), I would have to share in people's experience of work. The work assignments I received, on the other hand, were linked to my being a woman (personal self). Similarly, I am not typically conscious of "being an American" (personal), but in the setting I studied, this background feature of my identity was highlighted (situational).

---

[41] I have found it useful to reflect on people's descriptions of how they interview others. My approach is influenced by Glaser and Strauss, *The Discovery of Grounded Theory: Strategies for Qualitative Research* (Chicago: Aldine, 1967); Robert K. Merton, Marjorie Fiske, and Patricia L. Kendall, *The Focused Interview* (New York: Free Press, 1956/1990); Ken Metzler, *Creative Interviewing* (Englewood Cliffs, NJ: Prentice-Hall, 1977/1989); and Elliot G. Mishler, *Research Interviewing: Context and Narrative* (Cambridge, MA: Harvard University Press, 1986).

[42] Kibbutz members were uncomfortable acknowledging homosexuality. It is no surprise, therefore, that *Time Magazine*'s article, "Change on the Kibbutz," pp. 78–80, November 6, 1972, stated, "There is no known homosexuality on the collectives."

As I discuss various selves in the pages that follow, I will try to make these boundaries more blurred than they appear in this somewhat rigid initial categorization. One way I will do this is to jump back and forth among the large categories. For example, when discussing "research-based selves" I will analyze being sponsored and being a researcher, then move to the second category—personal selves—before returning to "being a good listener and giving feedback" and so forth. This approach reflects the fact that in the field, various selves were being created simultaneously and sequentially within these various categories. The multiplicity and simultaneity of processes are one of the challenging features of field research. The kibbutz (and other relatively closed communities) is a setting in which the multiplicity and simultaneity of these forces are particularly intense, particularly if the researcher lives in the setting instead of leaving each day.

One additional introductory remark is warranted. Fieldwork is a research activity that requires some combination of writing field notes, transcribing interviews, collecting archival and other material, and taking photographs or videotapes. All of these materials constitute the data on which a final written report is based. For the sake of scientific integrity, these materials must be stored and catalogued in a secure, accessible manner so that findings and interpretations can be examined and verified by other researchers. Researchers must provide substantial data to demonstrate and support the points they wish to make. Researchers who do not agree to do this cannot expect others to accept their interpretations. Thus, in this book I will attempt to provide the reader with sufficient data from field notes, interview transcripts, and other sources to understand how I reach particular conclusions.

CHAPTER 1

Developing Research Selves
The Desire, Opportunity, and Preparation
to Do a Study

People taking part in a kibbutz wedding.

The first phase of entry in the field—the phase I call "before entry"—begins with the **desire, opportunity, and preparation** to do a study in a particular setting. In my case, I wanted to do a field study in Israel, preferably of a kibbutz and preferably related to gerontology, an area of increasing social relevance and interest to me and an area I was teaching. My desire to do this study just as researchers' choice of their topics more generally—had intellectual and psychological roots as well as emotional overtones. I thought highly of kibbutzim[1] for philosophical, ideological, political, and spiritual reasons. I knew that a

---
[1] Plural form of *kibbutz.*

kibbutz was a popular research site because it allowed researchers to examine such important questions as "Is there a society in which young children do not live with their parents, thus modifying the definition of a family as a household?"[2] Or "Do women achieve equality with men in kibbutzim, and if they do not, does this demonstrate that women do not want equality with men but rather want to live as women, with unique characteristics?"[3]

Moreover, I suspected that kibbutzim might have some innovative approaches to dealing with issues of aging. These potentially useful ideas might be transferable to the United States. For example, gerontologists at the time had adopted the "disengagement" theory to characterize the process of aging.[4] Did this apply in the kibbutz as well, where the whole society was founded on the principle of mutual assistance? The particular kibbutz political movement, to which the kibbutz I studied belonged, had already established the Inter-kibbutz Department of Aged and Old Members, chaired by David Atar. In a 1975 article,[5] he stated that kibbutz members first began to discuss issues of aging in the 1960s but to little effect. "Members of old pioneer settlements [i.e., kibbutzim] discussed this problem [n.b., aging is defined as a problem] but their call to the agricultural settlements [i.e., kibbutzim] and the kibbutz movements [i.e., political umbrella organizations] found no understanding [because there was a lack of] a sufficiently large group of

---

[2] Two examples of such studies, both of which created storms in academia and the general public, are Bruno Bettelheim, *The Children of the Dream: Communal Child-rearing and American Education* (London: Macmillan, 1969), and Lionel Tiger and Joseph Shepher, *Women in the Kibbutz* (New York: Harcourt Brace, 1975). One of the first sets of articles on this topic was Shmuel Golan, "Collective Education in the Kibbutz," *Psychiatry: Journal for the Study of Interpersonal Processes* 22(2):3–15, 1959; "Behavior Research in Collective Settlements in Israel," *The American Journal of Orthopsychiatry* 28(3):17–22, 1958; and Shmuel Golan and Zvi Lavi, "Communal Education," *Ofakim—Quarterly for Education and Culture* 11(4):23–34, 1957, published as a single pamphlet, Shmuel Golan, *Collective Education in the Kibbutz* (Merchavia, Israel: Education Department of the Kibbutz–Artzi Hashomer Hatzair, 1961).

[3] According to Melford E. Spiro, "The founders of the kibbutz movement proclaimed as one of their historical missions the total emancipation of women from the 'shackles'—sexual, social, economic, and intellectual—imposed on them by traditional society," *Gender and Culture: Kibbutz Women Revisited*, p. 5 (Durham, NC: Duke University Press, 1979). The fact that this has not been achieved continues to fascinate researchers who try to explain it. Thus, there is extensive and continuing literature on the topic of sex-role equality on the kibbutz. See Selma Koss Brandow, "Illusion of Equality: Kibbutz Women and the Ideology of the 'New Jew,'" *International Journal of Women's Studies* 2(3):268–286, 1979; "Ideology, Myth, and Reality: Sex Equality in Israel," 1980, *Sex Roles* 6(3):403–419; Sylvie Foigel-Bijaoui, "From Revolution to Motherhood: The Case of Women in the Kibbutz, 1910–1948," in Deborah Bernstein (ed.), *Pioneers and Homemakers: Jewish Women in Pre-state Israel* (Albany: SUNY Press, 1992); and Michal Palgi, "Gender Equality in the Kibbutz—From Ideology to Reality," in Kalpana Misra and Melanie S. Rich (eds.), *Jewish Feminism in Israel: Some Contemporary Perspectives*, pp. 76–95 (Hanover, NH: University Press of New England, 2003). Other useful literature puts this question in the context of gender ideology in the society at large. See, for example, Eyal Kafkafi, "The Psycho-intellectual Aspect of Gender Inequality in Israel's Labor Movement," *Israel Studies* 4(1):188–211, 1999.

[4] Elaine Cumming and William E. Henry, *Growing Old: The Process of Disengagement* (New York: Basic Books, 1961).

[5] "Aging in Kibbutz Society," *Gerontologia* 1(4):1–8, 1975.

aged people whose problem justified attention or action." In the same article, Atar quoted Bergman, president of the Israel Gerontological Society, as having a much stronger view. "At first," Bergman claimed there was a conscious and unconscious rejection on the part of the kibbutz members [toward the problems of aging], together with an unwillingness to admit the very existence of the problem. Today, we are witnessing an almost feverish activity aimed at overcoming the lag of so many years." From denial to "feverish" involvement certainly suggests that kibbutzim were undergoing changes in attitudes and behaviors, both of which I planned to explore.[6]

I hoped that somehow I would have the opportunity to study elderly people in kibbutzim through traditional fieldwork approaches: living among them for an extended period and participating fully in their lives. My hope was to obtain empirical information (e.g., do nursing homes exist on kibbutzim?) while learning about the setting's own definitions of the situation (e.g., is there a kibbutz "philosophy of aging"?). If given the opportunity, I was interested in learning about the roles, activities, and feelings of elderly people in the context of kibbutz life.

My analytic perspective stemmed from cross-cultural gerontology, a field that asks how the experience of aging varies as a consequence of different cultural, economic, and social contexts. My methodological orientation reflected my training in qualitative sociology and grounded theory, and my theoretical perspective reflected my training in symbolic interactionism and social psychology. Instead of administering tests or questionnaires, I wanted to document interaction, collect records, interview people, and ask "What is going on here? How is meaning conveyed in interaction? What are elderly people doing and saying, how do they talk, how are they talked about?"

In preparation for a potential study I read literature about aging that had been produced by such kibbutz researchers as Dr. Uri Leviatan as well as relevant studies about the kibbutz published by foreign and Israeli researchers and journalists.[7] When I knew I would have time off from teaching, I applied for a U.S. government grant to carry out the study but was turned down. I did, however, tell friends and acquaintances in the United States that I would like to do such a project. Networking saved the day when one of my friends informed a kibbutz member friend of his

---

[6] Extensive research on the elderly kibbutz member since then focuses on problem solving and includes Monica B. Holmes, Douglas Holmes, and Simon Bergman, "The Israeli Kibbutz as a System of Care for the Elderly," Community Research Applications, Inc., March 1983.

[7] For example, Murray Weingarten, *Life in a Kibbutz* (New York: Reconstructionist Press, 1955); Yosef Criden and Saadia Gelb, *The Kibbutz Experience: Dialogue in Kfar Blum* (New York: Herzl Press, 1974); and Melford Spiro, *Kibbutz: Venture in Utopia* (New York: Schocken, 1956). I did not yet find articles specific to aging, although after I arrived on the kibbutz, I was given Url Leviatan, Gila Adar, and Zvi Am-Ad, *Aging in the Kibbutz*, 1979, a publication of the newly formed Institute for Study and Research of the Kibbutz and the Cooperative Idea, University of Haifa, Israel. For an overview of research before 1962, see Francis Horigan, *Psychiatric Abstracts Series No. 9, The Israeli Kibbutz: Psychiatric, Psychological and Social Studies with Emphasis on Family Life and Family Structure: A Survey of the Literature*, U.S. Department of Health, Education, and Welfare.

about my interest and showed him the book I had recently published.[8] I noticed that although there was a great deal of discussion about child rearing[9] and sex role differentiation,[10] there was almost no research about aging. This seemed perfectly reasonable at the time because kibbutzim themselves were just beginning to pay attention to the fact that some of their members had become elderly. Perhaps it was also evidence of denial because the kibbutz had an image of being young, healthy, and active.

It is not surprising, therefore, that this "friend of a friend" contacted me and invited me to do a study of aging in his kibbutz pending agreement by the relevant decision makers in the kibbutz. This kibbutz member was an Israeli academic temporarily in the United States, conducting research of his own with our mutual friend, a professor at the university where I was teaching. We met briefly to discuss my interests. I knew almost nothing about him but relied on the recommendation of my friend.

After the individual's return to his kibbutz, we began to correspond and then to negotiate more formally the conditions under which I would be able to conduct a study that would satisfy my intellectual needs as well as those of the kibbutz.[11] Thus, like the Adlers and many other researchers, I relied on a sponsor to gain access to the study site. Without his help, the study would most likely never have taken place. As it turned out, the sponsor had a profound impact on my study.

After a few months, this individual brought a proposal to the *sichat kibbutz* of the kibbutz, which I will call "Kibbutz Emek."[12] Doing so gave him the status not only of my informal sponsor but also of the formal sponsor of my study, which in the eyes of kibbutz members and institutions gave him a relation with me. Although in theory the *sichat kibbutz* consists of all kibbutz members who gather every Saturday evening[13] to discuss and decide on matters of general concern, individual participation is entirely voluntary, as is true of nearly everything on the kibbutz. Participation is like voting in the United States—encouraged but not mandatory.

---

[8] Shulamit Reinharz, *On Becoming a Social Scientist: From Survey Research and Participation to Experiential Analysis* (San Francisco: Jossey-Bass, 1979).

[9] Melford E. Spiro, *Children of the Kibbutz: A Study in Child Training and Personality* (Cambridge, MA: Harvard University Press, 1958); A. I. Rabin and Bertha Hazan, *Collective Education in the Kibbutz* (New York: Springer, 1973).

[10] For example, Yonina Talmon, *Family and Community in the Kibbutz* (Cambridge, MA: Harvard University Press, 1972); Menachem Gerson, *Family, Women, and Socialization in the Kibbutz* (Lexington, MA: Lexington Books, 1978).

[11] Nowadays I would have had to have my study approved by an institutional review board. Such a board did not exist at the time. For a discussion of the impediments that such boards pose for fieldwork, see Stefan Timmermans, "Cui Bono? Institutional Review Board Ethics and Ethnographic Research," *Studies in Symbolic Interaction* 19:153–173, 1995.

[12] Kibbutzim are not stand-alone communities but rather are part of what is called "kibbutz movements," that is, a group of kibbutzim that adheres to a particular set of ideals, defined at a particular time by a particular leader(s) and drawing its members from a particular youth group. Ha-Shomer Ha-Tza'ir was the feeder youth group of Emek, and the founding philosopher was the Russian ideologist Ber Borochov. See his "Our Platform" (1906) in Mitchell Cohen (ed.), *Class Struggle and the Jewish Nation: Selected Essays in Marxist Zionism* (New Brunswick, NJ: Transaction Books, 1984). Emek was one of the early *Ha-Shomer Ha-Tza'ir* kibbutzim.

[13] This particular kibbutz chose this time, but the day and time vary among kibbutzim.

However, because the kibbutz is a small society, everyone knows whether you participate or not, and many people have strong opinions on the topic. The following minutes, which I have translated,[14] were officially recorded during the meeting when the proposal for my research was discussed. At the time, I was still in the United States:

> 20.1.79 (date) Research team on old age in Emek:[15] Proposal of [my sponsor]. We are talking about 3 researchers with their families: a neurologist, a social worker and a sociologist. The work would be conducted free-of-charge . . . . The intent is that the researchers together with a parallel staff would study the elderly only of Emek and would focus on the problems of Emek. 'I am interested in the future of Emek.'
>
> Conditions for selection of staff: a) Every one would know some Hebrew; b) They would live in the kibbutz for a certain period; c) They would study the people of Emek only.
>
> The neurologist would come to the kibbutz for a period of a month in order to prepare the research plan. After the completion of the plan, the financial arrangements concerning his travel would be arranged using U.S. resources. A parallel staff would be established in the kibbutz to help implement the project. The researchers want to test community life, not in terms of questionnaires, but rather using the method of community anthropology. At the end of the year, a final practical report will be delivered with practical suggestions for the kibbutz. The researchers will be permitted to use the research for their own purposes, without the disclosure of names. Members who are affected by this topic are requested to take part. We must provide one room[16] for a year or two, and a second room for a half-year. People with young families will have their children in the children's house.[17] At the moment, only one child is involved.

Discussion:

M:[18] The demand for rooms of the type requested is very great. A building with 5 rooms [in one area of the kibbutz] is about to be torn down. We don't have sufficient space to house our soldiers[19] who are released from the army. And in the [certain neighborhood in the kibbutz], there are no available rooms. Thus, if this proposal is accepted, it will compete with the establishment of a neighborhood for young people.

A different M: There are three problems.
  a. Problem of housing.
  b. The cost of caring for the child.
  c. Will this research be specific to Emek?
I personally am not enthusiastic about this research.

---

[14] Except where noted, all translations are mine.

[15] *Emek* is a Hebrew word meaning "valley."

[16] The word *room* refers to a one-room apartment, not a room in an apartment.

[17] Collective child-rearing buildings.

[18] Seventy-five-year-old man.

[19] All eighteen-year-old kibbutz young people serve in the army for various lengths of time, and individual housing is provided to them when they are released.

T:[20] The topic was brought to the *mazkirut*[21] more than a year ago. The financial aspect is not really a factor. It is likely that this project will provide means for solving problems of the elderly. There is a technical problem of housing but we should solve it for the sake of the larger good of the research.

Z:[22] Advises acceptance of the proposal and points out that the *vatikim* are the first generation of older people on the kibbutz, and there is alienation between the *vatikim* and the younger generation. Every effort that attempts to solve this problem is desirable.

D:[23] Accepts the idea but asks who are the anonymous people who will do the research? It is clear that someone will be affected by the housing shortage. With regard to the research, expresses doubt from the last experience that the researchers will end up not working in the kibbutz and that in actuality, we will have to support the researchers and that will cost us money.

T:[24] It seems to me that old people are not a problem, but rather the real problem is the next generation.

M:[25] I was elected to the "absorption committee" and I was warned that we have no rooms and from this perspective, the research will cause an additional difficulty.

Outcome of the vote: 26 in favor, 6 opposed. The research proposal was endorsed.

Only thirty-two of the more than two hundred kibbutz members voted, and only five people's opinions were recorded, only one of whom was a woman. Twenty percent of those who voted were opposed, and 80 percent were in favor. Yet, the minutes communicate the sense of a meager kibbutz endorsement, reflecting both the small number of people who thought the subject was important enough to show up at the meeting and the lack of forceful positive arguments. These minutes show that although the project had gained formal approval at this *sichat kibbutz*, there was probably not much interest in it. The opposition hinged on cost, space, questionable relevance, and negative previous experience with researchers. I have no way of knowing how many people actually attended or if other important comments were voiced because those facts were not recorded and no one I asked seemed to remember. In retrospect, I could see that some people believed that the kibbutz had concerns that differed from issues of aging. This would become a constant theme in my discussions with kibbutz members.

The implication of these minutes to me is that I clearly would have to show that I was worth the kibbutz's allocation of a room. Thus, the first perception that kibbutz members probably had of me before I even arrived was as a kibbutz member-sponsored person who would cost the kibbutz services and would take up valuable space to do a project of questionable value. That was how I was imagined. My sponsor did not send me the minutes, nor did I know to ask for them. I discovered them after I arrived. Rather, he simply wrote to inform me that "the project

---

[20] Middle-aged woman.

[21] The management group of the kibbutz, composed of kibbutz members and rotated every few years.

[22] Elderly man.

[23] Middle-aged man.

[24] Elderly man.

[25] Middle-aged man.

was approved." At this point he and I referred to the endeavor as *the* project, not his, ours, or mine. The issue of control grew rapidly.

WARNING STORIES

One reason why there may have been little enthusiasm for the project was the kibbutz members' experience with previous researchers who had come to stay with them. From the start, like all participant observers, I was concerned that I would be *acceptable enough* to the members of the kibbutz that I could remain in the field long enough to study aging. But I did not know exactly what would make me acceptable. One hint I received early in my stay was embedded in frequent comments about *other* researchers. During the *sichat kibbutz* discussion prior to my arrival and in my first conversation with the two *mazkirim*[26] after I arrived, people told me about Emek's negative experiences with previous researchers.

> 3:1: The *mazkirim* told me they have not had good experiences with researchers. Over and over again (day 3) I was told the story of T, a "researcher from England who is Jewish" and who initiated research on the kibbutz. [Being Jewish is relevant to the *mazkirim*, because Jews should not have done what T did.] Nevertheless, when the Six-Day War broke out (in 1967), he apparently fled the country in response to his embassy's instructions. At the same time, another visitor from France did not do so, but 'stood by the kibbutz.' When the war was over, T wanted to return to Emek, but people didn't want to speak with him.

Obviously the implication of this story was that researchers are expected not to be cowardly (i.e., leave the country) if there are military problems. If the kibbutz would let me in, I was expected to stand by even if the going got rough. I was not to abandon the kibbutz and evade the dangers it was facing.

In some cases, kibbutz members told me that the findings from previous researchers were not helpful.

> 17:1: S said (with a disdainful tone) that every one of the anthropologists has told them that the way they build the houses creates a situation where everyone's back and not the front faces each other, so that it prevents relationships from forming. [I would certainly have said the same thing. The implication here was that kibbutz members situated their buildings the way they did for some important reason that the anthropologists did not take into consideration, thus demonstrating their incompetence.]

These oft-repeated stories taught me that kibbutz members would be judging both my character (would I be a coward?) and my findings (would I make the same senseless suggestions?). Clearly these stories were not-so-subtle ways to shape my behavior on the kibbutz and to share the values of the members with me. I also felt that by telling me these stories, kibbutz members were *preparing me for failure* in the sense that they would most likely reject my findings. At the same time, they were teaching me what I would have to do to avoid failing.

As time passed, I was told additional stories about their experiences as research participants. Whenever I heard such stories, I tried to extract from them what the

---

[26] Kibbutz managers or coordinators. *Mazkirim* is plural, and *mazkir* is singular.

kibbutz members perceived the problem to be and to reassure them that I was doing something different.

> 23:2: N told me he had participated in a research project before. People sat around a table in the communal dining room filling out questionnaires about whether or not they were satisfied, their family relations, etc. They got *no* feedback except perhaps a general one to the kibbutz as a whole. I contrasted this with myself in that I will base my work on *interviews*, will live in the kibbutz and will give feedback to the kibbutz immediately. I told him I invite people to my room to talk and gave as an example C. He was surprised that C would have anything to say that I would be interested in, but I said we talked for hours and it was worthwhile.

In other instances, I learned that individual kibbutz members wanted me to express appreciation for their assistance and to be specific in what I wanted from them.

> 55:2: I went up to Z and asked him if he knew who I was and if anyone had talked to him about my asking him for help. He knew, but said he couldn't help because he had helped so many researchers 'recently.' He mentioned a British and Belgian person whom he had helped get their doctorates. I said I already had my doctorate, but if he didn't want to help, fine. He gave them hundreds of hours of his time and not even a thank you! They wanted to know everything. Who was married, who was separated from whom, etc. He doesn't want to get into that again, but if I have specific questions, he said I can write him a note and he'll let me know if he can help or not.
>
> 57:2: I guess my note was ok, Z will meet with me at 9:45 tomorrow.
>
> 58:1: I was having lunch with S and her husband, the beehive keeper, when Z came over with lists of information for me.

Without ever saying so, Z had become my research assistant in the sense that he gathered the data I needed. Perhaps my clarification of my way of doing research helped him. Over time he had also seen me in many other roles, and perhaps that, too, persuaded him to cooperate. When I finally gave my feedback to the elderly club toward the end of my stay, Z got up and made a speech about how I was "not like the other researchers," specifically commenting on my interviewing and willingness to interest myself in the broadest possible picture. If this is true, it is gratifying to suppose that the community would be open to other researchers in the future. As I told my students subsequently, one should leave a field setting in a way that does not spoil the possibilities for future research.

TELLING ME WHAT TO DO

Comments about these phantom "other researchers" kept cropping up. Perhaps these comments were also a way for the kibbutz members to let me know that they were familiar with research and could tell me how it *should* be done.

> No Date: Today I went to the cosmeticist (kibbutz member) thinking may be I'd ask her for an appointment tomorrow, to have my eyebrows done. I've never had them shaped in my life, but I saw other women doing it, and may be my eyebrows would look pretty that way. I felt comfortable asking her since I've had lunch with

her a few times. When I arrived at the salon, she asked me if I wanted tea. She told me that E had told her I was studying the elderly. She had sort of known, but not really. She then told me she used to belong to the committee on the elderly and while in this function someone from another kibbutz asked her to help him collect data for his dissertation.

M: "It was very difficult. People didn't feel like opening up. I think it's much better to observe and see what people actually do. Like the fact that you work in the kitchen is good."

Me: "I talk to people all the time, but only those people who want to talk to me. I observe and everyone knows that I'm observing. I'm trying to understand this kibbutz from the inside by living here."

M: "The members were really alienated from the other style of doing research because they felt they were doing it *for him* and weren't getting anything in return. They had no intrinsic reason for helping him. They had no motivation to be open."

Clearly this member was telling me about the norm of reciprocity. Not only should fieldworkers give something in return, but also if members do not believe that reciprocity will be possible, they are unlikely to permit access to themselves in the first place. I think this member was saying that I should respect members' knowledge by letting them guide me through my research.

M: "You should try to get to know people who are completely 'alone' (by this she meant widow/ers with no children on the kibbutz). For instance you could learn a lot from J. He's very bright and he loves to talk. But since you're doing research, you have to be selective in what you accept from him (meaning that not everything he says is truthful). F is 'alone;' P is very well liked. He lives next door to S who takes care of him in a wonderful way. He is completely alone here."

People told me what to do all the time, just like they tell each other what to do. My research role was being formed.

Lunch with Z on Sunday, November 4. He asked me how my work was going and I said "fine." I told him I had stopped interviewing for a while. He called what I do *pigishot* (meetings) rather than *ra'ayonot* (interviews). He thinks I should continue with the *pigishot*, which are more important than talking with the coordinators of committees. Those are not worth my time, according to him.

I found myself responding pretty much as they do to constant advice giving—I accepted part of it, I explained away part of it as something I could not do, and I objected to part.

No date: I have to fashion my own existence here and can't be pushed around completely. Part of this "advice giving" is probably a way of testing me, may be also of criticizing me and minimizing my work. On the other hand, it is a way of showing some interest, engaging me.

194:3: Z said I should read *Bameshek* and *Hedim*. I said I would.

Fortunately, because he told me to do this, he supplied me with the journal issues.

I also began to feel that there was some competition among people about who had the best insight into kibbutz life—who could really tell me what life was all about and could tell me what I should do in order to get that superior understanding. If I talked to the "wrong people," it would show that I was "stupid."

> E said I wouldn't get much out of the facts that Z gave me. On the other hand, he thought it was good that I talked with H "who is critical but deep." Also T can tell me lots of stories about how he got into carpentry, he said. "Those are very worthwhile." [As the advice piles up, it's going to be difficult to do everything, and then, I'll end up disappointing some people.]

Because some people were perceived of as smarter than others, my own intelligence was judged by whom I perceived to be intelligent. Whom I associated with became a way of judging whether or not I was an intelligent person and a good researcher. On the other hand, I was not interested in interviewing only those people who were considered most knowledgeable. Rather, I was interested in everyone's views—from those on the margin to those in the center. This was a difficult idea to get across to kibbutz members. "Why would you ever want to talk to her? Or to him?" was a common comment. Only gradually did people realize that everyone and everything were interesting to me.

> S: "You should watch out for people who like to talk a lot because you don't want to just get a lot of nonsense. You want to get a little deeper." This of course made me feel insecure. Was I just getting superficial nonsense from people, or was the everyday conversation worth noting?
>
> Me: "I just want to hear what people tell me; they might hide or even lie, but I accept everything."
>
> S: "Oh I didn't mean to imply that there was such a thing as objectivity."
>
> Me: "In addition, I can also see what goes on, I don't just interview people. Today, for instance, I haven't interviewed anyone." (Am I explaining or defending?)
>
> S: "From working in the kitchen you can learn only so much. You should also work in the *communa* (clothing repair, folding and distribution center), the *kolbo* (store for members' needs), and the children's houses."
>
> Me: "I agree."

The comment that I should watch out for people who talk too much reinforced an observation I later made at the *sichat kibbutz* when some people stood up to make speeches. Typically these were older people, whose long speeches were not appreciated by people in other age groups. I came to the conclusion that each culture projects its fears onto its old people in accordance with a particular set of values, just as it projects onto its young its aspirations with regard to a particular set of values. For instance, in the kibbutz I deduced that the bad things that can be projected onto old people, things that are seen as particularly abhorrent, are not being a good worker, being a hypochondriac, wobbling around, preaching, and being excessively concerned with ideology.

An obvious advantage of conducting this field study throughout the course of a full year was the opportunity to act in terms of the community's definition of time and process.

> No date: I've noticed that many people seem to like to say "no" first when I ask them for an interview. They seem to want to be asked again or to take their

time and come around and say "yes." By doing this, they can appear to not be over-eager, and they can judge how sincere I am in my requests. I have to understand that a "no" means "ask again." Or as I like to say, "no is half way to yes."

Gradually people began to recognize that I would understand the kibbutz best if I had the maximum amount of information. They then switched gears and wanted to make sure that I knew *all* the stories.

> No date: He said I should interview RS who was chair of the internal review committee of the entire kibbutz movement and very insightful. There's a long story about this unusual man who carried out the unprecedented act of leaving the kibbutz when he had already become old. People had gone to see him on the kibbutz and in Tel Aviv to convince him to return, but he didn't.

It turned out that I did, in fact, interview this man repeatedly on his occasional visits back to Emek. And when he acknowledged this relationship by shaking my hand demonstrably and publicly whenever we would meet in the dining room, people began to realize that I was talking to people and "getting stories" that *even they were not getting* because I was not in conflict with anyone.

SYMBOLS OF ACCEPTANCE

After a while it became obvious to the kibbutz population that I was in contact with many people on the kibbutz. Their willingness to talk to me privately led to my being given approval to participate in more exclusive activities. To me, one of the potent symbols of acceptance was the permission to attend the *sichot kibbutz*. I received this permission by day 73, and the conditions included even taking notes at the meetings. I believe that people saw me as someone who had become a good researcher *because* I had *taken people's advice*. I also think I achieved the status of a "good researcher" because I was *serious*, as evidenced by the fact that I attended meetings regularly and took notes publicly rather than just "hang out." Here are the notes of the first *sichat kibbutz* I attended:

> 79:3: At 9:30 p.m. went to the *sichat kibbutz*, held in the dining room, where a half hour ago we had just eaten dinner. The tables were not arranged differently. All the young and middle-aged women sat embroidering or knitting at a long table near the back wall facing the chair (man) of the meeting. Older and middle-aged people sat closer to the chairman, and at the back wall, or standing near the doorways and edges of the room were the young people. T (E's husband) served as chair of the meeting. Next to him sat the two current *mazkirim*, S who was taking notes, plus N, the *Merakez Meshek*. The printed agenda had been taken off the bulletin board on the wall downstairs, and was referred to by T, who chose people to speak, organized the voting, and occasionally delivered an opinion (he seemed effective).
> Agenda:
> 1. Changes in the general budget allocation for members
> 2. Application to be a member by a new family
> 3. *Mazkirut* nominations; other elections
> 4. The "A" case

In my opinion, this was a highly charged agenda. About seventy people showed up, not all at once. Most stayed until the end, as far as I could see. I sat next to my sponsor. Y rose and asked that something be put on the agenda, something about an item in the newspaper. He was told that it would be placed on a future agenda. The atmosphere was somewhat chaotic: People interrupted and yelled out, and there wasn't always quiet when someone was speaking. This clearly was an informal democratic process, closer to the British parliamentary culture than to *Robert's Rules of Order.*

> N got up and explained the current family budget system and something about the future system. Then there was a need to vote on whether or not the deficit that members might accrue would be linked to the cost-of-living index at the time it came due. Voted in favor of this linkage after a long debate about vacations, committee functioning, deficits, etc.

These were sensitive financial issues. Having this information was extremely useful to me, particularly in striking up conversations the following day. In this way, it reminded me of football at the University of Michigan, where I was teaching before and after I lived on the kibbutz. If you didn't go to the games, you couldn't be part of the conversation. In my case, I began to be joked about as the person who "really knew what was going on" (in contrast to the kibbutz members who did not) because of the range of people with whom I spoke and the range of activities in which I participated (in contrast to the smaller range of conversation partners and activities of kibbutz members). People watched me during the meetings, just as I watched them.

> 266:1: H: why do you take notes in the *sicha?* [I think she meant, I should just participate.]

During one vote at a *sichat kibbutz* later in the year, when slips of paper were being distributed on which people could indicate their vote, the *mazkir* jokingly gave me a slip of paper and said, "You may as well vote, since you know what's going on." Gradually people began to come to me to ask me *what I thought* about many phenomena because I had earned the status of "knowing what was going on" and "knowing the important stories." The more I was able to observe kibbutz members engaging in important discussions with each other, the more I was able to understand how they interacted with me and what they expected of me. I began to understand the connection between the *sicha* and the other committees on the kibbutz and, once again, to appreciate how intertwined were informal life and organized kibbutz administration. And I was able to see the role that older people played in shaping kibbutz opinion.

Being allowed to participate in rather private committee meetings did not necessarily clarify kibbutz life for me. Sometimes the more I experienced, the more confused I became.

> 84:3: Got back home and typed a little, and then went to the meeting of the nominations committee. Those present included R (chair), N, Y, and G. When I arrived, M was present because he had been asked to be *sadran avodah.* He did not accept the position, but he also didn't appear to have stated any reason for

rejecting this responsibility. I asked Y if I could remain in the room during this discussion. I did not want to intimidate M. Y said that if I were problematic, he'd let me know. M seemed embarrassed by the whole topic and close-mouthed. He wouldn't say what the problem was, but only that there *was* a problem, and he couldn't accept the job. He said that if the committee brought it to the *sicha* and they wanted him to do it, he would take the responsibility, but he wouldn't last more than a month or two. (C had told me that the problem is that M fights with everyone; my sponsor said that that is what M would not reveal to us.)

D and N called me out during the middle of this meeting to tell me that my two-and-one-half-year-old daughter was crying. When I got to her *peuton*, she had stopped. When I got back to the meeting, M had left. There was a discussion as to whether or not to put forward his nomination to the *sicha* anyhow. There was also some speculation as to what his problem was.

> 84:3 R said the explanation has something to do with husband/wife relations, but there's no point to try to intervene with wife since if she were *against* his nomination, she wouldn't let M do it at all. R pointed out that if he said he would accept *sichat's* decision, they should put that proposal forward.

I was learning their secrets, and they did not seem to mind. Most of the secrets were stories that people told me about each other behind each other's back—ostensibly for the purpose of having me "understand."

> 205:1: L reminded me about tomorrow night. He said he leads a complicated life, and I included as one of the components his being a *"kibbutznik."* But he said he *wasn't* such a kibbutznik. Not, for instance, like K who feels guilty all the time that he is teaching in a university (and does not work in the kibbutz itself). Feeling guilty for not doing what one should do apparently is a sign of being a good kibbutz member. L doesn't feel such guilt at all. Perhaps it's because K travels a lot overseas, whereas L is always here (in Israel) close "to the scene of his crime." K first taught in *Givat Haviva*, which was seen more as kibbutz-serving "movement activity." He even had an apartment connected to the college. He was afraid he wouldn't be accepted as a professor at the university (as opposed to the kibbutz college) since he is a Marxist. Not true. L said K is very competent, but he is always trying to do something visible in the kibbutz because he feels so guilty about not being on the kibbutz as a regular worker.

As time passed, people "remembered" the original reluctance of the kibbutz toward the project, as expressed in the *sichat kibbutz* minutes discussed earlier. I believe these comments express the former ambivalence that people felt, ambivalence that had been converted into acceptance. Perhaps they were still ambivalent, but at least they could now safely talk about their mixed feelings as "memories." On the other hand, the "remembered," as opposed to the "currently experienced," reluctance might have been a way of expressing the relief or trust that people felt as time went on.

> 161:3: M told me again of the original reluctance of the kibbutz to participate in my study. "Why should we be an object for someone else's purposes?" I think she told me this because she did *not* feel that I was treating her as an object. Actually her comment raises a terrible moral dilemma for me—because I do

consider the people here "objects of my research" and at the same time, as "people who are unique individuals to me." May be I should just remember that we are all always objects and subjects to one another.

> 251:1: N told me that people said, 'What if she says bad things about us?' I think he said this to me because either a) he trusts that I won't; or b) it doesn't matter to him any more if I do because I am a person to him and whatever I feel like saying is fine.

The idea of harm—saying bad things—came up frequently. Would I do harm? Would I embarrass anyone? Would I malign the kibbutz? I began to wonder if sociologists should adopt the Hippocratic oath to do no harm.[27]

> [from an interview] Shula: do you want to ask me any questions, or do you know who I am and what I am doing here?
>
> M: I don't know, but I am not asking. I suppose it will not be harmful (to the kibbutz movement).
>
> Shula: No.

I never made a secret of the fact that I was studying the kibbutz, and, in fact, I tried to be a very overt observer so that people would help me do my work. From every indication, people accepted my identity on the kibbutz as some sort of a researcher who was studying the elderly. They agreed to be interviewed individually, allowed me to attend committee meetings, and made sure I knew about events of interest.

Perhaps the most dramatic proof of the acceptance of my researcher role came at a meeting of the old age club that occurred after I had been on the kibbutz for ten months. Approximately fifty people were present to hear me deliver some findings from my research. In some ways it was very awkward for me because I was giving them public feedback about themselves. In other ways it was very comfortable because by that point I knew everyone personally, and my talk was a kind of extension of our conversations. After I spoke for about an hour (albeit with continuous interruptions and wisecracks from the audience) on the topic of the advantages and disadvantages of aging on a kibbutz, there was a question-and-answer period. At its conclusion, one elderly man stood up and said the following:

> I want to bring up a few points. Shula's view is so broad, we could have a discussion for hours about what she said. [Someone shouted out "we could have several meetings."] In the last few years, we know that many people have studied the kibbutz—some lived the kibbutz life and some never even came to a kibbutz. They were all experts on analyzing such material. They wanted to dissect and expose all the problems of kibbutzim, including the problems of old age . . ..
>
> I want to also say that Shula's job was to study the problems of old age, but she made every possible effort to investigate and penetrate kibbutz life in general, and also to read and to interest herself in the history of the kibbutz and the kibbutz movement. I want to state that what she was able to do in these 10 months deserves our great respect. She had intended to study only old age, but she was *able to uncover additional problems*. To study the kibbutz way of life, and to

---

[27] I propose this idea as something different from the bureaucratic process of receiving institutional review board approval.

understand it, requires more than 10 months. There are many advantages and deficiencies that Shula still doesn't know about. [Someone shouts out: "She should come for another 10 months."]

I had the opportunity 13 years ago to help someone who did his doctorate on the kibbutz and then fled during the Six-Day War, and another person who sat with me and wanted information about demography, and another researcher who came from Belgium. [Of course, he is making himself very important here.] If I compare these people with the openness and charm of Shula (G—did you hear that?) when she met with people, then this all speaks well for her. I wish Shula the best of everything and thank her.

The story ends well—but it almost didn't. It almost collapsed midstream. The problem was one I had not anticipated because I had so little knowledge about this particular kibbutz. The problem was my sponsor himself.

RELYING ON MY SPONSOR

To express the significance of the "sponsor" in this project, I have to return to the beginning of the story, although I have just mentioned "the end." After I had been on the kibbutz for a little over two weeks and had gotten to know a few people, I asked for their recollections about what happened at the initial *sichat kibbutz* meeting when members debated whether or not I should be allowed to come. During one such conversation, I received a surprising bit of information:

> 18:4: I asked S, a *mazkir*, to tell me who had been in favor of, and who had been opposed to, the project. He said that at the general meeting no one spoke against it [this is an error, if one is to believe the minutes], *even though my sponsor ... had introduced the proposal!*

The *mazkir*'s comment confirmed what I was already feeling—that affiliation with my sponsor was going to become an important factor in how I would be perceived. As it turned out, the person who had invited and sponsored me had the reputation of a person who was difficult. Many people disliked him, and soon after getting to know him, I disliked him as well. Instead of my sponsor being my guide and protector, he became an irritant and real liability.[28] Thus, one of the selves I quickly had to create in the field was a person who could function independently of my sponsor even though he had made the whole project possible in the first place. I had to become a person who would demonstrate publicly that I could cope with this individual. I was dependent on him; neither I nor most others on the kibbutz could bear his company; and people saw us as a team. It was like being stuck in a bad marriage that I couldn't get out of until the children were grown.

In retrospect, I recognize that I actually benefited experientially from this exceedingly difficult relationship because many, if not most, kibbutz members

---

[28] The classic case of the seemingly ideal sponsor-researcher relation for a man was that of William Foote Whyte, whom a social worker introduced to Doc and with whom he gained access to all aspects of street corner society. See William Foote Whyte, *Street Corner Society: The Social Structure of an Italian Slum*, fourth edition (Chicago: University of Chicago Press, 1993); and Carol Stack's relation with Ruby in *All Our Kin* (New York: Harper & Row, 1974).

have at least one very strained relation on the kibbutz. On a kibbutz, if you have a strained relationship with someone, you nevertheless must live with him or her, and most likely you will see him or her many times a day. In fact, on a kibbutz people must remain in deeply interdependent relationships even with those individuals they despise. (Another analogy might be the possible negative relations among some tenured members of a university department, except that faculty members can find a way to keep their distance from one another.) Thus, because of problems with my sponsor, I could understand and empathize with the interpersonal problems of many kibbutz members. I now had such problems myself!

During the course of the year I learned about who was not speaking to whom now and who did not speak to whom in the past. I observed many people fighting with one another psychologically. Certainly a few people got along with everyone, but that was the exception, not the rule. Although I found my association with my sponsor to be very difficult at the time, in retrospect it may be have been useful in helping me empathize with others. I also began to marvel at the psychological stamina and coping mechanisms of the older kibbutz members who had lived with each other for years under these conditions. I also hypothesized that different kibbutzim probably have different psychological climates—both members and outsiders told me that Emek kibbutz members were particularly hard on each other.

Although my sponsor seemed to be undermining my work as much as supporting it, my husband, daughter, and I shared a table with his family every single Friday night of the year we were on the kibbutz. Sitting with this family in the large dining hall of the kibbutz each week when nearly everyone ate together reinforced to onlookers that the relationship between my family and his was solid. This was not the case. Nevertheless, I felt that to break the commitment to share our Friday night public meal together would have signaled to him that I wanted to make a serious, public statement. Neither could I afford to do this nor do I know who would have "taken us in" as a substitute family. If we had requested a change, we would have had to explain why—a very unappealing prospect.

At the end of my stay, I reviewed the steps I had taken to gain true social access rather than the simply bureaucratic access granted by the committee to this kibbutz. I listed ten steps, the first of which I have discussed here; the remainder I will refer to in subsequent sections. These steps include the following:

1. differentiating myself from the previous researchers who had studied this kibbutz and listening to advice about how to do my research;
2. freeing myself from my sponsor and getting new allies;
3. getting my daughter integrated into her children's house;
4. finding suitable workplaces for myself;
5. gaining permission to attend the *sichat kibbutz*;
6. obtaining invitations to attend committee meetings;
7. demonstrating that I trusted kibbutz policies and would adhere to them;
8. being very visible (e.g., using the pool nearly everyday with my daughter);

9. earning the trust and cooperation of each individual separately;
10. developing friendships.

As I will show, freeing myself from my sponsor's psychological grip and from the public presentation of ourselves as a working team was essential to my project. Unfortunately, it would take several months of hard daily work to achieve this goal.

From a methodological perspective, I learned about the significance of what happened before my entry, understanding the warnings that the members gave me, letting people tell me what to do, separating myself from my sponsor, getting other allies, and being tested (to be discussed in the next chapter). Only as this process unfolded would I begin to see symbols of acceptance. Entry into the field is circuitous and multifaceted rather than linear. It is not like walking into a room. Entry into a field setting is a continuous process of entry and reentry and, in my case, a continuous process of departure as well.

CHAPTER 2

Becoming Independent
of the Sponsor

Yali pouring a drink for my friend Ruth Gruschka (whose earrings Yali just borrowed).

Defining a research role for oneself is not entirely in one's hands. Instead, as I was to learn, it is tied, in part, to the person(s) who facilitates one's entry into the field and to how close that interpersonal tie is. In the next few pages, I explain the way this phenomenon developed in my project. Following the positive outcome of the vote taken at the *sichat kibbutz* that granted me entry to the kibbutz, one of the *mazkirim* began an exchange of letters with me in which we specified the conditions under which I would live in Kibbutz Emek. Seven months following the approval of the project, my two-year-old daughter and I moved to Kibbutz Emek with the formal status of "temporary members" for six months, renewable for another six months if the kibbutz and I agreed.

Each person on a kibbutz has a formal status. At the time of the study,[1] there were at least seven statuses on this kibbutz: (1) member (typically for life), (2) child of a member (under eighteen years of age), (3) soldier (currently serving in the army and not residing on the kibbutz), (4) parent of member, (5) Ulpanist (foreign Jewish volunteer learning Hebrew half a day and working in the kibbutz at an unskilled labor job the other half), (6) volunteer (typically non-Jewish individual from abroad who does not attend Hebrew classes), and (7) hired laborer (employee). A person's rights and responsibilities in the kibbutz are tied to his or her status. My category was unique—resident or temporary member—and thus required definition in terms of my duties and the services I would receive.

A few days after I arrived, I met with the *mazkirim* (two men, one about five years old than me and another about fifteen years older than me) and with my sponsor to work out the agreement and draw up an informal contract. We decided that the services I would receive included the following: a one-room apartment (called a *cheder*), daily meals, laundry service, child care, health care and health insurance, pocket money at the rate received by a member of my age and family status, telephone tokens, an English-language newspaper subscription, and haircuts. I would also receive some research help such as audiocassettes, photocopying, and bus fare for travel within Israel. (I never used the latter.) I would receive work shoes and work clothing and a clothing and shoe allowance for my daughter. As I was to learn, using these necessary services helped construct my *situational selves* while also enabling me to form relationships with kibbutz members that could aid in the research. As a resident (or, alternately, a temporary resident), I had role relationships with a broad range of kibbutz members and kibbutz institutions. My contract entitled me to use one of the kibbutz cars for occasional research-related local transportation if needed. (I did not use a car.) I would also receive weekend lodging, meals, and laundry service for my husband on the days he came to the kibbutz. I could bring guests to the dining room and have overnight guests in my room.

In exchange for this support, I agreed to work in a varied set of kibbutz employment branches[2] according to negotiations between the *sadranit avodah* (women's work organizer) and myself. We used the scale of eight working hours per day (generally 6:30 A.M.–2:30 P.M.) six days per week (not Saturdays), as was required of kibbutz members of my age and sex. They agreed that the six days

---

[1] This kibbutz's archives state that in 1965 the statuses were members, candidates for membership, children of members, young people who came from outside the kibbutz, young people from abroad, parents of members, temporary people, and people attending the Ulpan. There is now a new status—resident. This is a person who has bought a house on kibbutz land adjacent to the kibbutz and who may send his or her children to kibbutz schools. See Arik Mirovsky, "The Kibbutz Movement—Round Two," *Haaretz Weekly*, p. A7, March 28, 2008.

[2] Had I received the research grant, I still would have worked on the kibbutz as a way of learning about the kibbutz way of life and of meeting people. I don't believe the kibbutz leadership would have accepted payment for my stay, nor did I ask. At the time, there was little cash exchange among kibbutz members, and because they were asking for a report, one could just as well have argued that they could have paid me. In any case, I was not paid, nor did I pay anyone for my stay. Generally, in kibbutz society at the time, one paid in hours of labor.

would be divided between four days in regular kibbutz work and two days for research-related work. I also did all the "service rotations" required of women my age, including guarding the children's houses at night and taking care of groups of young children every fourth Saturday afternoon. My other Saturdays (Shabbat) were free to use as I wished. My work obligations made me similar (not identical) to a female kibbutz member my age (thirty-three years old). They also differentiated me from a guest who has no work obligation and from a volunteer who usually works in one branch only (typically requiring no Hebrew language skills, e.g., fruit picking) and does no guard duty rotations.

At the end of six months, I requested and received a few extra days "off" in order to prepare an *oral* report. (As it turned out, I also received, per my request late in the year, a month off from the regular work branches in order to prepare a *written* report for the kibbutz before my departure at the end of the year.) Upon my return to the United States, I offered individual kibbutz members copies of audiocassettes I made of my interviews of them for their use or for deposit in the kibbutz archives. The *mazkirim* gave me complete autonomy as to my research procedures, my report(s) to the kibbutz, and any publications that might ensue.

At the first meeting among the *mazkirim,* my sponsor, and myself, I realized that a problem might be brewing. (I will provide about thirty brief excerpts from my field notes to illustrate the evolution of this problem over time, with each field note labeled by the number of the day in the field.)

> 3:1: To my surprise, my sponsor opened the discussion with the *mazkirim* by announcing that I would say something about what I intended to do, and that we would then discuss practical matters. This threw me off guard, because I had not known I would be asked to present anything.[3] Nevertheless, I tried to rise to the occasion and spoke (in Hebrew) about doing a project whose goal would be to describe the situation of the elderly in Emek, to give the kibbutz suggestions as to what its problems are and how they might be resolved, and then to take the material and publish it for an outside audience. I talked about the first stage being used to develop relations with individuals on the kibbutz and with kibbutz institutions.
>
> A discussion ensued as to whether there would be contact with outside institutions, such as the kibbutz movement as a whole, research institutes, etc. They expressed the fear[4] that the research would become generalized and not specific to Emek. I assured them that I was doing a case study and would contact outsiders only for advice and consultation. For example, I might want to ask what arrangements there are for the elderly on other kibbutzim. They did not want the research to be "basic and statistical"; they preferred applied and practical.[5]

---

[3] In retrospect I see I was not assertive enough to simply say, "I'd like to discuss the 'contract' today and the project in a few days." Rather, I tried to be accommodating. My acquiescence to my sponsor's definition of the situation also reflected my newness on the kibbutz.

[4] I later saw that this fear was also expressed in the original discussion of the research project, held at the *sichat kibbutz.* Their concern was that this kibbutz not be exploited for a research project that would produce "useless" generalizations rather than "useful" material specific to this kibbutz.

[5] In retrospect it is interesting that in this conversation, only the sponsor, the *mazkirim,* and I were defining the research project. No one suggested that I convene members of a group of elderly people and find out what preferences *they* had!

I told them that I could not assure them that I could solve their problems. Also, I said that from my initial observations, they were doing some good things with regard to transportation, which severely hampers the ability of the elderly in urban and rural areas from getting the services they need. My intention was to say that they were probably doing something things very well and that they probably needed help in other areas. One of the *mazkirim* then told me about two problems he has noticed with regard to the elderly. . . .

The discussion seemed to be concerned with the *mazkirim* letting me know what they want and trying to decide whether or not I would conduct the research in a trustworthy manner. There was a certain wariness on their part and perhaps a testing of my ability to express myself (in Hebrew) and to demonstrate what my research values were. I felt that my character was being examined. I now know what their difficulty was. I had been on the kibbutz for only a short time, and they had witnessed no behavior of mine that would allow them to judge my character. All they knew about me was that I was being sponsored by this particular member.

The subtext of our conversation was that even though the *mazkirim* and I were trying to develop a clear agreement about the research, a problem had arisen already. This concerned whether or not I would be collaborating with my sponsor. From an ethical perspective, one could make the argument that we should have collaborated because that would have avoided the common practice of U.S. researchers studying communities in other countries without giving scholars in those countries the opportunity to participate. My sponsor was interested in collaborating; I was ambivalent; and the two *mazkirim* were opposed. From their perspective, the argument that it was fairer to the kibbutz to involve my sponsor was wrong! All three were members, and I was already caught in the middle. Sponsorship was becoming an ethical, methodological, and interpersonal problem even before the project had begun.

The following field notes demonstrate how the issue evolved during the first few days of my study:

> 2:1: My sponsor raised with me the question of our collaboration or my working alone. Also the issue of my research budget from the kibbutz. He wants to talk about these matters.
>
> 3:1: I went to my sponsor's house to tell him I had decided I would like to collaborate with him on the project. (I feel awkward rejecting him after he had made it possible for me to come here and I am not sure I can do the project without his assistance.) I said my major reservation, however, was confidentiality, in that one of my assets is my position as an outsider to whom people might feel able to speak freely. This asset would be lost if he were present during interviews or if people knew that everything they said would be available for his scrutiny. He seemed to understand the problem and had some suggestions:
>
> a) he does not want to interview everyone;
> b) he could be present at initial discussions and I could then have private in-depth ones;
> c) I could develop a code to preserve the anonymity of people I interview;
> d) If I made tapes, they could be transcribed so he wouldn't be able to identify the voice.

These are not effective solutions, and the problem loomed very large ahead of me. My next idea was to suggest that he be involved in aspects of the project other than the interviews, such as helping to examine the records in the *mazkirut*, working in the archives, leading me to appropriate literature or teaching me about history, etc.

Four days later:

7:1: Interview/discussion with my sponsor. Wide-ranging talk about what general activities we should undertake and what he should do for me. I asked him to provide me with the following:
  a) list of the committees of the kibbutz
  b) list of where everyone works
  c) map of the kibbutz
  d) list of cause and date of death of kibbutz members
  e) history of this kibbutz

I was using him as a highly informed research assistant, but then he began to try to carve out a role as my supervisor. He suggested I read all the articles on "old age and dying" in *Hedim*, the literary and social science journal of the kibbutz movement. I told him I had read the piece by Rachel Manor while resting. [I should try to finish reading it.] In the article she states that she "would like to die as she lived," but she didn't specify what that meant. She is a psychologist who taught at Oranim and who has recently retired. On the occasion of her retirement, people (including my sponsor) gave talks in her honor. His talk is published in *Hedim* as well. He respects her and wants me to meet her.

My sponsor described the "mourning committee," the cemetery, "the health committee," the bringing of parents (of members) to the kibbutz. He told me what he perceives the problems of the elderly to be:
  b) the differences between elderly members and non-members;
  c) the "social committee";
  d) whether or not the elderly are active in committees;
  e) the "culture committee." [He set up an interview appointment with Z and the two of us for tonight.]

This was a helpful interchange.

8:4: My sponsor set up an appointment for me to meet the founder of the kibbutz. . . . He also asked R of the "health committee" to meet with me concerning both her role and the experience of her father who lives in an old age home in Tel Aviv. [My sponsor] is carrying out a lot of the things I've asked him to do for me.

Five days later we carried out our first "joint interview" of a kibbutz member. In addition, my sponsor began to convey information to me from the *mazkirut*. Both made me uneasy.

13:1: Reminder to myself: Ask my sponsor to get me *Shdemot* (a journal) and to not interrupt or disagree when a person is speaking during an interview.
My sponsor said the *mazkirut* has two questions for me:
  a) how can I assure confidentiality given *his* participation; similarly, how can I assure objectivity;

b) where can I work? [since I should be effective in my work] We decided that when I meet with them, I would say that my sponsor would be involved in all aspects of the study except the interviews. He will not have access to the tapes.

The sponsor and his wife were my only contact on the kibbutz in the early phase. But soon that was to change.

[15:1: My sponsor and his wife had cake with my husband and me.[6] My sponsor then left on a one-week study trip abroad.]

Unconsciously perhaps, I took advantage of my freedom and the opportunity to talk to the sponsor's wife without his presence.

[16:2: My sponsor's wife brought me the map her husband had given her to give me . . . I asked her how she feels when her husband is away and she said she enjoys it.]

16:3: I spontaneously invited C to come for an interview and he did. The entire interview is recorded on tape.

In hindsight, the significance of this "spontaneous invitation" was that I was testing whether or not I could approach people and set up interviews on my own. I also "unconsciously" chose to interview a man who, in addition to being a neighbor, was the father of a *mazkir*. Thus, if the father accepted and even enjoyed the experience, I presumed he would tell his son, and this information would reverberate on the official meeting I would have with the son in his role as *mazkir*. Things worked out as I planned. And, as it turned out, I was not the only one taking advantage of my sponsor's absence.

17:1: I was called to a meeting by one of the *mazkirim* who came into the *beit yeladim* [a building where groups of 6 young children live] where I was washing dishes with Yali's *metapelet* [my daughter's day care worker]. The *mazkir* abruptly asked me to stop what I was doing and come to a meeting.

Unbeknownst to me, the *mazkir*'s "agenda" was to have me function separately from my sponsor. The *mazkir* was taking advantage of my sponsor's being abroad, just as I had unconsciously done. This may account for the fact that the meeting was called so suddenly.

17:1: On the way to the impromptu meeting, I walked home quickly to get the list of points I had been accumulating for discussion and to pick up my tape recorder. When I got to the meeting, I discovered that the other *mazkir* opposed my taping, although the *mazkir* whose father I had interviewed didn't mind. That *mazkir* said, "Here on the kibbutz we try to influence each other and not to stand on tapes of what we have said to one another." [In other words, he interpreted my desire to tape as my lack of trust of him! Although I wanted to tape in order to make sure I would follow through on all the agreements and be trustworthy!] I decided not to tape so as to avoid offense.

---

[6] This is a typical Saturday afternoon ritual—visiting someone in his or her home and having cake and coffee. The woman typically bakes the cake or cakes herself.

We then began to review the contract among my sponsor, the kibbutz, and me.

> 17:2: The *mazkir* who preferred not to be taped explained that he had talked to my sponsor in the kitchen[7] about the problem they were going to raise, and I, too, said I had discussed it with him. Basically, the *mazkirim* are opposed to the research being done as a partnership between the sponsor and myself. They said it had not been presented that way to the *sichat kibbutz*,[8] nor did they see that arrangement serving the interests of objectivity. They were concerned that every suggestion my sponsor makes to help me will influence the way I see things. Also, the sponsor is perceived as a 'theoretician' and not as someone who is good in practical matters. Conclusions presented to the kibbutz in both of our names will not be as well received as if just I presented them alone. Moreover, the social worker flatly refuses to participate in the research partly because of him. She didn't even answer his request to participate and told one of the *mazkirim* about her decision. Clearly she can't get along with my sponsor.
>
> I explained that my sponsor and I had talked about the issue of his role and he had agreed that he would help me
>
> 1) in the first stages to get to know people and to set up appointments with them; and
> 2) to prepare questions. I gave the example of Z and A.*

Even with that, the *mazkir* claimed that my sponsor might suggest certain questions and not others. The *mazkir* did not come out and say that if they had been presented initially with a joint project, they would not have accepted it. They want someone to come "from the outside and see what's going on." The *mazkir* said that if my sponsor published in *Hedim*, where it is expected he would publish, it is possible that some people would be hurt by what he writes. They don't want him to be involved in joint publication.

This meeting gave me the push I needed to resolve my ambivalence. I could distance myself from my sponsor "because" of the *mazkirim*. Little did I know, however, that my sponsor would reject the *mazkirim*'s perspective and try to continue to collaborate with me. He was not a pushover, and he believed I owed it to him to allow him into the project.

During nearly the entire duration of my time in the field, I tried to establish a self as independent as possible of my sponsor. In the early part of the year, this was quite difficult because kibbutz members justifiably saw my sponsor and me as having important ties. One kibbutz member, for instance, told me he assumed I was a Marxist because my sponsor was known to be a Marxist. Fortunately some members queried me about my relation to him rather than assuming they knew what it was.

> 31:3: Lunch with M. He asked if my sponsor and I are doing this project together and I said that he is helping me, answering my questions and providing me with information, but not getting involved in the interviews because of

---

[7] On the kibbutz, people discuss business with each other wherever they happen to meet, in this case in the kitchen of the kibbutz.

[8] I do not know why the sponsor did not present this structure at the *sichat kibbutz*, but the project might have been aborted from the start if he had.

professional confidentiality. I don't report to him what I say or hear. I gave as an example that I asked him for a list of all the committees.

Because the question of my relation to the sponsor seemed important to the community, I actively tried to spread the news about our actual arrangement, stating it very carefully in case what I said got back to him. I tried to be meticulous about acknowledging that he did have a role but that the role will not jeopardize the confidentiality I hoped to be able to establish with kibbutz members. I believe that because I succeeded to a large extent in conducting the study in ways that conformed to the expectations of the *mazkirim* and that satisfied my desire for independence, my sponsor was frustrated and retaliated by undermining me in subtle ways.

> 48:2: My sponsor came by my *cheder* at 2:30. He wanted to see my library, i.e. the books I had brought with me. Talked about what the *mazkirim* had said. He thinks that we should operate "as usual" until the *mazkirim* demand otherwise. He agrees that I can sign alone the conclusions I will write. He still wants to remain involved, even to attend some interviews, but I tried to indicate it would be best for me and for the kibbutz members if I did the interviews alone.
>
> I told him what one of the *mazkirim* had said he sees as the purpose of the project, i.e. a list of the needs of the elderly. My sponsor thought that was silly, since a simple questionnaire, or a suggestion box, or talking to one of the people who works closely with the elderly could handle it. . . .
>
> He said he could guess what everyone I interviewed had said. He asked why I had spoken with the *mazkir*. Was it in his role as *mazkir* or as the son of the man I had interviewed? He also asked why I had interviewed C.
>
> In order to steer the conversation back to what the *mazkirim* and I had agreed on and get him back into the role of research assistant rather than research partner, I told him I'd like help with:
> a) Ages of all members and residents;
> b) Work assignments of everyone;
> c) Family relations;
> d) Where everyone lives;
> e) The percentage of people leaving the kibbutz at different times. We agreed that group should measure this.
> f) Who has the power on the kibbutz and what age group holds the positions of power?

Clearly I was trying to negotiate roles for each of us. I was trying to free myself from my sponsor and establish an independent research role, relying on him for help that did not involve his interacting with kibbutz members while I was interviewing them.

> 54:1: At the home of A and R. A opened the conversation by asking if I was working alone or with my sponsor. I answered, 'I am working alone, but my sponsor is helping me as a . . . mediator [A's term].' R asked if my sponsor would sign the report that I would give. I said, 'No.' I gave the example of asking my sponsor for the list of committees since I didn't want to bother the *mazkir* all the time. People want to know how I met my sponsor in the first place. I tell them about my book.

57:2: My sponsor came over to my room and gave me a book on large kibbutzim.

59:1: My sponsor's evolving roles:

a) Fighting battles for me;
b) Setting up special interviews (e.g. the kibbutz founder; a prominent sociologist);
c) Interpreting events for me that I don't understand;
d) Informing me about what's going on;
e) Helping me prepare questions before I interview people whom I don't know.

62:1: My sponsor came over to my *cheder* from about 2:30–4:00. He gave me various materials I had requested, including the birth date of everyone on the kibbutz membership list. I asked him to read the few pages of Tiger and Shepher's[9] book that are concerned with the political system and tell me what is different here in this kibbutz from the one that Tiger and Shepher describe. I asked him if minutes are kept of meetings, telling him that I think it's a good idea. But he kept on saying that things are informal here, and that it's unnecessary to increase the bureaucracy.[10] It makes me wonder what kind of suggestions he [or the kibbutz] could really implement. His rationale is always "I know it from experience." He's hard to convince of anything. I'm worried that I'll never be able to get any suggestions past him that he doesn't agree with . . .

64:1: My sponsor said he had dictated all of the *mazkir's* letters to me (implying that I had no special relation with the *mazkir,* and that my sponsor was omniscient). He also said that the things written about me in the kibbutz's internal newsletter don't have much weight because the *mazkir* wrote them. In other words, he is undermining my thinking that I have an independent relationship with the *mazkir,* while also undermining the *mazkir* himself for being unintelligent, i.e. not worth having a relationship with.

I asked my sponsor about people who have parents that live outside the kibbutz. He provided me with a list, also containing some names that he wasn't certain of.

I showed my sponsor a letter I had received from a U.S. scholar who had studied the kibbutz and showed him his paper. Gave these to him to read.

Asked my sponsor for *Israel Statistical Yearbook.* The fact that he's a professor helps me in the sense that he has access to a library.

Later in the day he stopped by with a book he has just received—a bibliography on utopias. He asked me if I wanted to give a talk at a one-day conference in January. I agreed. (He seems to want to establish himself as a co-professor in my eyes.)

He told me his problems. He is trying to arrange for another researcher to come, but this person (whom I know) thinks he can just deposit his daughter in the *beit yeladim* and then go off and do his thing. Impossible. He wants to consult with me on the arrangements for this person's visit. I gave my sponsor my book and an article I had written.

---

[9] Lionel Tiger and Joseph Shepher, *Women in the Kibbutz* (New York: Harcourt Brace Jovanovich, 1975).

[10] He was right. 173:3: The *mazkir* came into the *communa* [public laundry] while I was working there and I told him I wanted to extend my stay on the kibbutz since there was so much to do. Thus, in this informal way, my contract was extended to a year.

I was trying hard to define a type of professional collaboration, to please him, and to do things "right" because he had enabled me to do the project in the first place. But it wasn't working.

66: 1: My sponsor criticizes me for working too hard. He thinks I don't enjoy myself enough. Am I trying to prove to him that I am working hard? Am I suffering from some sort of guilt? Or is he simply undermining me so that I will depend on him more?

Dinner with my sponsor and his wife. Later in the evening he introduced me to K, the archivist who works 6:30–8:00 a.m. and 8:15–11:30 a.m. I said I would like to talk.

67:1: I am very sick with the flu. My sponsor's wife was very helpful to me and to Yali.

68:1: My sponsor came at about 8:30 a.m. and we talked for 3 hours. Taped our conversation. He wants to conceive of the project as a joint one with a co-authored paper at the end. [He is still talking about this although 2½ months have passed!] He said he would approach an academic colleague for a budget and will get someone to transcribe/translate the tapes. We spoke about a wide range of subjects including the fact that, according to him, women are not fulfilling their potential because they have so many children.

My relation with my sponsor is continuously evolving and terribly confusing. He said we will have many more discussions about our collaboration. He picked up cues from me that I think of myself as working alone in this project. That was the way I presented myself to Shepher when we went to visit him. This is becoming one of the worst parts of the project. How did it turn out this way? I was suspicious from the start since he seemed like an abrasive character. Yet, he is also helpful.

77:7: I had the idea of observing classrooms, and my sponsor's wife immediately asked permission of a teacher for me.

80:3: My sponsor came over to me while I was eating and brought paper and pencil, so I could take notes later at the Erev Yom Kippur[11] meeting [actually so he could take notes for me since he thought I would not obtain permission to attend the meeting.] He implied that the reason he was going to take notes was that he "knew" I didn't trust his telling me what happened. But then he said that he agreed I needed to form my own opinions.

We then got into what I considered to be an unpleasant discussion concerning a difference of opinion. He said, "Who are you to tell me about the kibbutz?"[12]

---

[11] Kibbutz Emek had eschewed religion, yet it did celebrate Jewish holidays in redefined ways. Yom Kippur is the holiest day of the year among Jews, and Erev Yom Kippur is the evening before the day. On this kibbutz, an open discussion is held on Erev Yom Kippur during which people try to assess how things stand on the kibbutz.

[12] As early as 1958, Eva Rosenfeld published an article on this topic, entitled "The American Social Scientist in Israel: A Case of Role Conflict," *American Journal of Orthopsychiatry* 28:163–171, 1958: "A social scientist from abroad is essentially a stranger to the kibbutznik, a potentially dangerous person who, himself uncommitted, tampers with sacred things, and might touch on repressed doubts and spark off anxiety. This observer may experience expressions of oversensitivity or 'touchiness' on the part of the kibbutznik, whose discomfort is often related to criteria of judgment. The kibbutz members pose this question to the sociologist: 'Do you really believe that someone who does not accept our way of life is capable of judging how successful we are?' . . . The kibbutznik often

What annoyed me were his argumentativeness and his idea that neither I nor anyone else can tell him anything. Am I not here in order to tell him things about his kibbutz?

Later, one of the *mazkirim* informed me that I was welcome to attend the Yom Kippur meeting. I took my own notes. The discussion that ensued was heartfelt and revealing.

Like many relationships in life, my relation with my sponsor was never entirely one thing or another. As hard as I tried to remain separate from him, we were always linked in people's minds. When I met with people, even informally, they frequently brought up his name.

> 96:7: N: "I think your sponsor is vulgar although he did impress women, including me, formerly. Do not show this transcript to him."

He and I occasionally continued to have dinner together, adding new layers of complication.

> 88:4: Dinner with my sponsor and his wife. He asked how my interview went with H. I said 'interesting' in order to be non-committal. But, also I said it was "all an introduction." She said, "With him it is always an introduction; he never gets around to the essence." I said, "He understands my method better than anyone else." She said, "He is intelligent." She wanted to know if he told me *his* background, by which she meant about the death of his wife. She also wanted to know what questions he asked me. I said (vaguely) that he talked about the past, present, and future, his work and his family. But even though I was vague, I wonder if I was divulging too much even in these generalizations. What is my sponsor's wife's role in this project? Later that day I went to his house and participated in an argument with him and his wife about the cause of his wife's excessive fatigue. My sponsor visited me constantly in my *cheder*. He is draining my energy.
>
> 101:4: My sponsor came over and gave me more materials. I told him that I would be meeting S again tonight and he said this would lead to trouble if I interviewed people twice, although some people are worth it. He suggested that for S the relevant topics were—the fact that all his children are off the kibbutz, and the nature of his work. My sponsor said he does not know what S does. He told me about last night's *sichat kibbutz,* which I had not been able to attend. . . . A new "absorption committee" was voted in, but my sponsor says it doesn't matter since there aren't any people to absorb.[13] I said maybe they could continue to work with those who have already been absorbed but who still need extra help such as learning Hebrew. My sponsor said that a club for this purpose was set up last year, but one person refused to attend if a certain other person did attend, so it fell apart. My sponsor disagreed with the *mazkir's* statement that everyone is working to capacity. Rather, he felt that some people are "parasites" (the worst reputation one

---

teases the observer by challenging his ability to understand collective life truly, without being so committed."

[13] In kibbutz terminology, "absorption" refers to helping newcomers (i.e., new potential members) to get integrated into kibbutz life.

could have on a kibbutz).[14] He told me about other controversies that arose during the meeting. We then planned when we would be going to the university together. Finally, he gave me newspaper clippings concerning aging on the kibbutz, including one describing "Yom HaVatik" (Senior Day) in a different kibbutz.

Although my sponsor continued to assist me by providing information and resources, he gradually became more removed, which was painful to him but necessary for me and for the viability of the project. I tried to be cordial but distant. Other people who don't get along on the kibbutz typically still agree to help each other within the kibbutz framework. That's what we did. Moreover, it would have been difficult for me to not have a reliable relationship with a family on the kibbutz in case I needed help. The dilemma of the creation of a responsible research self was thus exacerbated by my reliance on his family as a kind of adoptive family on the kibbutz. How could I spend some time with them socially without collaborating with him and without being perceived by everyone as allied with him? How could I deal with the fact that the person who made me miserable was the person I relied on?

> 115:9: Visited my sponsor and his wife after the consultation with the gerontologist. My sponsor's wife annoyed me to no end, as did he. I won't go there any more for social visits. All they did was argue with me. What the hell am I doing this study for if they pounce on me, saying everything I say is wrong? Either I won't say anything, or I will tell them to stop it. I left there feeling miserable. I want nothing to do with them because they do not treat me with respect.
>
> My sponsor set up a meeting with the *mazkirim* for Wednesday at noon. He didn't attend the meeting today with the gerontologist since all of a sudden he is "staying out of the research as requested by the *mazkirim*."

Messages started to come in from peacemakers.

> 139:1: R, a friend of my sponsor's, talked to me about him at length, as if to "explain" him. She told me how he came to this country at the age of 14 or 15 from an Eastern European country; how he was against education, went to agricultural school, and became very political, started lecturing but in a boring way. Never 'knew how to work well'[15] on the kibbutz. Started studying for a degree late in life, doesn't know languages well unlike his wife who knows Hebrew well, and unlike R's own husband. According to this friend, my sponsor is a clever man, particularly because he is so eager to find out what the latest developments are in everything. When he went to America, he didn't stick to his topic, but visited, learned, etc.

In the fifth month, we were pretty much stuck where we started.

> 172:2: Started typing notes about the book [I was reading concerning the origins of this kibbutz's founders] when my sponsor came in to my apartment to find out how I was doing. He brought my spirits way down since he said

---

[14] A parasite is a free loader, someone who doesn't work as hard as everyone else and yet receives all the benefits of a regular kibbutz member.

[15] This psychological phrase forgives a person who doesn't fulfill his or her job requirements on the kibbutz.

1) My mentioning to him that a little girl is sick is not what people are talking about; only those in her circle would talk about it. When a group of his friends met at her grandfather's, they talked politics, not 'who's sick.' Issues such as 'who's sick?' used to be printed in the kibbutz information sheet, but it's not coming out right now.

2) He thinks my reading on the origins of the kibbutz members is going too far afield. If I start doing things like that, I'll never finish the project.

3) One of the *mazkirim* wants me to make a presentation to the *mazkirut* since my sponsor did so in context of 'reorganization' talk he gave there recently. This is part of the *mazkirut*'s effort not to be reactive only. I didn't know about this. Did I get the newsletter?

4) Talked about medical records. He said I won't have access. Wants to get started on 'our paper.' Borrowed my book, *Aging and the Social Sciences.* Mocked my husband and me for planning our trip to Jerusalem in detail. When he left, I continued studying from the book about origins—with a defiant spirit.

The sixth month:

183:3: I left sponsor's house feeling undermined for every interpretation and comment I made. My sponsor said we should get together tomorrow so I can tell him what information I need.

199:8: I stopped by at his house to give him papers. He has been reading on aging and wants to know if we will still be writing. I told him about the fact that I will be interviewing E tonight. He said E's wife might have been more interesting. (So what else is new?)

204:1: My husband believes I am not handling my sponsor correctly. I should be nastier to him since he has a nasty way of talking to me. But I cannot respond quickly enough, and to respond slowly has no purpose. It's not my language or my style!

208:1: Got ready for my sponsor. Had a useful session with him.

The seventh month:

216:2: His wife came to invite my husband and me to stop by their home that evening . . . When we arrived, we first talked about the *sichat kibbutz,* the second meeting in a row that my sponsor missed. He asked what I would say at the *mazkirut* meeting and I gave him an outline, but he complained that it had no content. In front of my husband!

The eighth month:

240:3: Saw D. She said I should tell my sponsor that L, who is pregnant, needs to sit up front when we take the truck to the city; she wants to know who is driving, etc. The interesting thing here is that people still see my sponsor and me as some sort of a unit.

240:5: Went to my sponsor's house since he called me over while I passed by. He and his wife were entertaining his former students, R [high-ranking army officer] and N who wants to study psychology now that she finished MA in philosophy. My sponsor was bragging. I was not holding my ground. He tells them to ask me—in front of me—where they can study management. Her father is a member of a different kibbutz and is the organizer of all things concerning the elderly there. He takes courses, brings in lecturers on gerontology, visits places, etc. He is 66 and feels younger, loves it. My sponsor laughing that there will always be elderly. His wife said that I will help. Said situation is not bad here for them.

The tenth month:

> 322:1: Our friends from Jerusalem didn't visit us in part because their host at the kibbutz they are visiting hates my sponsor and wouldn't come. What problems has his sponsorship caused me that I don't even know about? Our friends' host on the other kibbutz told our friends that my sponsor has a terrible reputation.

Parting gestures:

> 352: Last day on the kibbutz. Squeezed in one more interview. Dropped off my report at my sponsor's. Thanked him for his help. He said this was "inappropriate."

My field notes outline several strategies I took to become independent of my sponsor and to develop an independent research self. I succeeded to a certain extent, but it was certainly unpleasant. The closest analogy I can find is to arrive in a foreign country to enter into an arranged marriage with a stranger from which there was no divorce option. This analogy recognizes that there is a structural element to the problem I encountered. In addition, the process I went through is unlikely to be unique to me because marginal people typically are the link with outsiders, including researchers. Having the researcher rely on the marginal person is a liability that requires work to overcome. But there is also a psychological or individual element. How my research might have been different with a different kind of sponsorship is a question I asked myself throughout. Was there anyone else who would have brought me in in the first place?

CHAPTER 3

Gaining Allies, Overcoming Antagonists, Being Tested

The director of egg production, working.

In order to get out from under the thumb of my sponsor, I tried to develop a strong relation to formal authority figures—that is, the *mazkirim*, people I hoped would have more power than he did.[1] Fortunately, the role they took aided me psychologically in the first stage of the project. I think it would have been impossible to extricate myself from my sponsor's imposing ways had it not been for them. Being involved in this process had the advantage of teaching me about the importance of

---

[1] The degree to which anyone has authority over anyone else in the kibbutz is open to question because the society is entirely voluntary. The elected *mazkirim* and all the committees make decisions, as does the *sichat kibbutz,* but there is no way to enforce them. As I was told repeatedly, "there are no police on the kibbutz. You have to persuade people to do what they are supposed to do."

kibbutz politics. Some elderly members told me—in a corroborating way—that sometimes they wait for an election of new kibbutz officers (e.g., *mazkirim*) so that they can deal with a particular *mazkir* when they are trying to solve a problem.[2] Given their lengthy experience on the kibbutz, the elderly have learned to work the system well.

A month and a half after I arrived, one of the *mazkirim* ended his term of office, and the kibbutz elected a new *mazkir*.

> 47:5: My sponsor told me that the new *mazkir* had been on the *mazkirut* last year and was opposed to "our" project. I am concerned. Therefore, although I have no formal obligation to renegotiate/review my contract with him, I decided to ask him to meet with me, simply for informational purposes. I want to make sure I had his cooperation.

At first it seemed that the cooperation I would receive from the new *mazkir* would be only grudging because I was told he (182:1) "has no patience for the academics who contribute 'nothing' to the kibbutz." Moreover, my sponsor liked to tell me how close he was to the new *mazkir* and how I needed *his* help to get the *mazkir* on my side. On the other hand, after I met the new *mazkir*, I learned that we had something in common—he had a graduate degree from a university in the United States.[3] He did not dismiss out of hand what I had to offer as long as I also worked in a kibbutz labor branch. But he was skeptical about me for another reason—he thought I would assume arrogantly that I knew more than I did.

In fact, I found that he seemed to actually enjoy talking with me privately in my role as an academic. What he wanted to avoid was public acknowledgment of this shared interest because association with me might have highlighted his own outsider status. As I was to discover, the distinction between public and private turned out to be highly charged on the kibbutz. Some people (my sponsor, for example) claimed that nothing is private on the kibbutz in the sense that everyone knows everything about everyone.[4] There are no secrets. If this is so, then people feel pressure to make their private selves "as good as" their public selves because a back stage is not available for hiding the "bad self." Goffman's term, *back stage*,[5] is useful because it points to the strong public space in the case of the kibbutz. I believe the claim that there is no privacy on the kibbutz is exaggerated. Even in prisons with maximum surveillance, inmates are able to create private spaces that others can't access. There likely is a range of degrees of privacy among social settings, and the kibbutz is surely in the section where privacy is limited. My arrival in the kibbutz may have allowed people to carve out a little more private space for themselves, a space where they could discuss things with me that were not be available to others. The elderly gain privacy on the kibbutz as they become less

---

[2] I was also told, but cannot corroborate that this is true, that women timed their pregnancies to coincide with the rotation into the job of a particular child-care worker.

[3] Later in the book, I will discuss the meaning of being an American.

[4] At the time, only personal effects were privately owned; all other property belonged to the kibbutz as a whole.

[5] Erving Goffman, *The Presentation of Self in Everyday Life* (New York: Anchor Books, 1959).

mobile and thus less public, but their privacy is vulnerable as others are compelled to enter their space to care of their physical needs. On the other hand, people do not join kibbutzim in order to gain privacy. Just the opposite. I observed the mobile elderly trying to be as public as possible so as to assert that they were still active and valuable kibbutz assets.

This new *mazkir* may have been concerned that because he was not born in a kibbutz, kibbutz-born members might perceive him as not a "real" kibbutznik.[6] He was new on the job and had to prove himself. Generally he seemed to accept my presence as long as I avoided unnecessary demands on him and was self-sufficient. As a new *mazkir,* and like any other organizational leader, he had enough work as it was and didn't need any superfluous burdens. Our conversation was bureaucratic in terms of redefining my rights and responsibilities, but he also revealed a few things about how he planned to carry out his role as *mazkir.*

> 186:2: I met with [the new *mazkir*] in his office from 9:00–10:00 a.m. I asked him if I was talking with the old *sadran avodah* or the new *mazkir* (i.e. in which role was he having this conversation?). He said he is trying to "force a crisis" on the kibbutz so that it will deal with the problem of not having a *sadran avodah.* On the other hand, "the kibbutz has a kind of inertia which allows it to continue to function even if certain tasks are not filled . . ."
>
> He wanted to know if I needed anything from the kibbutz. I said all was fine, but that I wanted to work only 2 days per week in the future and have 2 months off at the end. He said that was OK, but I must inform the "sadranit avodah." He wants to set up a meeting with the *mazkirut* and my sponsor and the coordinator of the "committee on elderly issues" in one month to hear an interim report. I recommended that we not have too many committees involved at once. Accepted. In terms of final report, I told him I would write it in English, and my problem was who will translate it and how it will be disseminated.
>
> I asked him whether or not a new social worker would start to work at Emek. [I would have liked to work with such a person.] He said that the previous social worker no longer works here because she has received only one day per week release time from her kibbutz and is using that time to work in a different kibbutz.
>
> He doesn't think social work is such a great thing anyhow, except may be for individual therapy. "To just 'listen' is kind of 'silly,'" he said. Emek has applied for a social worker from the social work department of the main kibbutz movement, but there is a long waiting list(!) He is interested in accepting only a social worker that is a kibbutz member since otherwise it takes a year for them to figure out what a kibbutz is. [I said "½ year" thinking of myself.] I asked to be kept informed re this and to meet whoever is 'hired.' He agreed to my keeping the tapes of my interviews until I translate them. He also agreed to meet on Thursday morning for a more personal discussion. He set aside from 9:00–12:00 although I had asked for only an hour or two!

Later when we had our private discussion in his home, rather than in his office, I recognized that he was torn about the fact that he was a person with an academic degree who was not working as an academic but had just become a *mazkir.* He expressed some of the historic ambivalence in kibbutzim toward academia.

---

[6] Informal way of referring to a kibbutz member.

He also expressed considerable disdain for the United States. He probably would have appreciated me more if I had been an Israeli social scientist, preferably a kibbutz member who was a social scientist.[7] My husband also got to know this new *mazkir* but found his extreme anti-U.S. attitude difficult to tolerate, particularly his attitude that (238:1) "All crazy things come from America." I tried to prevent my husband's attitudes toward the *mazkir* from affecting my relationship with him, recognizing that although my husband is originally an Israeli, his academic position combined with his lack of work on the kibbutz probably intensified the *mazkir's* desire to express anti-American sentiments. Also, the fact that my husband was born in Israel and is now an American did not enhance the *mazkir's* appreciation of him because emigrating from Israel was considered abandonment of the country.[8] Nevertheless, he invited me to give a brief report on my work to the head of the entire kibbutz movement, a man who was planning to visit Emek toward the end of my stay.

From my experience, I understand how important the cooperation of the *mazkirim* is. In general, *mazkirim* are interested in having the kibbutz follow through on decisions made in committees and in *sichot kibbutz*. Because my project had been endorsed during a *sichat kibbutz,* my case fell into this category. In order to sustain the *formal* authority the *mazkirim* exercised on my behalf, I engaged in continuous role-reinforcing conversations from the start of my stay.

> 9:3: I saw one of the *mazkirim* on the path. He asked me how things were going. I said "Well . . ." He then asked me a question about my research: Do I ask people specific questions or let them speak freely? When I said the latter, he said that people can talk a lot without getting to the point. For example, Z can take ½ hour to say something that should take a minute. I told him I want people to feel free to talk, although I might later want to ask them specific questions. He said he took a course for *mazkirim* and they had a lecturer come in and explain how you can actually learn something from what people tell you! I mentioned that I let people talk and that I interject 'why?' from time to time. He was delighted.

---

[7] Many kibbutz members are themselves social scientists who study the kibbutz. See, for example, Avraham Yassour (ed.), *Kibbutz Members Analyze the Kibbutz* (Cambridge, MA: Institute for Cooperative Community, 1977), although people who are not kibbutz members contributed numerous items to the collection as well. See also Zvi Lavi (ed.), *Kibbutz Members Study Kibbutz Children* (New York: Greenwood Press, 1990).

[8] In the 1930s, 1940s, and 1950s, those who lived in Israel sometimes defined those who left as traitors. The same was true for those who left a kibbutz for nonkibbutz Israeli life. In his article, "Becoming a Kibbutz Founder: An Ethnographic Study of the First All-American Kibbutz in Israel," *Jewish Social Studies* 46(2):13–130, 1984, John Snarey wrote: "It was the custom of the kibbutz for departing individuals to come before the general assembly meeting to explain or, as some felt, 'to confess' why they were not staying. As more people began to leave, and as those who were remaining became consequently more demoralized, many remember that these sessions became painful, cruel, and brutal. Incriminations were often unmercifully fired at the departing person, the 'traitor.' The departing person often felt guilt or remorse" (p. 122).

The positive feedback that the *mazkirim* received from others, including from their own parents, concerning my interviewing contributed to their ability to be supportive of me.

> 18:4: S came up to me in the dining room to say he thought I would need help, but he sees I'm managing very nicely because I talked to his father last night and saw his photo album. His father had asked him if I found what he said to be interesting. I told his son that I wanted to interview *him* (the son) next. We tried to set up a time but he has meetings in the evenings and he has to do something for the army. But he'll be in touch. I said I'd like to speak with T and he thought he'd be agreeable.

Clearly the *mazkirim* were helpful to me in carving out a research role separate from my sponsor, but I needed to find my own way around as well. Another equally effective strategy was to try to get other individuals as allies and friends so that I could replace my dependence on my sponsor. Fortunately I found that some individuals on Emek reached out to me from the start, just as I did to them. From the beginning, people approached me, enabling me to explain to each one individually what my project was about.

> 5:2: Met E at the swimming pool where she was taking care of her daughter just as I was of mine. She initiated a conversation about where I was from, etc. I explained the project. She immediately told me what she thought the problems of the elderly were . . . She said she would be interested to see if what she considers to be problems are also the problems others mention.

In other words, at the same time I was trying to deal with formal sponsorship, I attempted to gain the cooperation of each individual separately.

> 18:1: Played a little with the kids, while D watched. Since I was sitting next to her, I asked her if she knew why I had come, and she said that M had told her. Taking advantage of 'interviewing' one young person, I asked her what she thought of the conditions for the elderly at Emek.
>
> 22:1: Sat at lunch with M . . . Then two women and a man [I don't know their names] joined us and M left. I introduced myself to one of them who then asked me who I was—an Ulpanist? a volunteer? a guest? I said, "None of the above, but rather a researcher." I asked her if she remembers that the kibbutz invited this study. I told her I am not doing this for myself but rather for the kibbutz. That I already have my degree and a job. But that the kibbutz said there's a problem needing investigation. She remembered.
>
> I said it would be specific to Emek, that I am aiming for a description of the state of the elderly, including their health, work, etc. If I discover problems, I will list these and possible solutions. I told her my way of working is to invite people to drink a cup of coffee and tell me about their lives and perhaps to answer specific questions. Sometimes I tape the discussion with their permission. [We then talked about many different aspects of kibbutz life for about half an hour.] I told them I would be working half time on the study and hoped they would help me. The man wished me luck, and I invited the women to come some time and talk. I said I need their help. One said I should just talk to everyone and I'd find lots of different opinions.

23:1: For breakfast I plunked myself down next to a white-haired man . . . He eventually asked me if I was a guest of my sponsor's. When I told him I was looking for a place to work that would be best for my research, he said it wasn't worth my time working in the laundry since *only elderly women* worked there. I explained that I have had meetings with the *mazkirim,* and he said, 'But they are younger than you!' (not true). So he clearly did not grasp what I was talking about.

27:4: Got a phone-call while I was in the dining room. The guy who answered the phone said, "It's for you, Laura." But when I said I wasn't Laura, he said it was for the person who was taking care of the elderly. How did he know that I was doing it, and that it was me?

33:3: Lunch with B. She said she doesn't go to the *sichat kibbutz* any more, so she didn't know the circumstances around my coming. "May be it's just as well," she said, "so you can explain it to everyone individually."

38:4: When I visited T (an elderly woman) in the hospital, she told me she knew what I had come to Emek to do. She called the elderly, "people over 70" and asked me what I had concluded! She asked about me, where I learned Hebrew, whether I want to come to live on the kibbutz, etc. The (kibbutz) doctor came in and asked whether this woman was one of my statistics. I said I was interested in her, but not statistically.

41:1: N said she knew I had come here to do research on the elderly and I explained that it was *for* the kibbutz. She asked me how I was getting my information. I said, "I talk to everyone."

174:4: Talked with Y. She had been uneasy about the project, but now sees I'm not treating them like guinea pigs, but working and living among them. Why don't I become a member?[9] Other people say they've enjoyed talking with me. "Come again!" she said.

I worked hard to destroy the perception that I was an agent of my sponsor by nearly never mentioning him when introducing myself.

OVERCOMING ANTAGONISTS

In addition to their carrying out the decision of the *sichat kibbutz* and supporting my attempts to extricate myself from my sponsor, the *mazkirim* were helpful in other ways. One example is the case of antagonistic individuals who seemed threatened by my presence. These individuals actually attempted to undermine my work. I was surprised to learn that one of these was the kibbutz social worker! When I arrived at the kibbutz, she was about to end her term of helping its members. Nevertheless, she seemed to perceive me as a competitor. This social worker was a member of a different kibbutz and had worked a few days per month on Kibbutz Emek for the previous four years. She may have thought that bringing researchers to the kibbutz to study problems related to aging represented a criticism of her efforts on behalf of the elderly population. She might also have believed that my arrival represented an assessment of her not having accomplished enough. I later learned from one of my elderly interviewees that the social worker

---

[9] On the pressure to join a kibbutz one is studying, see Richard Schwartz, "Some Problems of Research in Israeli Settlements," *American Journal of Orthopsychiatry* 28:572–576, 1958.

had held a special meeting of their age group within the past year and asked them to discuss what the kibbutz should do for them. This informant was disturbed by the exercise and wrote a critical article about it for the internal kibbutz magazine.

41:2: The "health committee" coordinator and one of the nurses were speaking at a dining room table about having one of the kibbutz members admitted to the hospital. Accompanying the coordinator to the table was the kibbutz social worker who was getting progressively more irritated by the fact that the coordinator and the nurses, among others, were supposed to attend a meeting of the *mazkirut* shortly to hear a report of her four years of work on the kibbutz as a social worker. Since they were preoccupied with this person's illness, they would probably not come, or they would be late.

The health committee coordinator asked me to introduce myself to the social worker, which I did. I briefly explained my project. The social worker said that I am doing either 'consultation' (meaning therapy) or 'research,' meaning she was going to define what I was doing. Taking the ball in my own hands, I said that I will work on the kibbutz and talk to people and then I will report my interpretations and findings to the kibbutz.

"But who will follow through on the conclusions?" she asked. "Perhaps it will be stuck in a drawer somewhere," she said in a discouraging way. She feels I am encroaching on her territory, both in terms of the work she does and the research she did in another kibbutz. She argued with me about whether the kibbutz had invited me or I had asked to come. I insisted that the kibbutz had invited me by way of my sponsor. She then argued about whether or not there was a team. She asked if I would be here on Sunday. I said I'm always here. [Great answer!]

I said she is deeply immersed in matters whereas I view things from the side . . . [I became conciliatory.] I also said I'd like her participation and cooperation. Perhaps I should have used the 'nasty approach.' After the social worker left, the "health committee" coordinator said she wasn't aware of this conflict and thinks the social worker's attitude is related to academic competition with me.

Because the social worker was in the phase of withdrawing from this kibbutz, it is understandable that she did not want to invest any time in me. Thus, although we set up several appointments to meet, she cancelled each time except once, when she arrived late, leaving us very little time to meet.

61:4: I went to the social worker's office around 10:30 a.m. as we had arranged. She wasn't there and had left no message either there or with the switchboard. Very annoying since this is the purpose of my day off today. There was a note on her door from another kibbutz member who had waited from 8:30–?; and there were two other notes in her mailbox, plus the switchboard said she had two messages.

When I mentioned this to another kibbutz member, she said that reminds her she's supposed to see the social worker, and another member stopped by too, saying that several times appointments had been deferred. Annoying. The "health committee" coordinator said the social worker is probably sick. But why not send messages?

80:1: I got a phone message from the social worker that she couldn't make the Tuesday meeting because of a hospital appointment. I don't think her input will be important, except for recommendations I want to make to the new social worker, if any.

Although the social worker's attitude was not consequential for my project because she left her job at Emek shortly after I arrived, it was meaningful as an illustration of potential problems I might have with others. In particular, I was concerned with the way the *mazkirim* would deal with this matter.

> 45:2: The *mazkir* told me that the social worker had spoken with him, upset, that I had said I was going to do therapy with the elderly people. [And this after I had told her that this was *not* the case!] I said, and the *mazkir* knew, that that is not true. He told me that he has to talk to the social worker about it. She must have been so upset that she couldn't even grasp what I was saying. I told him I had left her a note saying I wanted to meet. He said it wouldn't work. I told him the project was getting more and more complicated. He seemed to understand what I meant.
>
> The subject of the social worker's departure came up at a breakfast conversation with the kitchen staff, several of whom were seeing her for counseling.
>
> 101:1: C said she likes the social worker, and E said that she used to like her, but no longer does. She didn't explain the reason for her change of heart. A said, "The reason the social worker is leaving is that Shula is interviewing people." I then asked A if that is gossip or something the social worker actually said. [I think I could ask this question only because I had learned how kibbutz members sometimes speak, i.e. not differentiating between deeply held conjecture and fact.] A said that the social worker did not say it, but that is what people believe. He also said that the social worker wants to leave because she wants to pursue her career and working here is "simply beneath her."
>
> When everyone but C left the table, I asked her, as a person who appreciated the social worker's accomplishments, why she thought the social worker was leaving. In her opinion, the social worker is leaving because the *mazkirut* has not been good to her, and that this kibbutz is a difficult place in which to work, particularly in comparison to another kibbutz where the social worker worked for 8 years and succeeded! I told C that I had heard from someone outside our kibbutz that the social worker has succeeded here. C concurred that the social worker has helped many people.

Because of this conversation, I decided to join the social worker at lunch when I saw her eating in the dining room. She was eating with one of the *mazkirim* and his wife.

> The social worker said that in the kibbutz where she is a member, people believe she cares more about Emek than about her own kibbutz (meaning she is a very devoted social worker). She then said I could come to visit her at her kibbutz to learn what she did here at Emek. (She seems to want me to defer to her.)
>
> Then the *mazkir* turned to her and said "Good bye." She retorted, "You aren't going to get rid of me that easily," meaning that they would see each other again. (This is a common Israeli expression.) He said, "Lots of people were sorry she was leaving and that they seemed to value her work now that it wouldn't be available to them any more, whereas at the time . . ." (He seemed to be trying to assuage her hurt feelings.) Then they all left the table, and several people stopped the social worker to make appointments.

The *mazkir* later gave me the following explanation for the social worker's negative attitude toward my project:

115:2: I think she was opposed since she felt uninvolved in the original decision-making process. She was not part of the *sichat kibbutz* decision to invite you. She is a very competitive person who doesn't want anyone else to work in this area, even though working with older people is not her specialty.

About a month later, one kibbutz member told me the following:

161:1: "I saw the social worker yesterday because she hitched a ride in a kibbutz car. The social worker was asking about you. 'Had you left yet, etc.' She is annoyed that the kibbutz isn't treating her properly, particularly that they didn't give her an elaborate send-off party after working here for four years. I was close to the social worker because I'm interested in psychology. I was the one who helped get her a room to work in. The gossip around here is that T, who is very smart and talented, tried to give the social worker a bad name. That's because T undermines anyone near her turf."

In other words, the more I would have "succeeded" in what I was doing, the more difficult that would have been for some people to take. My researcher status was clearly a barrier to my being acceptable to some and an asset to others.

The *mazkirim* also gave me tangible psychological support when a woman (kibbutz member) who was serving on the "executive committee" wanted to block my invitation to attend its meetings. My sponsor had made the request of the "executive committee," and the *mazkirim* had argued against the woman's rejection. They made the point that a research project that barred the researcher from the key decision-making groups' meetings would have only limited value. She was outvoted, and I was permitted to attend.

BEING TESTED

People on the kibbutz continuously requested that I give them informal feedback, particularly about other individuals. Many wanted to know what other people had talked about in their private interviews with me. Some simply wanted to know what I thought about the particular kibbutz itself or kibbutz life in general. These requests put me in a terrible dilemma. On the one hand, if I gave feedback, I could be "wrong" about what I said from their perspective. On the other hand, if I did not respond, I would be suggesting that I was superior to them and that I would not stoop to this behavior or that I was too stupid to have an opinion. They might not want to talk to me at a future date when I wanted to talk to them. I tried a wide range of strategies to get out of this situation. In the first example that follows, I deflected the conversation; in the second, I answered.

46:6: I sat opposite D at dinner. She started the conversation by asking me what I thought of N. I asked her why she asked.
316:2: J asked me what I thought of the former social worker, and I told her, knowing that a new social worker was about to come, and that it wouldn't matter.

Sometimes a person asked for an evaluation of herself or himself, but I just listened as the person answered his or her own question.

345:2: G asked me outright how I see her and T. I said that I marvel at her ability to stay in the kibbutz (despite all of her social difficulties) although

I understand that she was born on one. She said that she has taste and talent that others don't appreciate; that others like her have closed themselves off from the kibbutz or left to live elsewhere. And what remains is not quality. She said too that the "selection process" is bringing in lower and lower quality people. It was particularly hard for her and her husband when they came back from being emissaries overseas. "Everyone was jealous of us." But on the other hand, even though they both feel like strangers in the kibbutz, T is very attached to the physical setting and when they left for Switzerland, he had a hard time closing the shutters on their kibbutz apartment for the last time.

What does she have here, she mused, almost to herself. Her record collection, her garden, her studio, her talent and her students. She said that the standard of living is very high and she has everything she wants, except cash, which is something she would like. Without cash, she can't have a meal in a restaurant, can't buy gifts the way she would like. She spoke of a relative who bought a large record collection for G's daughter who lives abroad. And now she and her husband certainly can't leave because when you do, the money you get to start out is so pitifully small. I ended the "conversation" being deeply moved but not having said a word.

Aside from people making continuous requests for informal feedback and testing my willingness to give it, I was obligated to provide both oral and written formal feedback to the kibbutz. The first feedback session consisted of an interim report I gave to the *mazkirut* on the topic of "the elderly and work." The second formal feedback session was a talk I gave to the "old age club." This was the ultimate test because I would be talking to the very people I was studying. I was nervous about these presentations in part because my sponsor had become such an obstacle but also because I had learned that kibbutz members do not believe that anyone other than they can understand the kibbutz. I was not sure how well I understood it myself. I decided to handle my concerns by seeking advice from people I considered my kibbutz friends and from kibbutz members I respected and trusted. Frequently, however, my needs were downplayed in favor of theirs.

> 302:3: Sat down alone for lunch. Always awkward to eat alone in the dining room, even if you want some quiet time. In a few minutes R sat opposite me. Three days ago I had told her that I wanted to talk with her. She then started talking to me about what was on her mind, i.e. her fifth pregnancy, what her children think about it, and how she felt when she got a sister when she was nine years old. Z (male) came and sat next to us. I told R I had wanted to talk to her about my feedback to the kibbutz. I decided to persist even though Z was now there.

I asked another woman what I should do about the fact that I had about another month left on the kibbutz and that I didn't feel able to arrange *chugei bayit* (parlor meetings, plural) in people's homes to discuss what I had observed.

> She disagreed. She didn't like the idea of the *mazkir* getting the report, since then others would have to hear my views indirectly. She didn't think it would be a good idea if I left without people having a chance to hear what I had to say. They would ask, "she was here for a year, and what did she do?" Some people probably still don't know what I did.

I told her I had an agreement with the kibbutz to try to change things, but would need more time for that. We decided that besides the report, it would be a good idea to give some talks. To the health/elderly committee definitely, to a group of heads of committees perhaps, to the elderly club definitely, for the young (which she would set up for me!!), and an open meeting. She said it wasn't necessary to address the elementary school, and that the high school wasn't so necessary since they were so cynical.

What was striking about this conversation was my feeling of slight terror throughout. I feel strange asking people what I should do, and yet I keep on doing it. So far I have asked (four people). Something instinctive is telling me to keep on doing this. Perhaps I want them to share in the responsibility of what I produce (and fail at). Perhaps this is another way of getting data, even if it hurts.

Why do I feel so insecure talking to her? First, she is extremely intelligent and very articulate, so my Hebrew vocabulary feels inadequate. How about my intelligence?

Second, she is very successful, to my mind, as an initiator and innovator. I think of her as a community psychologist. (I'm not sure I can do as well as she does.) That's why I turned to her. She's accomplished a lot—she (achieved a particular amazing political feat), she got the *chugei bayit* going, and now she has the committee for the young in operation. She said they had three meetings so far, one on the topic of creating a *moadon* (an entertainment facility for young adults), one to celebrate the birth of someone's child, etc. And one political one—I think. Now they will have a *chug bayit* (parlor meeting, singular) on young people. (It's amazing to me that older people, such as R have to organize the younger ones. It's like they still need *metaplot*. Can't do things on their own. Can't build their own society. Pragmatically, the only way to get the young people here is to have them build their own kibbutz here. Somehow be separate.)

But I also felt terror since maybe I had done the study improperly, had not talked to enough people, or had not organized a committee or a group to work with, etc. And even if I had *done* things "right," perhaps I hadn't found the right information. R speaks with certainty when she says the attitudes of the old people to the clinic are such and such. The certainty that comes from living here. What can I say about their attitudes in general? What if she and I would come to different conclusions? Who knows better? And would statistics help? . . . I sat with R and Z until nearly quarter of two. When we brought our lunch trays to the dishwasher, he said, "good morning!"

I continued to prepare myself psychologically for the feedback sessions.

306:1: I told M that I was going to speak to the old age club, to the young people and give another talk open to all. She said she would like to come, even though she had been at the first (interim) talk. Then I told her I was working on the problem of how to present my material to people in addition to presenting the written report, because there is so much. As a case in point, when I gave the interim report, I spent 2 hours simply on one topic. She served me tea and invited D, her husband, to join us. Then, to my embarrassment, although I do this sometimes too, she asked him my question. "How should I present?" She fed him details so he could construct an answer. She was acting as a liaison.

On May 31 (307:3) I suggested to my sponsor that he set up a meeting with his age group and that I talk about my research. Of course, he disagreed. He suggested, instead, that it be done at the *sichat kibbutz*. I rejected that. He said it would be hard to get people to come to any talk unless it occurred on a Saturday night. Moreover, several people in his group would not attend because they would already have heard it as part of their other activities (e.g., head of the elderly affairs committee, the health committee, etc.).

I then decided to seek permission from a schoolteacher to devote a class session to the topic of old age. My doing so would be an opportunity both to collect data from the children and to give feedback to the kibbutz.

> 313:1: Went to class. All present except for R who came late. Have material on tape. Another teacher observed and found it interesting that children said they knew so many old people that they couldn't write all the names down. Stopped at quarter to 10:00 although not finished with all questions. Next day the teacher said that children went home and told their parents what had been done in class and the parents were very touched and pleased. She said this informal reporting led to discussions at home. H said it is so important to have free discussions such as these—true for all ages. Kids had a hard time recognizing that 'all answers were correct,' even 'I don't know.' I kept on repeating, 'Whatever you think is ok, we are just trying to find out what we think.'

Some of my uncertainty reflected the fact that I had internalized the kibbutz attitudes. "No one understands the kibbutz," they had told me. "You can't understand a kibbutz until you've been here many years," they had said. There were other reasons to be insecure:

> 322:1: I am not old myself, so it is presumptuous to explain to the elderly the feelings they have about themselves.

I knew that kibbutz members were critical of each other and of outsiders. I did not want to be humiliated. Later that day, for example, I saw G, an elderly woman who, I knew, would be at any talk I would give because we enjoyed each other's company and she was curious about everything. She said she had just attended a talk by an Arab member of Knesset. She already had a viewpoint concerning the talk, what he left out, what he said wrong, what he wants, and so forth. This was reassuring to me. There was no way I could be correct in the eyes of everyone, so I should just try to be true to myself.

In early June, I gave my talk to the elderly in their "old age club."

> 317:3: A said I was wrong in claiming that old people do not change their minds about people and bear damaging grudges. He has changed his opinion about 10 times(!) When he sees someone complaining about his or her life, he tells him or her to consider all that they do have. Doesn't hate anyone. He said that old people do get together with young—mostly at work, but not in committees. He himself does not understand the young; they live in a different world entirely; they went through wars. According to S, T said that the young don't love the old. She says they don't have to; only her son does. She says the worst problem of old age is the problem of hypochondria, which D and Z have.

H apologized. D was pleased.

318:1: K said that her daughter-in-law came to my talk yesterday because she is interested in the topic. She was impressed by the notion of parents teaching their children how to help them. She knows that U did not ask anything of her children formerly so now she has to ask others for help. H realizes she made a mistake in how she brought up her sons in this regard. No matter how many young people were in her house (with her 3 sons and the "adoptees"), she was always the one to serve, to get the bread or food from the dining room, to clean up. She never thought of asking them to help, and if she did, they refused. Now she sees 10-year-olds going to the dining room with a basket (to bring food home to the *heder*) and she thinks, "This is the way it should be." The reason the old-timers spoiled their kids was because they were abnormal parents; they had no parents of their own, no grandparents, had gone through hell and wanted to pour all their love onto their children, but then the children had no responsibilities. Now she thinks the families are more normal, they are 3-generational and each one can demand more of one another.

The amazing thing about presenting my preliminary research interpretations to the members was that I continued to live with the members afterward. Thus, their reactions to my talk became part of the data I was collecting.

318:1: Like everyone else, the teachers asked me at breakfast how it went yesterday. I told them to ask others, because it was like asking a groom if his bride is beautiful. U had said that her daughter-in-law said she sensed the things I was talking about in her brief visits to the kibbutz. I said it was a strange experience to give feedback to a group about itself. Iris said, "It is not so strange," that sometimes the teachers have a researcher who gives them a breakdown of their profile. M agreed that it was strange because they could guess whom I was talking about. Living in a kibbutz is like being a pebble in a stream; you are constantly rubbing against each other—and getting shinier in the process, they tell me. I would once like to hear two people agree on anything! It's like the *Talmud*[10]—everyone has an opinion and there is almost never a resolution.

318:1: Y came over to join me for breakfast. He wanted to make two points with regard to my talk:

a) The conditions that I described do not apply exclusively to the old people but hold for all the people in the society;

b) the value of the work old people continue to do is very high. He said that pension is equal to 30 years of work, and that people like S have worked 60 years, equivalent to 2 pensions and are continuing. The contribution of the elderly to society is greater than that of younger people, according to his calculations, because if you subtract the special services for elderly from the value of their work, and the special services for children from the work of their parents, you get a surplus.

318:2: I was sitting with Y, when we were joined by R and got down to the real business—gossip.[11] She told me that Z had praised my talk and given her a

---

[10] Books of Jewish law containing a wide variety of opinions.

[11] Max Gluckman has shown the ubiquitousness and utility of gossip to maintain values in small groups. See his "Gossip and Scandal," *Current Anthropology* 4(3):307–316, 1963.

detailed breakdown. She wanted to know who the two people were who I said did not participate in the interviews. (I would not tell her.)

318:3: T said he already knew everything I said except that kids who were 11 years old didn't know what old age was all about. Asked me why, if social insurance was better here than in the US (which I had claimed), how come the life span was lower? Asked me if things were so good here, why do people laugh so little, and laugh less than outside the kibbutz. Said one thing I could never do was to train kids to take care of other people's parents.

318:3: C came over: "Very interesting, the best part was people's reactions." "That's why I let them interrupt me; did you see how they contradicted me in the middle of a sentence?" "Horrible manners!"

318:3: N told me that Y said she didn't come to my talk since she already knows about being old.

Basically many of these people did not want to accept anything that they did not already believe to be the case. Rejecting the sociologist's interpretation is probably much more common than the opposite in field research. For example, in a recent article about the Lindy Hop dance scene in Chicago, Black Hawk Hancock provided this excerpt from his field notes:

> "Ironically, when I questioned Lindy Hoppers about what drew them to the dance, their responses were always based around pleasure. . . . When I brought up the issue of race . . . people flatly denied that the dance had anything to do with it. . . . Most dancers seemed defensive toward this questioning and would immediately ask me why I was 'bringing race into this' or thought that I was 'bringing up something that's not there' or 'making it into something that it's not.'"[12]

Those who came to the talk, I learned, wanted to satisfy their curiosity and have a new conversation piece. Some attended because we had become friends. The feedback session was both social and research oriented.

323: D told me that H had been over at her house last week and told her that I had delivered my report to the club. H had not "identified" with my recommendations. I said that I had recommended that people accept positions on committees when invited, rather than turn them down automatically. But D and I did not get a chance to continue the conversation re this point.

The more I took in the feedback with equanimity, the more I reinforced my role as researcher, I believe. The more feedback sessions I gave, the more the community saw me in that role as well.

327:3: T asked me how my work was coming along, how the group with the young worked out, etc. She asked if I would distribute a one-page list of recommendations in everyone's mailboxes. I said it was too early for that. I hadn't even analyzed the data.

330:1: G said she wanted to give me some feedback on my presentation to the old age club. She thinks I made a mistake in saying that people have unyielding reputations. Instead, she believes that everyone earns his/her reputation and that people get into various "periods" with the kibbutz and that their

---

[12] Black Hawk Hancock, "Learning How to Make Life Swing," *Qualitative Sociology* 30: 113–133, 2007.

reputation changes. [I'd have to be here a very long time to see that.] Also the kibbutz, she feels, is very forgiving and solicitous, unlike other societies. Here people have learned to live with one another. For example, R has a terrible reputation because of what he did (illustrates my point, no?), but the kibbutz didn't throw him out. She believes that people have particular characters. She also thinks that everyone knows everyone else extremely well—when she sees someone walking, she knows where they are coming from and where they are going. Like S said, she knows what everyone will say. (Again, doesn't that illustrate my point?)

323:4: R knew that I have been giving reports, but said she wasn't going to come to any of them. Told her what I was doing now is trying to analyze my field notes without the benefit of interview transcripts. I said she is probably interested mostly in health, so I could give her some feedback on that topic. I said, "There are a few complaints, although not about you."

And then she started talking for about half an hour and I couldn't get a word in edgewise. There was such a stream of words, I felt I had opened a faucet. I didn't understand everything she was telling me in part because it was so contradictory.

She said she knows people are not satisfied with the way the nurses treat them on the sidewalks (i.e. when they meet them informally), "not a friendly word," etc. "But what can you do? Some people are just bad, some have a personality problem." She listened to this kind of complaining when she was the head of the health committee but couldn't do anything about it. She knew that the kibbutz doctor would soon be speaking to the old age club. She does not accept the suggestion that she (a kind of health aide) listen while the nurses treat, since the people want to have attention from the nurses.

She knows they now praise B, but she was a "witch" despite her dedication and three visits per day to sick people. "She would throw open the windows, give orders, etc. There are no angelic nurses and people here are spoiled. The health clinic was open all the time when the community was smaller and there was a different age structure. Here they don't have to wait in line. Sometimes nurses are rude, but people are too sensitive. The nurses might say, 'Get your medications at 10:00,' but the person finds it more convenient at 7:00. Instead of accepting it, the person complains. N is particularly sensitive and wants attention. When she was coordinator of the health committee, she asked Z to pop in on N even though the clinic staff said he longer needed it. She told this to N's daughter and created a storm, because Z doesn't know how to do things tactfully, has no life wisdom. Although it is true that people had a preconceived notion about her even before she started working; they thought she's stupid." Wow!

The common characterization of kibbutz life as a pressure cooker or a hothouse came to mind. My little troubles of insecurity were nothing in comparison with the psychological anguish many were feeling.

324:1: Lunch with K: He knew that M was one of the two people who did not cooperate with my request for interviews, "As I predicted." He asked M why people rejected what I said, and she said, "because I wasn't right." He thinks I could have been much more critical, that I said "zero," could have multiplied it by 1000.

I said that people's notions (e.g. absorption has not been good) are not based on data. Instead of generalizing, people should examine the cases. But he said, ignoring my point, that the kibbutz should not absorb individuals, just groups.

He asked me if I noticed that Israeli speech is very I-centered. "I think this and that," whereas Americans say, "Perhaps you should consider this and that."

I mentioned R's notion that Israelis typically say, "you are wrong and I will explain why," implying that a person doesn't even know why he is wrong, and has to have it explained to him.

329:4: D told me that S had said that the old people beamed when I praised the system but objected when I criticized. I told him about my meeting of the young and how they know how the old speak of them.

In the last two weeks of my stay, I gave many feedback sessions. I did not expect to be agreed with. Nor did I think I would feel humiliated. It would simply be part of the unending conversation that characterized kibbutz life. I knew that kibbutz members would instruct me as to what to think until the minute my car would drive out through the kibbutz gates.

337:1: S says I shouldn't think that when they were young, the current old were any better than are the current young. She "got sick" when she saw Y (an old man) and others vote on issues that concern the young. "The old have no right to intervene since they don't understand what's going on among the young people who work in the factory. How can they vote on things that affect our (young people's) lives, and will continue to affect us after they are dead and gone?"

Wait a minute, I thought to myself. Isn't this the essence of democracy? Do we vote only on things that are germane to us as individuals? But there was no time for rebuttal. My ultimate equanimity despite the intense psychological turmoil of entering the kibbutz and the swirl of ideas upon leaving it can be summarized in one way—I had learned to cope like a kibbutz member while establishing an identity as a researcher specific to this setting. In particular, I had overcome the stranglehold of my sponsor by forging alliances with powerful individuals and large groups of friends; I had overcome antagonists and undergone testing. People agreed and disagreed with me, and I had incorporated their responses into my understanding of the kibbutz.

CHAPTER 4

❦

Personal Selves

Helping Yali become accustomed to kibbutz life.

The first part of this book dealt with the evolution of researcher roles. Continuous negotiations around autonomy versus dependence and restrictions characterized the process for me, as is evident in the field notes about my attempt to free myself from my sponsor. Repeatedly explaining to community members what I was doing and gaining the cooperation of individuals, one by one, were part of the role as well. Tapping into the power structure and gaining allies to get access to events and organizations were crucial. Developing a research identity was, therefore, a highly political act, requiring strategic moves and power plays. Finally, giving feedback to the community while trying to retain self-confidence emerged as a struggle toward the end of my stay. All of these tensions and more were components of a research self I created in the field, and it is the variegated self that, as mentioned in the introduction, was the key research tool.

In this part of *Observing the Observer* I leave researcher roles behind and address a second set of roles. These stem from the personal characteristics of the individual that she or he brings into the field. These, of course, vary among researchers and could include physical appearance, language abilities, and many more personal traits, most of which are part of who a researcher is before he or she enters the field. I call these "personal selves." In my case, I will discuss nine of them, choosing only those that were salient in the field—mother, woman, wife, thirty-three years old, daughter, American, academic, dance enthusiast, and Jew. All of these personal characteristics became lenses through which I examined my topic—aging on a kibbutz.

BEING A MOTHER

When the opportunity arose to conduct this fieldwork study, I was the mother of a two-and-one-half-year-old daughter named "Yael," whose nickname is "Yali." In my naiveté, I never asked the question, "Can a mother do fieldwork and bring her child(ren) into the field?" But I now realize that even if I had looked in the research literature for information and guidance on this topic, I would have found almost nothing because so few researchers bring their children into the field with them or write about doing so.[1] An alternative explanation is that most female field researchers are not mothers or are not mothers at the time of their fieldwork.[2]

For those who are mothers,[3] some, such as anthropologist Elsie Clews Parsons, who had four children (and two who died at birth), were wealthy enough to employ caretakers and keep their children at home while they went to the field. Parsons

---

[1] For example, a review of Peggy Golde's *Women in the Field: Anthropological Experiences* (Chicago: Aldine, 1970) reveals that Jean Briggs was alone in the Arctic; Laura Thompson was alone on the Papago Reservation; Peggy Golde was alone in Guerrero, Mexico; Laura Nader was alone in Mexico and Lebanon; Ruth Landes was alone in Brazil; Helen Codere was alone in Rwanda; Gloria Marshall was alone in Nigeria; Ernestine Friedl went into the field with her husband; and Hazel Weidman was alone in Burma. Cora Dubois describes the fieldworkers who have studied Orissa, India: "Of the seven Americans who have worked in Bhubaneswar, two men and I were unmarried . . . Three were newly married but childless, and one had two children. None of the three wives and one husband was professionally involved" (p. 235). The only exception was Ann Fischer, who had just married when she entered the field in Micronesia and became pregnant. Her children and husband accompanied her on her subsequent research trips. She writes, "It is not usual to have an opportunity to have a family in the field, and in this respect my own experience is exceptional. Anthropologists' wives who are not themselves anthropologists often do this, but women anthropologists generally do not. The responsibility for a large drop-out rate for women in anthropology rests perhaps on this one problem" (p. 270).

[2] This was the case for Margaret Mead, who wrote about postponing having children in order to complete her graduate studies and then to undertake her field research, then having multiple miscarriages in the field, being told she was unable to bear children, and ultimately having a child when she no longer did fieldwork. See *Blackberry Winter: My Earlier Years* (New York: Pocket Books, 1972), especially chapter 18, "On Having a Baby." Mead's daughter, Mary Catherine Bateson, wrote *With a Daughter's Eye: A Memoir of Margaret Mead and Gregory Bateson* (New York: William Morrow, 1984), to describe the life of the daughter of fieldworkers (among other topics).

[3] See Nancy Scheper-Hughes, *Death Without Weeping: The Violence of Everyday Life in Brazil* (Berkeley and Los Angeles: University of California Press, 1992), who writes that she went on four field expeditions with her husband and children (pp. 15, 537–540).

almost never took the children on her field trips and turned to her mother to care for the children when they were young. As her biographer, Desley Deacon, discovered, Parsons and her husband came to an agreement "probably at the time she began to work seriously in anthropology, that she should have primary responsibility for the children until the age of twelve. After that, their everyday care and major decisions such as schooling were [his] responsibility."[4] The children ranged in age from three to thirteen, with one in boarding school when she started her anthropological fieldwork. Deacon has also noted that Parsons advised Esther Goldfrank to leave her five-month-old daughter with a good nurse and return to the field.[5] Mothers who do not have to travel to do their fieldwork can, of course, have children who are cared for by others, like any other children of working mothers.

If we look at writings about ethnography from twenty years ago, such as John Van Maanen's *Tales of the Field*,[6] written in the decade *after* I left the field, there is no reference to women researchers at all. As Van Maanen wrote, "Those readers familiar with the recent writings of Clifford Geertz, George Marcus, Howard Becker, George Stocking, Joseph Gusfield and particularly James Clifford will note that the concerns of these writers serve as the focal point for much of this book."[7] Not only are nonmothers the primary source of theorizing, but also the way that the family of a male writer is described reinforces the idea that children do not belong in the field. They hardly belong in one's life!

> To my family . . . must go the greatest appreciation for putting up with one who at this very instant still writes rather than lives. Casey, Patrick and Nicole have learned to cut left on the big ones and drop down the expert's slope while hearing little more from their pasty, hunched-over father these past months than such endearing remarks as 'put that down,' 'leave me alone,' or the tired and always false, 'just a couple more days.' Their mother, kind soul, has managed to read and correct both my prose and demeanor with remarkable good cheer while maintaining a traveling heart and home.[8]

It is not my intention to disparage Van Maanen, nor is he unusual in his expression of gratitude to his family for leaving him alone and to his wife for editing his book.[9]

---

[4] Desley Deacon, *Elsie Clews Parsons: Inventing Modern Life*, p. 281 (Chicago: University of Chicago Press, 1997). Parsons was also innovative in doing fieldwork with men to whom she was not married.

[5] Deacon, p. 291.

[6] John Van Maanen, *Tales of the Field: On Writing Ethnography* (Chicago: University of Chicago Press, 1988). In Carolyn D. Smith and William Kornblum's edited volume, *In the Field: Readings on the Field Research Experience* (New York: Praeger, 1989), the female contributors are Carol Stack, Ruth Horowitz, Barbara Meyerhoff, and Claire Sterk. Only Stack brought her child into the field, and his role is unclear. Horowitz, Meyerhoff, and Sterk studied local communities. In his book, *Learning from the Field: A Guide from Experience* (Beverly Hills, CA: Sage 1984), sociologist William Foote Whyte writes that "Kathleen King Whyte had been with me for two years in the street corner study, and she and our four children joined me in [. . .] first foreign field project [in Venezuela]," p. 16.

[7] p. xii.

[8] p. xvi.

[9] In a footnote, Buechler writes, "Thanks also go to my wife Judith-Maria Buechler for editorial help in writing this paper and for permitting me to use examples from her own experience [in the field]," Hans C. Buechler, "The Social Position of an Ethnographer in the Field," in Frances Henry

In fact, the paragraph quoted earlier can be found almost verbatim in many books by fathers, except that the names and the specifics of the ski slope vary. Rather, my point is to draw attention to the way the researcher handles the responsibilities of parenting while also doing fieldwork. This problem is not limited to anthropology. In the classic overview of sociologists' field experiences, *Reflections on Community Studies*, edited by Arthur J. Vidich, Joseph Bensman, and Maurice R. Stein, there is no woman among the authors of the eleven chapters and therefore no opportunity to explore mothering in the field.

Until recently few women wrote much about this topic. Helen Lynd mentioned it briefly in the Middletown studies, and Nancy Scheper-Hughes offered a much longer account about her research in Brazil.[10] Carol Stack, author of *All Our Kin*,[11] wrote that when she did her research in 1969, she was "twenty-eight, a white, working-class, politically active, single mother—with a young son who was with me round the clock."[12] In the acknowledgments to her book, she thanks John R. Lombardi as a co-researcher, and in an "About the Author" passage at the end of the book, she describes a new project of "comparative research in urban white ethnic communities in the United States, where once again she and her co-workers, her son Kevin, and John Lombardi, also an anthropologist, will participate as a family in the daily life of the community."[13] I could not find any information about what that meant. But what did Kevin do as a child while she interviewed? How was he involved? What was Lombardi's role?

Joke Schrijvers offers a positive chapter in which she asks this question: If women combine work and family in other contexts, why not in fieldwork?[14] Sociologist Carol A. B. Warren has also analyzed motherhood in the field:

> Motherhood is another part of the gendered field through which entrée is negotiated; Fleur-Lobban and Lobban (1986:188) note the significance for their fieldwork in the Sudan of both their marriage and their daughter Josina. Women

---

and Satish Saberwal (eds.), *Stress and Response in Fieldwork*, p. 7 (New York: Holt, Rinehart and Winston, 1969). But in the body of the text (p. 8), he writes, "At every step I shall compare my own experience with that of my wife. She was studying child-rearing patterns and market relations. Her position in the community was different from my own because her informants were primarily women and children, while mine were for the most part men. This provides a comparison of male and female channels of communication. In conclusion I present the importance of this method."

[10] Nancy Scheper-Hughes, *Death without Weeping: The Violence of Everyday Life in Brazil*, pp. 537–540 (Berkeley and Los Angeles: University of California Press, 1992).

[11] Carol B. Stack, *All Our Kin: Strategies for Survival in a Black Community* (New York: Harper & Row, 1972).

[12] Carol B. Stack, "Writing Ethnography: Feminist Critical Practice," in Diane L. Wolf (ed.), *Feminist Dilemmas in Fieldwork*, p. 97 (Boulder, CO: Westview Press, 1996).

[13] See also John R. Lombardi and Carol B. Stack, "Economically Cooperating Units in an Urban Black Community," in Peggy Sanday (ed.), *Anthropology and the Public Interest: Fieldwork and Theory* (New York: Academic Press, l976).

[14] Joke Schrijvers, "Motherhood Experienced and Conceptualized," in Diane Bell, Pat Caplan, and Wazir Jahan Karim (eds.), *Gendered Fields: Women, Men & Ethnography*, pp. 143–158 (New York: Routledge, 1993).

ethnographers have also found that motherhood is a potentially powerful source of mutual identification between women respondents and researchers.[15]

In my experience, motherhood is much more than that. At it turned out, my daughter's presence became a more significant component of my fieldwork experience than I ever imagined and gave me the additional role of mother-in-the-field. Because Yali was my first child, I might have paid particular attention to her. But if I had had two very young children at the time, I don't think I could have conducted this study. It would have been physically impossible. It is important for readers to understand the barriers (and advantages at times) to intellectual productivity for mothers whose research relies on fieldwork. The research on mothering in general shows that in many cases it is difficult to combine with any kind of work situation, a problem with which many societies are still struggling.

Being a mother is a sine qua non in Israeli society, particularly in ultrareligious communities and in kibbutzim, which are societies that have higher birthrates than do other Jewish communities in Israel.[16] Israel has the highest birthrate among Western countries.[17] Thus, having a child made me "normal" in terms of Israeli society. But I was only barely normal because I had only one child at my age. Not having "at least one child" while being a married woman in her early thirties would have raised continuous questions about me:[18] Was my husband or I infertile? What were we waiting for?[19]

---

[15] Carol A. B. Warren, "Gender and Fieldwork Relations," in Robert M. Emerson (ed.), *Contemporary Field Research: Perspectives and Formulations*, second edition, pp. 211–212 (Prospect Heights, IL: Waveland Press, 2001). She is quoting Carolyn Fleuhr-Lobban and R. C. Lobban, "Families, Gender and Methodology in the Sudan," in T. I. Whitehead and M. E. Conaway (eds.), *Self, Sex and Gender in Cross-cultural Fieldwork* (Urbana: University of Illinois Press, 1986). See also Cecilia Van Hollen, "Epilogue," in *Birth on the Threshold: Childbirth and Modernity in South India*, pp. 215–220 (Berkeley and Los Angeles: University of California, 2003).

[16] On Israeli pronatalism, see Susan Martha Kahn, *Reproducing Jews: A Cultural Account of Assisted Conception in Israel* (Durham, NC: Duke University Press, 2000); and Susan Sered, *What Makes Women Sick? Maternity, Modesty and Militarism in Israeli Society* (Hanover, NH: UPNE, 2000).

[17] Israel's birthrate of three children per female is the highest of any of the world's developed nations and is actually closer to the rates for developing nations, such as India and Peru. It is higher than the birthrates for Algeria, Turkey, Lebanon, and Brazil.

[18] M. N. Srinivas, *The Remembered Village* (Berkeley and Los Angeles: University of California Press, 1976), writes, "My bachelorhood was also a subject of frequent comment. By village standards, I should have been a father of several years' standing. Why had I remained single? I tried to explain that I had not thought of marriage till I had completed my studies and obtained a job. A man needed a job to maintain a wife and children. But the villagers were amused that a man whose family owned a good quantity of rice land (according to them), and who was educated should trot out an excuse such as not having a job in defence of his remaining single" (p. 27). The author continues discussing this topic at length.

[19] Carolyn Fluehr-Lobban was asked these questions outright while doing research in the Sudan. "Are you married or not? Do you have children? Why not? It was difficult to explain why I did not have children in 1970–72 and again in 1975, after several years of marriage. Many women were kind enough to intimate that the problem was with my husband and not me. Yet when we had our daughter Josina with us, women and men would freely opine that one child was not enough." Carolyn Fleuhr-Lobban and R. C. Lobban, "Families, Gender and Methodology in the Sudan,"

Because I carried out this study as a "temporarily single" mother of a young child with the intermittent presence of her father, I could not proceed with my work until I had made arrangements for her care. Women with young children can do extended fieldwork away from home only if the issue of the child's care is taken into consideration. Being able to undertake fieldwork that takes one's children away from their home is not an easy matter for the mother or the children. Perhaps women are more likely to conduct fieldwork close to home for this reason. By "arrangements" I mean more than having someone watch over the child. It means medical care and psychological comfort, clothing and food, and everything else a child needs. Taking care of my daughter's needs was not something I could "put off" while I did other things, no matter who else was caring for her. Rather, my role as mother began as soon as I arrived on the kibbutz and immediately exposed me to a wide variety of kibbutz norms. I began to understand how difficult it must have been for women on the earliest kibbutzim when children first began to be born. And I understood how difficult it is for women and men to achieve that elusive "equality" on the kibbutz unless the care of children is fully equalized as well.[20]

My previous knowledge about kibbutz life had prepared me for what I believed would be Yali's child-care arrangements. She would live in a children's house (*beit yeladim*) appropriate for her age group.[21] During her first week on the kibbutz, I soon learned, Yali was not permitted to "enter" (i.e., move into) the *beit yeladim* because of the kibbutz's understandable quarantine policy designed to protect kibbutz children from the illnesses of newcomers. When that period ended, I would begin the laborious and unfamiliar process of helping her move away from me, in keeping with the kibbutz policy. Anthropologist Hortense Powdermaker, a pioneer in writing about the fieldwork experience, starts her description of her first study with these words:

> This was my first night in Lesu alone. As I sat on the veranda of my thatched-roofed, two-room house in the early evening, I felt uncertain and scared, not of anything in particular, but just of being alone in a native village. I asked myself, 'What on earth am I doing here, all alone and at the edge of the world?'[22]

Being home alone was something I craved. Instead I was usually burdened and tired.

To give the reader a sense of what it felt like to have my daughter accept the child-care arrangement, I have included a lot of (but not all) the field notes I took on this topic. The tedium and repetition in reading through all these notes are intended to convey the difficulties I encountered. Although I wanted to start the process on day 1, I soon realized that the "quarantine" made a lot of sense because

---

in T. I. Whitehead and M. E. Conaway (eds.), *Self, Sex and Gender in Cross-cultural Fieldwork*, p. 189 (Urbana: University of Illinois Press, 1986).

[20] See Michal Palgi, Joseph Raphael Blasi, Menachem Rosner, and Marilyn Safir (eds.), *Sexual Equality: The Israeli Kibbutz Tests the Theories* (Norwood, PA: Kibbutz Studies Book Series, Norwood Editions, 1983).

[21] See the film, *Children of the Sun*, directed by Ran Tal, 2007.

[22] Hortense Powdermaker, *Stranger and Friend: The Way of an Anthropologist*, p. 51 (New York: W. W. Norton, 1966). She seems to have been alone on every one of her field trips.

I took Yali to the health clinic almost every day in the first couple of weeks for her various ailments. After all, she was a two-year old, and we had moved to a foreign country with a new climate for her! Thus, because I was a mother, the clinic waiting room was one of my first observation sites.

> 5:1: Visited the nurse because Yali complained of pain while peeing. The nurse knew that earlier in the day we had left the medical line after waiting ½ hour. She said that in the future we should be prepared to wait even longer. I had thought kibbutz members were spared the misery of lines, waiting and hassles. But perhaps not in this case. How good are the social services here? Do the elderly have to wait, too?
>
> 8:1: Woke, ate, went to clinic. Doctor looked at Yali's throat and listened to her chest. She has somewhat red tonsils, he said. He didn't request the records of her immunizations that I had carefully prepared and brought with me. How good is the medical care here? What does one do if one is not satisfied?[23]

One useful outcome of these early clinic visits was that they challenged any romantic notions I might have had about kibbutz as utopia.

Being the mother of a young child meant that I needed to deal with the infirmary, nurses, and other health care providers and health issues a great deal. Through this connection, I learned how confusing the infirmary was for some people.

> 75:3: Played with Yali all afternoon. I tried taking her to the doctor at 7:00 p.m. since N said she had coughed badly during the afternoon nap. But there was no doctor on call. Don't know what the schedule is. Not posted there or on the bulletin board.
>
> 200:6: Went to Yali but she was already asleep. X said she hadn't felt well. Had M check her ears since B had left a note saying Yali cried in the night complaining of her ears. B had also told me that in the dining room. Yali didn't eat; she complained of stomachache; she didn't have a b.m., etc. Why didn't they take her to the doctor? What are they waiting for?

As a mother of a young child, I learned about attitudes toward child rearing but also how the medical system functions.

> 200:7: At 4 in the afternoon, I went to pick up Yali. The young D girl was the *mekima*.[24] I stayed with Yali a long time, making her bed, feeding her oranges . . . Took Yali home and read to her. H came by with nuts for her. Took Yali to *chadar haochel* where I talked to Jehuda on the phone. She stood outside the phone door making a b.m. in her pants. Afterwards I went upstairs for food to take back to my room. U wants to know why I'm eating in the *cheder*. What else should I do if Yali is not feeling well? This multi-tasking is overwhelming.
>
> 327:3: I'm worried about Yali. She's grouchy, negativistic, and not really happy. Doesn't want to go to the pool when she gets home to my *cheder*, although

---

[23] During our interview, an older kibbutz member who had lost his sight in both eyes (except for some peripheral vision) claimed that his problems could have been averted if he had had quicker care and earlier diagnoses.

[24] Person who comes to the children's houses a little before four o'clock to wake the children from their naps and get them ready for the parents, who pick them up around that time.

when she gets into the pool, she is happy. Cries a lot. Frustrated by mosquito bites, constipation . . . Perhaps frustrated that her father is not here.

Where one eats, just as where one has her child sleep, is a political statement—the old-timers think everyone should eat in the *chadar haochel,* but younger families find it a burden and prefer eating in their apartments. Eating at home diminishes the collective quality of kibbutz life, but it is perceived as convenient by families with young children. And because the birthrate is high, families might spend years not eating their evening meal in the *chadar haochel.*

> 217:2: Yali is sick. Brought her to the *cheder* in the middle of the night. J guarding alone till 2 a.m. and her son wouldn't go to get us. A drawback of this system.
> 219:1: Yali is quite sick with the chicken pox. I tried to entertain and distract her from 4–9.

For the week before Yali started moving into her children's house, I had her with me at all times, and I had to defer the start of my research except for short periods of times when she was napping. And even then, I did not want to leave her alone. Thus, I saw the kibbutz world through the eyes of a mother with no time for herself.

> 6:1: My sponsor introduced me to D in the dining room. When I told him I was studying old age, he said he was willing to meet and talk right away. But we put it off till next week, as I still have to watch Yali. I am learning, however, that the dining room is clearly a key institution and opportunity for communication in the kibbutz. At least that!

As each day passed, it became increasingly important to have Yali enter successfully and happily into her *beit yeladim.* On the other hand, I did not want her to sense my urgency.

> 6:1: I met with the education coordinator. She explained the process of getting Yali into the children's house. Today she will speak with the *metaplot* and get back to my sponsor about where Yali should go. [Why does my sponsor have to be involved?]

While we were waiting to have Yali move into the children's house, I discovered that she loved the Olympic-size swimming pool on the kibbutz. To my surprise, its vastness did not overwhelm her. Thus, I spent a lot of time with her at the pool to help her get used to her new surroundings. The pool became my third research site after the clinic and dining hall.

> 5:2: Met E at the pool as we were both taking care of our children. She invited me for tea (I think this was the first invitation I received). She has 4 children; her twins are Yali's age. She said I should come with Yali to visit her. Seemed helpful and friendly.
> 8:1: Swam with Yali.
> 8:4: Yali and I went to the new housing section to visit E. That whole lower area is really quite pretty, particularly in the evening. Lots of visiting among families. Yali is making me "normal," because I am not just a woman, but also a mother. Taking her for walks is a wonderful excuse for exploring the kibbutz. Walking around alone would have appeared bizarre.

8:3: In the swimming pool one grandmother said to me, "bli ayin hara (no evil eye intended), Yali is cute." Yali's been wonderful. She's been a real asset to me in making initial contacts with people. She's as easy to talk about as the weather.

Little did I know that life would become much more complicated. I spent so much time with my daughter at the swimming pool that S later said (307:2) I could have had a second career in swimming lessons. It turned out that Yali became an excellent swimmer and was able to swim the width of the pool under water. She jumped off the diving platforms and in general loved the water. Perhaps she loved being at the pool because we were there together, and I didn't leave her with others.

To have Yali "enter" the *beit yeladim,* the children's education coordinator first had to identify the most appropriate group for Yali to join. Each group lived in its own little building or section of a building. At least two possibilities were available to Yali. After choosing the appropriate group, I had to ease her gently into the selected group and have her feel comfortable enough for me to leave her with the group of children and the *metaplet* for long periods of time, including overnight. The day eventually came, and I brought Yali to her *bayit* (another word for *beit yeladim*). Immediately I was concerned about her potential placement.

(n.d.) The children seem young, babyish, and in fact they are younger than Yali. Will they speak clearly enough for her to learn Hebrew? Will she adopt childish habits? e.g. they swim in a kiddie pool, but she swims very well in the adult pool. I'd rather she continue learning to swim in the regular pool. She did play happily with Lego's and with the hammer and pegs.

Should I visit another group? I did convince them to accept her now and not wait until after X (the *metapelet*) returns from her vacation in a week. Do all the mothers worry about these things?

X met Yali and asked her if she'll be happy in the group, instead of saying she hopes Yali will be happy in the group. I'm not used to that way of speaking to children.

What, after all, is the quality of the kibbutz education? Particularly at this age level. Are the women motivated to care for each other's children? Someone told me that in the past, education was very important; it was an honor to be a teacher or a *metapelet*. But now everyone wants to be an engineer. Why? The answer I received was that "people don't like being evaluated by others, which occurs between parents and the teachers of their children." And here I am doing it already!

8:1: I brought Yali to her children's group of five children. The head *metapelet* is X, a loud, bossy woman. Her assistant, N, is phlegmatic—just the types of people to drive me crazy. N read a newspaper most of the time. I thought she was supposed to be taking care of the children. She intervened in fights among the children and emptied the potties when one of the mothers pointed out to her that they needed to be emptied.

This particular mother seemed very nice. She too is a *metapelet* and is responsible for an older group (4-year-olds). She has 4 kids of her own. There is an incredible network of roles and relationships here among mothers and *metaplot*! This woman's child cried bitterly when she tried to leave. She had brought one of her daughters, too, to visit her little son. Someone came to visit N while I was there and schmoozed with her for a long time. The whole time I was questioning what a *metapelet* should act like. Should she be active and involved all the time? Is it good during 'free play' to really let the kids be more on their own?

Clearly I was questioning how sensible it was to have Yali enter this particular group and, even more broadly, what I was doing by having her be part of this whole child-care system. But if I didn't place her in a *beit yeladim*, then I certainly couldn't conduct interviews at night (unless I left her alone in my *cheder*, which I would not do). On a kibbutz, there was no such option as hiring a baby-sitter. The collective child-care arrangement had to work.

> 9:1: Went to the *peuton* (house for infants and young toddlers) with Yali. At first there was nothing about it I liked. The children were crying, they had runny noses, they seemed to hurt themselves a lot, and the *metaplot* seemed only to reprimand or yell. How can you reprimand an infant? So far I see nothing special about this education. The *metaplot* give things to the children to play with, rather than play with the children. Children in Yali's group—if she stays here—are A, Y, N, V and O. Yali is more developed than they are, but she really wants to play with them. I think the children are cold. They lie naked on the cold floor, after swimming, with fans blowing. At least classical music is playing. I enjoyed playing with the babies. I could see myself working here as a *ganenet* (kindergarten teacher), probably because I already want to improve the system. X said she'll stay with the group till the *gan* (until they reach kindergarten age) since she spent one year studying young children (meaning she is skilled in dealing with this age group).
>
> 9:2: In the dining room in the morning, the children whom Yali got to know in the swimming pool gathered around her and made a huge fuss . . . I think the on-looking parents gain more trust in me because of this.
>
> 11:1: Took Yali to the *beit yeladim* for breakfast rather than have her eat with me in the *chadar haochel*. I stayed with her till 11:00. Each day I feel somewhat better about the group, but I'm still not pleased. I didn't like the way X poured the food down A. X told me she's divorced and her former husband and son are here. She's remarried and the two men are cordial, "because we are cultured people." I noticed how parents and grandparents take their children out of the *beit yeladim* at all times. There seems to be no discipline or rules. The role of grandparent seems important both in terms of loving the child and helping out the parents.
>
> My sponsor's wife thinks it's good that *metaplot* don't really play with the children, but rather give them materials to play with, supervise and clean them. Perhaps I am too adult-centered. Is it wrong that I go into the pool with Yali instead of simply watching her? The system is making me question myself.
>
> 11:1: Swam. Lunch. E volunteered to watch Yali while I got food. Swimming again. Spoke to the head of the education committee about visiting a second group house, which would perhaps be a better alternative for Yali. She said that X and N are good *metaplot* because "they give to the children." What does that mean? Clearly I was being cooled out of the idea that another group would be more suitable for Yali. I would have to take it or leave it, or make a big scene. But who knows if anything would have been better?

Chaos and self-doubt became themes in my field notes.

> 14:1: I took Yali to her *beit yeladim*. Her *metapelet* went to her son's *bayit* to help celebrate his birthday! [When she returned, I went to the dining room and

ate breakfast alone which was very uncomfortable. I arrived after everyone had already started eating with someone.] What a chaotic morning.

13:2: Yali was making too much noise while I attended the old age club meeting, so I had to leave. It was so chaotic. Am I jeopardizing my relations with the elderly? Am I rushing Yali?

These are some of the many examples of conflict between my role as mother and researcher, with role as mother taking priority. I have found that ethnographies convey a sense of order and control. I felt neither.

13:3: Talk with S and her sister T, both elderly women. S started the conversation by mentioning she noticed I couldn't stay at the old age club because of Yali. Clearly, Yali is both an asset for meeting people (like E), and really a problem sometimes. Yali doesn't like it when I go to my worktable to write field notes in my room. She wants to play with me, read a book, etc. She never lets me nap with her.

16:1: X told me that the little boy, Y, creates a lot of work for her by hanging on to her, while another one is very close to the other *metapelet*. What kind of a way of assessing children is that? Am I talking about Yali the same way? X said that Yali eats chicken and potatoes "without limit." I think that's good, but who knows?

16:2: Took Yali swimming. Some women don't really interact with each other at the pool. They just watch their children, like the *metaplot* do. I am trying to fit in by imitating them. But I'm finding it hard to do. I prefer to play with my child. I wrote up Yali's list of Hebrew words, which is very limited.

16:3: Took Yali to the children's house. She loved watching the kids go to bed. Then she loved going home with me. How ironic.

Although Yali was content playing with the children during the day while I stayed around, it took several more weeks before I could get her to sleep in the *beit yeladim* and several weeks before she could part from me during the day without crying. She had periods of aggressive behavior and other typical two-year-old tantrums. But I worried that my trying to leave her was making her angry. I was always sensitive to how she coped with separation from me, particularly when others were watching.

16:1: My husband left for Jerusalem after taking Yali to the *beit yeladim* with me. I spent the morning there trying to make Yali comfortable. I am learning that the trick of getting Yali used to the *beit yeladim* is having her be there a lot.

18:1: Yali woke up with a stomachache this morning, I was told by a *metapelet*. I took her to the infirmary . . . Then went to her *bayit* . . . Then one of the nurses made her rounds through the *batei yeladim* and looked at Yali's throat, nothing. Then Yali threw up her morning juice. Wouldn't eat breakfast . . . After lunch I put Yali to sleep in the *beit yeladim* . . . When she woke up I brought her to my room, she threw up all over me . . . Took Yali to dinner with my friend Ruth who had come for visit. While I was eating, my husband called. I went downstairs from the dining hall to take the call. I couldn't talk long since Yali was with me . . .

19:1: Went to the *beit yeladim*. Yali wouldn't stay by herself there during breakfast. Meals are the hardest times for her. She copes with my leaving by going to bed, whatever the time of day. At first D and Yali's *metapelet* said I should leave anyhow since they saw no progress in Yali's ability to cope with my leaving. Then I suggested they take Yali for a walk and I would clean up. After more discussion, we decided I would stay with Yali and leave only when I felt comfortable. That is really the wisest decision. Yali's *metapelet* invited me to come to her home on Friday afternoon to tell her what happened since she is going on vacation now (again?) for a few days! Yali and I went to visit the horses.

19:2: I left Yali playing in the *beit yeladim* and went to my room . . . Gave Yali lunch in the *beit yeladim* . . . Then I went for lunch in the *chadar haochel,* then returned to *beit yeladim* to put Yali to bed. I (over)slept in the *beit yeladim* till 4:00 since the person who was supposed to come at 3:00 to wake up all the children and get them ready to go home with their parents didn't show up. N's mother said this is very unusual. Sometimes it happens with the older kids. In their case, they know that at 4:00 they can go home and so they just do it.

So I(!) tried to get all the kids organized for their parents who would pick them up at 4:00 . . .

Took Yali swimming. Saw Yali's *metapelet* who inquired how Yali was doing. She wanted me to start working in the infants' house. (I can just imagine how much conflict that would have created for Yali—to see me working with other children and not her.) I told her I wasn't able yet to help out with the infants. She asked if I'd like to work in the kitchen. Do I know how to cook? (for hundreds of people!) I didn't express much interest but said I'd give it a try if need be. Went back to my room with Yali and then to the home of my sponsor and his wife since she had invited me for coffee, but she wasn't there . . .

I learned that balancing mothering and working on the kibbutz is not resolved once and for all but rather persists and evolves.

67:2: O took Yali and her group on a field trip [to the kitchen] where I was working. I had no idea they were coming. Should I hide behind the door to the pantry so Yali won't see me and get upset when she has to leave? The children received affection from lots of people, e.g. candies from E, hugs from everyone. Miraculously, Yali didn't cry when she left, even though I had decided not to hide.

67:4: C put Yali to bed, and I sat next to her for what seemed like an eternity until she fell asleep.

68:1: Yali is getting more and more aggressive—bites clothes, toys, me; throws things, picks up stones.

72:1: Yali had another "fit," then I left for lunch.

117:5: I came back from the university and picked up Yali at her house. I played with her and with the other parents and their children who were picking up their children. I became embarrassed when she became bossy and cranky. M invited us to his house, but Yali didn't want to go, so we didn't. I would have loved to go.

And then the day came when I tried to have Yali sleep overnight in the *beit yeladim* rather than in my *cheder.* On this particular kibbutz this is done when one of the parents of the child sleeps on a cot next to the child's crib in the *beit yeladim* to make the child feel secure. This process was an incredible ordeal and was a public performance on which many people could comment. Parenting is observed and evaluated.

19:3: T told me where I could get a bed for the night to sleep in the *beit yeladim.*

19:4: Took Yali for a walk to look at the sunset . . . The *shomeret laila* (the female night guard for the children's houses) from 8–10 p.m. tonight is D's wife,

T. I find her rather cold. A somewhat younger pair of women takes over from 10 p.m. to 6 a.m. I put Yali to bed for the first time in the *beit yeladim* rather than in her bed in my *cheder*. No fuss.

20:1: Spent the night with Yali in the *beit yeladim* . . . The night was very hard on me because the *shomrot* have their office in a room adjoining and they made so much noise, talking and arguing until 2:00 a.m., since, after all, it is their work-day . . . I think they ate a meal as well. When I finally said something to a *shomeret,* she said they were simply not paying attention to the volume.

But I was quite pleased with how quickly the *shomeret* came out to comfort a crying child. Of course it would take longer for her to arrive at a more distant children's house. She only said 'shhh' and the child quieted down. It seems to work, although T told me that sometimes the older children run away from the houses and go home to their parents when they are afraid of something, particularly in the winter when there is a lot of noise from the weather. She remembers one time when her son came home soaked up to the waist.

It was imperative to be there [Yali woke up twice], and I'll do it again tonight, but I'll try to sleep in a different spot and tell the *shomrot* to keep it down.

D asked me if I really intend to have Yali sleep in the *beit yeladim* at night because she thinks it is very difficult for the mother! Her mother had a very hard time with it when they arrived on the kibbutz, although she (the child) was old enough to enjoy the independence. Mothers are fearful that something will happen to the child.

. . . I saw T on the path and she said she had thought about the fact that I was doing it rather easily, whereas for some kibbutz mothers it was so difficult!

Clearly people were mothering me to help me mother Yali. Because a child is not the sole responsibility of its parents, one could say that the whole kibbutz (or anyone on the kibbutz) is responsible. The child is truly the product of the kibbutz and not just of his or her family. The same, I discovered, is true for the elderly. They are not the responsibility solely—or even primarily—of their adult children but rather of the kibbutz as a whole. One implication of this idea is that the care may be given (to the child or to the elderly) in a way that the parent or adult child does not entirely endorse.

25:1: Woke, went to Yali. She was crying. It was after 7:00 . . . G (the older woman) said she was so pleased that Yali had spent the night well in the *beit yeladim.* She said she has lots of experience. And you have to be consistent with the children. Even if they cry, you have to take a no-nonsense approach and they have to learn what is expected of them. It's interesting to me that N, the assistant *metapelet*, thinks of me as being nervous, I believe, and tells me to calm down and relax with Yali in terms of not trying to leave all the time. This morning I didn't leave once.

20:2: D told me his wife had told him I had slept at the *beit yeladim*. [Apparently this is newsworthy.] I told him Yali consumes all my time. And he said 'Don't I know!' I guess I am sharing experientially some of the most significant facets of kibbutz life.

20:2: When I came to see Yali, I asked her what she did before I got there, and she remembered having sung with the children . . . She seems happy. I had lunch with the six children . . .

S would have been able to talk with me tonight, but I called it off since I have to be with Yali. That didn't sound right when I said it, as if I resented being a mother. I don't. I adore my child. I'm proud of her. But it's nearly impossible to be both a mother and a fieldworker, at least for now.

22:1: Spent the night in the *beit yeladim* again. This time the *shomrot* were quiet but the children weren't. But I was very impressed with the way the *shomrot* dealt with the children, knowing exactly what they wanted, changing their sheets that were soaking wet, etc. They should be called *metaplot laila* (night child care workers) rather than *shomrot laila* (night guards).

I had a hard time falling asleep after they took care of B who arrived(!) in the middle of the night, so I wrote some notes. Yali did well in the morning. I went back to my room exhausted. Saw T and told her what I was doing. She advised a few more nights of my "sleeping" in the *beit yeladim*.

Having my daughter become part of the group and not be with me twenty-four hours a day, and particularly not during the nights, was a long, uneven process. Some days were positive, and others were awful.

22:4: Spoke with the education coordinator about being pleased with the way things are working out.

23:1: 1:15 p.m. Have a few minutes before going back to Yali. I'm very tired and headachy all the time. Yali was very whiney this morning. Couldn't leave her at all.

23:3: Slept with Yali in the afternoon in the *beit yeladim*. Children dressed nicely awaiting their parents. Came back to my room with Yali and straightened up, waiting for my husband who showed up with guests! Gerontologists from the US. My husband and I were then invited to Yali's *metapelet*'s house for tea. We spoke a lot about Yali's adjustment and how the sleeping arrangement should be tonight. Even when I'm not dealing with the issue, I'm talking about it!

27:1: Back at the *beit yeladim*, Yali's *metapelet* told me she's been thinking all the time about how to integrate Yali, and she sees such a positive difference in her behavior now. She wants to take credit—fine with me.

31:3: Slept a little and went for Yali at 2:30. She slept till 3:00. So, I sat on the floor with the *metapelet* reading a magazine while the children slept. Returned to my room and then brought Yali to her *metapelet*'s house so I could go to the meeting. Yali's *metapelet* took her for a walk to E's and then met me in the *chadar haochel* for dinner. Amazing that this plan worked!

G, the women's work organizer, came over to discuss with me where I would work . . . My one-month time allocation for getting Yali acclimated is up. Now I have to so-called start working.

31:4: Put Yali to bed after a story. O told me that in fact Yali had woken up at 5 a.m. and O had given her a bottle. I felt reassured.

35:2: After I prepared salad in the kitchen, my work assignment, we started scooping out tomatoes for "Friday night vegetarians." Then I went to Yali who was just fine, even ate breakfast by herself! She again woke at 5:30 a.m. and O quieted her without any trouble. She made an elephant out of Lego's.

38:5: Went to visit Yali. She was in fine shape. Didn't fuss at all.

49:6: In the afternoon it was P, a sweet kibbutznik, who was taking care of the children. She reported no trouble with Yali. I sat on the side watching all the parents picking up their children. I'm getting to know the parents, but we just chat and don't feel like friends.

53:2: Went to Yali. She cried when I left.

59:2: Went to Yali. Saw her playing nicely, so went to speak with her *metapelet*. Yali plays nicely with N all the time, I am told. They played doctor with N speaking Hebrew. Yali's *metapelet* asked Yali what she was doing and she said, 'I'm the doctor,' meaning she understood what was going on.

She also asked her *metapelet* for juice in a cup rather than a bottle. X gave her some meat so that she wouldn't eat only chicken. When I went to the playroom, she was sitting at a table with O and N. The table was covered with a blanket (pretend tablecloth), and they were singing and pounding their hands as if it were Shabbat. She seems very well integrated. Yali's *metapelet* claims that Yali understands everything said to her in Hebrew!

Later that day I overheard a conversation between the mother of a child in Yali's group and the *metapelet*:

"Isn't it amazing how quickly Yali is learning Hebrew?" Yali's *metapelet*: "What do you mean, amazing? Both of her parents are professors!"

On the kibbutz, people frequently attribute children's behavior to their parents' values and teaching because they know each child's parents well from living closely in the community. This attribution has both positive and negative implications for the parents. If an adult child leaves the kibbutz, for example, people wonder why her or his parents did not instill love of the kibbutz sufficiently in him or her. It's always the parents' doing, they think. I took Yali's difficulties to heart as my failures, while the *metaplot* took her achievements as their successes.

284:4: Dinner with Q, R and Yali. She was misbehaving and Q said that R's father would never have permitted him to get away with this without a slap on the cheek. [Hint.]

84:3: Went to the kibbutz theater performance with R and Yali. Yali was uncontrollable, so in the middle of the play, I ran back to the children's house to get her a bottle. I felt very uncomfortable and wondered how other parents control their children.

In the evening I went to a meeting of the "nominations committee," and in the middle of it, D and N came in and told me that Yali was crying so I should go back to the *beit yeladim*. When I got there, she had stopped. But when I got back to the meeting, the subject they had been discussing was completed.

285:6: X "let me in" (to the *beit yeladim*) if Yali and I went to another room and Yali didn't cry when I left(!) From there I observed X screaming at the kids to be quiet. Tomorrow is the party for Y's 3rd birthday. Later, X told me she is proud of how disciplined the kids are when they go for a walk, and how they learned to cross the street. She told me doesn't reprimand children for masturbating unless it gets way "out of hand." She is proud of Yali for being dry (i.e. using the potty), promised her gum as a treat, and will go to her house to get it. She lets Yali hand out forks at meals!

Like many mothers, I learned, I had occasional flare-ups and arguments with my child's *metapelet*:

131:2: Worked till a few minutes before noon, swept the floor, and told L that I wouldn't be back today. I went to see Yali. A's grandmother was there and told me that yesterday Yali cried when I didn't come for the *sha'at ahava* (love hour).

I had an initial reaction of guilt, but now, after some thought, I believe that it is not I who must alter my behavior every time Yali cries, but it is she who must learn to accept reality, even though she is only a young child. Moreover, the *metapelet* must support me in this. Yali's *metapelet* wanted to speak with me and said

a) Yali might be getting sick since she is crying a lot.

b) Have I been getting her into her pj's at home as the *metapelet* had suggested?

c) Yali is aggravating A at night. I should tell Yali to stop.

I told the *metapelet* that sometimes Yali bothers A and sometimes vice versa. I said that Yali's *metapelet* should help Yali more. She said NO, she works 'all day' anyhow. I said "How about C next door (in the next children's house)?" She said "There's a special problem there, in that the children were moving into a children's house after sleeping at home for a long time." She also said that the parents want to put their kids to bed by themselves. T was there and said that her son wouldn't go to sleep for anyone else but her. Yali's *metapelet* corrected her and mentioned others whom her son will obey. Everyone is arguing today.

She then said that Yali has me wrapped around her little finger, and I said she has not. Then Yali's *metapelet* suggested that R and I discuss ways we can coordinate putting our children to bed, e.g. one sits with the kids, the other sits in the bathroom, both decide what time they will go, etc. Sounds reasonable to me.

I left there feeling very bad, mostly because Yali's *metapelet* seems accusatory rather than helpful or questioning. I also think she doesn't want Yali to be assertive, but Yali is assertive, and she is also the oldest in the group. N, the assistant *metapelet*, always says that everything is fine, which is also unhelpful.

85:2: Went to see Yali after work. There was thunder and lightning, and I was concerned that she could be frightened. J (not a mother) said I need not be concerned, "They get over it," she knows from her experience as a child-care worker. Yali was fine, but the assistant *metapelet* asked me to tell Yali that she may not play with the light switch or the door.

132:3: R came up to me and asked me what it was like to put Yali to bed last night, since we are now trying to coordinate things. I told her that I had the impression from X that X was irritated. But R said it is not so, 'She would have told you if she were.' It is an Israeli norm to be blunt and honest.

At the *bayit* today, Yali's *metapelet* said that Yali was sweet. I think Yali's *metapelet* has an image of children as management problems rather than little people.

240:4: Went to Yali at 12:15. She was asleep. All children were sleeping. Yali's *metapelet* had gone and had left a note for C to take care of the children. [Is this right?]

281:1: Told Yali's *metapelet* to put the cream on Yali if her pants were dirty. Yali's *metapelet* seemed to think I was crazy to mention it, since she would do it anyhow. What can you say to people here? Can a mother give a *metapelet* instructions, or is it only the other way around?

284:4: P, who always passes me on the path without saying hello, stopped to talk when I asked her how Yali was doing. She [had been the *mekima*] and said that Yali is completely independent, dresses, organizes herself, etc. Independence is valued. A compliment about Yali is a compliment about me.

Having a child while doing fieldwork means that people can assess you by the behavior of your child, if assessing each other is what one does in that culture, as it certainly was in the kibbutz.

Unbeknownst to me, having my daughter sleep in a children's house was more than a matter of convenience for me or an interesting educational opportunity for her. It turned out to be a highly political act. While Yali and I were going through the typical ups and downs of a family relation, and I was excited to be a relatively new mother, kibbutz members told me that I had walked into a minefield for which I was unprepared. I did not realize at the time that child-care arrangements were the most highly charged issue on the kibbutz. I did not know that the question of where children would sleep deeply divided the kibbutz members and that by having Yali sleep in the *beit yeladim* I was making a strong statement that endorsed one of the sides![25]

People made comments about my decision nearly until the day I left the kibbutz.

> 310:1: H (an elderly lady) started telling me how wonderful Yali is, but that she saw Yali walking around on Shabbat as if something was wrong. I told her about how Yali brought her bike to the *bayit* instead of to the *cheder* (my room). Since I didn't know where the bike was, I thought it was lost or stolen. H appreciated the story that Yali brought the bike "home" to the *bayit*. This meant she feels that her *beit yeladim* is her home.

The *mazkirim* in particular felt I was doing the kibbutz a true service because I was demonstrating to them, as a foreigner and as a researcher, that I approve of the kibbutz method of child rearing. Inadvertently I had gained political and social power in one group by the way I handled mothering.

---

[25] Kibbutz society has gone through many such radical changes that are widely reported in the press, including the establishment of factories, the hiring of foreign workers, and most recently, the selling of land. See Joel Brinkley, "Kibbutzim, Israel's Utopias, Develop a Flaw: Debt," *New York Times*, p. 13, March 5, 1989.

CHAPTER 5

Understanding the Elderly as a Consequence of My Mothering Role

Kibbutz factory workers eating breakfast on the job.

As mentioned earlier, the lack of literature on the trials and assets of being a mother in the field probably reflects the fact that few mothers have tried it and perhaps the fact that those who have tried it employed people to care for their children. Because so much of the methodological literature in the social sciences seems to assume that the social scientist is a male or a person without dependents in the field, there is little guidance on how to combine the roles of participant observer and mother. From my own experience, I conclude that to understand how a community functions, the researcher can actually benefit from being a mother.

My decision for Yali to move into a *beit yeladim* turned out to be a statement with significant consequences. If Yali didn't adjust well, for example, it might mean that I personally hadn't handled the matter well (I was a "bad" mother) or that the system didn't work and therefore that opponents of this child-care system would be validated and vindicated. If Yali did adjust well, it meant not only that she was a great child (and possibly I was a good mother) but also that the system worked. Politically, my decision (to have Yali live in a *beit yeladim*) represented the endorsement of traditional values, the values of the pioneers, the values that stood for the uniqueness of the kibbutz way of life. If I had chosen to "keep Yali at home" (i.e., she would sleep in my *heder* and spend only the daytime hours with the children), I would be endorsing a new, antikibbutz, profamily, anticollective education stance.

At first glance I thought the old system of collective care was very poor, particularly in terms of the quality of care given by the *metapelet*'s assistant. If I truly believed that was the case, then I would have to remove Yali from the system and find alternative arrangements in order to do my research. I probably couldn't find any alternative, and therefore I wouldn't be able to carry out my study. Also, if I withdrew Yali from the *beit yeladim,* that would be a slap in the face of all those kibbutz members (I presumed the vast majority) who supported the existing childcare arrangement. Clearly I was in a no-win situation. On the other hand, I would be a terrible mother if I sacrificed my daughter's upbringing for a whole year because of my selfish needs to do research. This ethical/political dilemma was extremely painful.

As it turned out, when I arrived in the kibbutz, a group of mothers who wanted their children "out of the system" had formed. They were going "on strike" (their words), which meant they were simply not obeying kibbutz rules and were letting their children sleep at home. The questionable merit of this group was the most important and most pervasive topic of discussion on the kibbutz at the time. People expressed the opinion that the strike would "bring down the kibbutz," whereas others thought the people who made that dire prediction were mistaken alarmists. To me, a key element of the "strike" was that mothers (not couples or fathers) were agitating to increase their opportunity for mothering. This was not a protest by women who wanted more political power to hold office, as we might find in other countries; it was a protest to have their children sleep at home.[1]

> 20:4: R told me that eight parents are keeping their children home at night against the kibbutz's wishes and in defiance of the formal rule. The parents have promised to put the children back in the *batei yeladim* after the new building is completed. "Perhaps my willingness to have Yali sleep in the *beit yeladim* will influence the group," he said! R said he slept many nights in the *batei yeladim* helping his children get used to sleeping away from their parents.

During the course of my year on the kibbutz, there were a few other "strikes" (e.g., by kitchen workers). In some cases a strike occurred when an individual or a group wanted the kibbutz members as a whole to pay attention to a problem that the striker(s) had alerted them to but that had not been dealt with. This type of strike

---

[1] Maya Narash Gleser, "Kibbutz Women as Office-holders and Their Social Status," *Kibbutz Studies* 31, pp. 22–24 (Efal, Israel: Yad Tabenkin, 1990). See also Bijaoui, Sylvie and Avrahami, Eli, "Co-optation and Change: The Women's Sections of the Kibbutz," in Michal Palgi and Shulamit Reinharz (eds.), *One Hundred Years of Kibbutz Life: The Arts, Ideas, and Reinvention* (in process).

was an attention-getting device. The striking mothers, on the other hand, were not just trying to draw attention to their personal concern; they were striking in order to challenge a basic tenet of this kibbutz's life.

> 23:3: E asked me why I'm putting Yali in the children's house—"it's because you want your evenings free, right?" [In other words, my decision reflects what's good for me rather than what's good for Yali.]

> 23:4: Sat on the bench in front of the dining room and B stopped by. He talked about how he has slept occasionally with the children, that he grew up in a children's home and how he thinks it's a fine system.[2] Nevertheless, when the mother is opposed, he commented, somehow her child is also opposed. And there is a whole group that is opposed and it's a real problem because it represents a problem of control by the kibbutz over the individual (a fundamental issue in collective life). The two *mazkirim* don't want to bring the matter to the *sichah* because they want to avoid a confrontation.

The striking mothers challenged the ability of the *mazkirim* to keep kibbutz life orderly and peaceful. In addition, on another level, the *mazkirim* tried to keep decisions taken by their kibbutz members in line with the policy of the larger kibbutz movement to which they belonged. Of course, some of the mothers were opposed to the strike.

> My sponsor's wife thinks it is very important that I put Yali in the children's house. She would like me to write about my *satisfaction* with the system. "If parents take their children home," she said, "then each family's housing has to be expanded, which is too large an expense for the kibbutz to undertake. If some mothers bring their children home at night, then it influences the other children in the family to want to go home."

Without her understanding the implications of what she was saying, children—if given the choice—clearly would prefer to sleep in their parents' home. Thus, the collective child-care arrangement, although adhering to kibbutz ideology, was not in keeping with the desires of children and parents. Both generations needed to exercise discipline over their own wishes.

> 41:2: Talking to a woman my age in the kitchen. She asked me about Yali's adjustment. She said that sometimes she misses her children in the middle of the night and walks across the kibbutz to see them. As a mother, I can understand that.

At first the heated opinions about child care made my own project on the elderly seem less significant. Little did the kibbutz members or I realize at the time, however, how interconnected the two issues were. For example, if the mothers did not get what they wanted, then perhaps they would leave the kibbutz with their families, with dire consequences for their elderly parents who would be left behind

---

[2] Holmes, Holmes, and Bergman focused on this issue as well: "while most older persons . . . supported the maintenance of children's houses and personally rejected family care for children, they felt that it is up to the current younger generation to make its own decisions about the nature of child care. Even on an issue so central to the ideology of the founding generation, an issue that cuts to the heart of the socialization to collective life and the collective identity, the older generation has been willing to stand aside in favor of the decision-making needs of the younger generation" (pp 1–6).

with fewer economic and personnel resources to care for them.[3] The departure of young families from kibbutzim can be compared with young people in the United States not contributing to Social Security. Old people in the kibbutz had to make sure that the young were happy so as not to have a society that was top-heavy among the elderly.[4] At the same time, the collective child-care arrangements were a component of the founding generation's ideology; in many ways it was what the kibbutz was all about.[5] As one elderly kibbutz member, founder, and theoretician told me, "The kibbutz was an attempt to create a system in which each individual would have a relation to the kibbutz institutions independent of his/her family."

It is well known that a summary of kibbutz ideology is "from each according to his[6] abilities; to each according to his needs." This slogan implies that there will be a balance between needs and abilities in which abilities (productivity) will outweigh needs (costs of services). As this man told me, the principle of "to each according to his needs" means that the kibbutz as a whole takes care of "the weak, the sick and the old." He continued: "In old age, a person is freed from worrying about income, freed from dependence on their children." And I would add, "just as they were freed from taking care of their children when they were young." As he said, "In the kibbutz, everyone enjoys complete independence from one's [adult] children . . . He lives in his room; his standard of living and the satisfaction of his needs are established by the whole society."

At the same time, family members do assist each other, he told me. "Grandparents help parents deal with their children. Adult children [who live on the kibbutz] help their parents in small ways, but the great burden of care falls to the kibbutz as a whole. These 'small ways' are seen as expressions of love." What the oldest generation—the founders —did not expect, however, is that many of the adult children would leave the kibbutz. Founders do not expect people to leave utopia. When commenting sadly on the current departure of their adult children or their friends' children, they ignore the fact that there has always been a trickle of outmigration. Of the sixty-three founders of Kibbutz Emek in the late 1920s, 25 are current members, 23 have died, and 15 have left the kibbutz. Fifty-four members currently aged sixty-five or older joined the kibbutz after its first year of existence. In a sense, the ability to leave is an important positive hallmark of the kibbutz. In this way it is a socialist society without being totalitarian.

Many of the radical changes that kibbutzim have been undergoing, and to which the elderly objected at first (e.g. increased privatization) have actually

---

[3] In no case in this kibbutz was an adult couple accompanied by the parents of either the husband or the wife when the couple left the kibbutz.

[4] Currently many older kibbutzim have a skewed age distribution with an abundance of older people and paucity of younger people.

[5] In his *The Children of the Dream: Communal Child-rearing and American Education* (New York: Macmillan, 1969), psychoanalyst Bruno Bettelheim attributed many aspects of kibbutz members' character to their being raised collectively by a *metapelet* as contrasted to being raised individually by their parents.

[6] Hebrew is a gendered language. It is probably the case that this individual meant "he or she." My translation, however, will use "he" when that is the translation of the Hebrew word that an individual used.

benefited the elderly. The introduction of factories, for example, created new work opportunities for older people who were no longer able to work in agriculture because of the physical strength that agricultural work demands. The widely publicized story about the successful soy-products factory in another kibbutz specifically reported on the benefit to older people in addition to the provision of a workplace: "Besides creating a source of income, the enterprise also provides financial security for aging members and an incentive for the next generation to stay."[7]

An elderly female kibbutz member, who was not a professional analyst of the kibbutz as was the man I quoted earlier but nevertheless did publish articles on aging in the kibbutz,[8] focused on the individuality of elderly kibbutz members. "There's no problem of old age—there's a problem of old people. And old people are so different from one another, the problems must be solved individually, and that's almost impossible." What I deduced from this statement—building on my comparison of the elderly and children—was that whereas children might be treated as a group (collective child rearing), old people must be seen as individuals.

Fortunately the striking mothers were not mothers of the children in Yali's group. If they had been, I would have been left without evening child care and would not have been able to conduct interviews. I would have had to go on strike myself!

> 24:2: She and I talked a long time about the education of the kids. She is working with the group of children whose striking parents took them home. She wants to help them bring their children back to the children's house.
>
> 25:5: Took Yali swimming at 4:00 . . . Came back to my room and just rested. I'm so tired. Yali didn't let me sleep of course . . . After dinner, took Yali for a walk and then to the *beit yeladim*. As we walked around outside in the dark, I taught her the Hebrew word for "moon." Although that was a lot of fun, it was also the case that I could not do anything of my own in the evening. That is not the case with the other mothers of young children. Thank goodness I don't have to go on strike.
>
> 27:1: Again I wasn't called during the night. Arrived at Yali's at 9:00 a.m. She had been perfectly happy when, in response to her whimpering, Yali's *metapelet* said I would come "soon."

My tiredness and my mood were closely related to Yali's ability to sleep through the night at the children's house.

> Saw R from the "health committee." She said in a tone of false complaining, 'See, you slept all night while I was up sitting with P and G at the hospital with inflammation of the nerves [probably shingles] and lungs[?].'
>
> 31:1: Yali not only slept through the night but I didn't go to the bayit till 10 a.m. She did very well without me. Yali's *metapelet* told me that E asked her when

---

[7] Jessica Steinberg, "In Soy Food, Kibbutzim Find Manna for a Modern Age," *New York Times*, pp. W1, W7, April 20, 2004.

[8] Kibbutz Emek, like all kibbutzim, usually publishes an internal newsletter to which kibbutz members contribute articles.

I could start working. She thinks I can tomorrow, but I should come to Yali between 10:00 and 10:45 for the time being. Now the *real* work is going to begin . . .

38:4: Visited P in the hospital as part of my attempt to learn about the proximity and use of the hospital. This was the first time I had met P. She was very interested in Yali's quick adjustment to the *beit yeladim!* How did she know anything about this when she is in the hospital? Why is this topic a source of interest?

I think the answer is that kibbutz visitors to this woman brought her gossip and updates. I might have been the subject of both because I was a newcomer and thus a novelty. In addition, as a researcher I was considered intelligent, and therefore my decision in reference to Yali's sleeping arrangement warranted some attention.

41:6: Brought Yali to bed. Went dancing. Spoke to [my husband] on the phone. Checked Yali. Went back to my room. Wrote field notes. Then I was called around midnight to take care of Yali. The *shomrot* said she doesn't sleep deeply and cries out, asking for me. May be this is too much for her. At 1:30 a.m. I went to sleep.

43:2: When I told Yali's *metapelet* what the *shomrot laila* had said to me, she said they were '*lo beseder*' (out of turn). They should have told the *metapelet* and her assistant—rather than me—that Yali wasn't sleeping well. Clearly, [Yali's *metapelet*] believes in (or at lest adheres to) the collective child-rearing system.

45:5: A (a young mother) says she is opposed to the system. Her 6-year-old daughter is at home (and not sleeping in the children's house as she was supposed to); her 10-year-old son had stayed home till he wanted to go to the *beit yeladim* at age 8. [I was incredulous but didn't express it.] She said it's not natural [but what is?]. She wouldn't have agreed to it as a child. All the problematic kids are at home, she said, so it appears that there are no problems in the *beit yeladim*. The children are fearful. Parents sometimes sleep with the child but it doesn't help. Most parents are unwilling to get up and sit with their children through the night. But, she said, "You must have read a lot about it and know what you're doing." I said I don't know about the influence on the mother. I am relatively calm, not worried; she isn't.

46:1: Woke up at 6 a.m. after going to bed at 4 a.m. Not to say I fell asleep at that hour.

46:3: Yali's *metapelet* now thinks it might be a good idea for Yali *not* to sleep with the kids unless we are going to stay permanently on the kibbutz! She said I should come over to her house one evening to discuss it. Oh no! Are the rules of the game changing?

46:4: Sat down next to the woman who I think is the launderer's wife, who was the *shomeret laila* this past week. She asked me how Yali was doing and I explained about last night.

48:2: The *shomeret laila* of last night came by and said Yali had been very good and had asked for two bottles and drank them without any problems.

49:6: Put Yali to bed with no trouble except that *other children* prevented her from falling asleep. Also the *shomrot* were noisy, playing with their grandchildren. She would have fallen asleep quicker if I had had her at home in my little apartment.

52:1: At dinner, the music teacher stopped by to say I was "brave" to have Yali sleep in the children's house. I am definitely earning prestige in some people's eyes because Yali is sleeping there.

59:2: Yali's *metapelet* said that the *shomeret laila* had to change Yali's bed because she was soaking wet. We should give her less to drink at night. She got my note about coming late. She let Yali know, and it didn't disturb Yali at all. Sometimes I feel that the *metapelet* is my ally and other times, my opponent. I hear that it is the same for other mothers.

59:3: Z said she took it as a 'major compliment' that I trusted her so much to be the *shomeret laila*.

I think Z's comment two months into my stay marks a significant stage. Because kibbutz members know there is nothing more valuable than a child, they took it as a sign of trust on my part that I entrusted my child to them. Nevertheless, as far as my research went, even the collective child-care arrangements did not meet my needs for time to do my work. Being a single mother must be very difficult on the kibbutz, and that may be that is one reason why there aren't any on Kibbutz Emek. After half a year, the arduous process of getting Yali to go to sleep and remain asleep continued.

204:3: Put Yali to bed. It takes forever.

232: Interviewed Y in her home. We had gotten into a state of real understanding. I had raised the thorny question of whether or not she felt it was right for elderly people to take their own lives. She said, "Yes, if they have the courage" and was about to elaborate, when there was a knock on her door and the *shomeret laila* said, "Shula, your daughter is crying and throwing up." I excused myself and left..

233:1: Yali wouldn't go to bed. I couldn't dance.

233:3: The *shomrot laila* didn't call me, so I suppose Yali slept right through the night.

284:5: Put Yali to bed. P leaves at 8:30 p.m. regardless of whether or not her child is asleep! She knows that her child will now be taken care of by whoever else comes. It makes sense for her, since she has to go off to put her other children to bed in the other *batei yeladim*. But it means more work for me since I have to deal both with Yali and the kids whose parents have left. True, I don't have other children of my own to put to bed, but I do have other work to do! Probably balances out in the long run. Would have been nice for her to mention it to me, though.

From this last note it is evident that by virtue of being a mother on the kibbutz, I was responsible for many of the other children from time to time.

Although fortunately, unlike a previous researcher on this kibbutz, I was not put to the test of how I would act if war was imminent, the kibbutz members actually tested me in terms of the child-care decisions I made and in terms of my mothering behavior more generally. Would I adopt the kibbutz system of having my child live separately from me? My placement of Yali in what actually was the kibbutz's normative system (although undergoing radical transition) signaled to kibbutz members that I had confidence in the kibbutz way of doing things. I believe that ultimately Yali was interpreted as a gift I brought to the kibbutz, a gift in which we could all share for a year. There is enormous love of children on kibbutzim, and Yali added to the pool of children to love. Thus, most of the time people were tolerant of the chaos a young child can generate, even if it inconvenienced them.

> 289:7: M said, "I used to be a *metapelet* myself. I remember standing on the porch after the children were in bed and listening to them talk. Now I like to watch Yali play and sometimes I stand by the fence to do so." I was so touched by her appreciation of Yali.
>
> 322:3: T told me that when he was walking to the dining room in morning, he had passed Yali walking alone to our room, singing. He got pleasure in it, he told me.
>
> 303:5: S invited Yali to her house for a piece of gum, which she went and got, and then returned to the dining room—all by herself!
>
> 322:3: A passed our table at lunch and tried to get Yali to say hello to her, unsuccessful. How does that make A feel about me?
>
> 327:2: Z commented to me that sometimes Yali stands in the *hadar haochel* and examines everyone deeply without going up to them, with self-confidence, while I talk to others.
>
> 330:5: She thinks Yali is wonderful; she liked the way I accepted what the *va'adat chinuch* [education committee] said about placing her in a *beit yeladim*, whereas mothers here don't accept their judgment.

Clearly Yali was both a source of utter chaos and a social bridge, just as children are for their parents elsewhere.

> 136:6: My sponsor says that the members of the old age club don't want me to bring Yali. It's difficult enough for them to hear the speaker, let alone have to cope with the noise a child makes. Also, they generally take care of their own grand-children in the afternoons and this is their one chance to get away. They don't want other people's grandchildren there. This makes sense to me. If I bring Yali, every-one would bring grandchildren! (The domino effect of grandchildren!) Is this his opinion or theirs?
>
> 81:2: [My husband] was eating with the men he had been working with; Yali pulled him away so he would eat with her and me. He left to go to work. Then Yali saw 75-year-old G, went over to her, and started talking. I was not able to eat while simultaneously watching Yali running around talking to everybody. Even-tually I moved my chair over to G. [I am very much aware of the extent to which women have extreme obstacles in doing their work since their children tug at them continuously. And this with only one child!] S joined G and me. I attempted to talk to them about the meeting we had attended last night. Yali interrupted all the time. We couldn't talk, but Yali and G could!
>
> 205:1: Went to Yali after lunch. She no longer takes her medicine willingly. No one had put socks on her. I then left Yali to go back to the *heder*. Typed a letter, picked up a kerosene heater since I'm cold in my room, worked a little and went to sleep for the kibbutz's afternoon nap time. R brought Yali with A. They played together awhile. Then R came to pick A up and invited Yali to watch TV. I went with them. R said Yali could stay there so that I could attend old age club. Ironic since it's for her age group, but she was in role of grandmother and thus did not attend.
>
> 205:1: After the old age club, ran back to R where Yali was, in order to bring her to the *hadar haochel* for dinner, but she didn't want to leave. So I returned to the *hadar haochel*, got food, brought it to R's and we all ate together.

As a mother, I was public and normative. But as a thirty-three-year-old with only one child, who was only three years old, I was deviant. No child in Yali's group was a single child. Whereas by virtue of being my first child, Yali was my oldest, all the other children in her group were the youngest in their families. Each had two, three, or four older siblings. With all the child-centeredness of the kibbutz, it is probably inevitable that I toyed with the idea of trying to have a second child while in the field, but that would have been completely unmanageable for me, although possibly welcome in other people's eyes.

As mentioned earlier, being a mother of a three-year-old forced me to enter into and take sides in the contentious debate between the older policy of communal child rearing (and sleeping) and the newer, rebellious activism among supporters of family-based residence of children. Most important for this study, however, was my ability to learn that the conflict between *one's commitment to a kibbutz policy* and *to one's own offspring* was not limited to young children. Rather, it persisted throughout the life of some kibbutz members. As it turned out, seventy-three adult children of the people over the age of sixty-five are no longer, or never became, members of Kibbutz Emek. These are seventy-three people "lost" to the kibbutz. Another way to put this data is that of the people over the age of sixty-five, three never had children; forty-two families have at least one child living off the kibbutz, either permanently or temporarily; and only fifteen families have no adult children who live off the kibbutz. Thus, it is normative to have children who have decided not to join Kibbutz Emek, and it is atypical (and thus prestigious) to have all your adult children become members of your kibbutz. As the elderly continue to age, they need the assistance of individuals who remain on the kibbutz.

Parents with an adult child who resides permanently "off the kibbutz" have defined certain requirements that need to be met by the kibbutz in order for them to feel content, just as is true of parents of young children, although the specific needs are dissimilar. At the time of this study, four items were paramount.

1. Time off from work to travel to visit the adult child. Most of the workplaces are flexible and enable the older person to take time off. On the other hand, this very flexibility demonstrates to some that the work they are doing is not vital to the kibbutz and that, unlike in the past, the kibbutz cares more about its members' needs than its economic well-being. The parallel issue with regard to child care is the fact that parents (usually mothers) have an hour off work each day to visit their children in the *batei yeladim*. This hour is called *sha'at ahava* (love hour).

2. Telephone communication. At the time of this study, telephone communication was limited and awkward. Few members had a private telephone in their homes, and most phone calls had to be made at a public switchboard, located on the ground floor beneath the dining hall and immediately next to the mailboxes where members gathered continuously. During my year on the kibbutz, the public telephone was frequently broken; the switchboard was open only from 6:30 A.M. to 2 P.M., the normal work hours of the switchboard operators and everyone else on the kibbutz. In addition, because there were only one or two public phones, people frequently felt rushed and under pressure to limit their conversations out of consideration for others waiting to use the phones. They also limited their calls for financial reasons because they were not paying for the call themselves; they were incurring a cost for the kibbutz. The fact that some members have access to telephones in their workplaces or have private phones in their homes because of

their work arouses jealousy and resentment. The fact that other kibbutzim have arranged to keep their switchboards available throughout the afternoon and evening hours increased people's annoyance with the system at Emek. Only during the wars, I was told, did Emek extend the hours of the switchboard's availability to members. It is likely that none of this matters today because of the ubiquity of cell phones. The question might have arisen, however, as to who pays for the cell phone bills—the individual or the kibbutz?

3. Facilities to host the adult child (with his or her family) in the parents' home or in a separate building when he or she visits the kibbutz. The design of the members' rooms made it difficult to host overnight guests. Sometimes a "free room" somewhere on the kibbutz could be used temporarily, but then one had to chase down the person with the keys to such a room and clean the room oneself in advance of the guests' arrival. In my recommendations to the kibbutz, I suggested it would be advantageous to organize arrangements for guests in a more convenient manner. The question is whether the very presence of these adult children reminds the kibbutz that they have not become members. It is possible that kibbutz members are not eager to put themselves out for people who left, and even more crassly, they are not interested in putting themselves out for those who have left their parents behind for other kibbutz members to care for.

4. Some kibbutz member parents feel the responsibility or the desire to help their adult child financially when the adult child leaves the kibbutz or when the adult child is about to make a big purchase, such as a new home, or on a regular basis if the adult child has financial difficulties. In Israeli society, it is normative for parents to either purchase an apartment for their adult child at the time of the adult child's marriage or at least to help with the purchase. The parents living in a kibbutz can use all or a portion of their personal budget for this purpose, and many older people do so because their own need for cash is quite limited. They can also get some extra money by "cashing in" their vacation subsidy or applying to the *mazkirut* for special assistance.

Some older people and some younger ones as well consider the inability of members to aid their children who do not live on the kibbutz to be a major problem. If this is the case, then people who think that their children might leave will consider opening bank accounts (secretly) for this purpose, or they will find some other procedures in order to acquire funds to help their children in the future. The loyalty to adult children who have left the kibbutz trumps—in most cases—the need to comply with kibbutz rules that the members had agreed to abide by concerning individual accumulation of funds. The desire to help adult children is creating new pressures on kibbutz values and practices. To my mind, it is part and parcel of the concurrent issue of young parents not wanting to have their children sleep in children's houses, despite the fact that to "keep them at home" violates kibbutz policy. The attachment to one's children—whether when they are young or grown—has proven to be very strong.

> 211:1: A stopped by during the party to show her husband the mail they had received, which included two letters from prospective volunteers in England, and one from the daughter of his cousin in the U.S. Both letters were in English and

her husband read them quite well. This elderly couple has frequent visitors from among the volunteers—current and former. They have not taken a vacation in years because the husband has saved the vacation subsidy, wanting to give the money to his daughter. He has already bought her a heater and helped her buy her house.

The desire to have cash to help family members and the need to find a system to meet this concern are new phenomena, arising because of the changing age structure of the kibbutz. As Josef Shatil wrote in 1972, "In the small commune of the first kibbutz, with an undeveloped economy and only about fifty or sixty members, there was no need to have a set division of responsibilities. Every evening the entire kibbutz sat together to plan the work for the next day. A member who needed a little money to travel to the city knew to which desk to go to find it. But the kibbutzim grew. Their economies developed and their needs became more varied."[9] Kibbutzim are larger now and have new intergenerational needs.

5. Travel abroad to visit adult children and grandchildren is considered a legitimate need by most kibbutz members, although there is resentment against the adult children who have left Israel to live elsewhere. Even during the year of my study, when, for cost-saving reasons, travel abroad was restricted except for special circumstances (e.g., assisting parents and taking work-related dance and sports trips have been approved), an older person's request to travel abroad to visit an adult child and another to visit an elderly relative were approved during a *sichat kibbutz* without discussion. Again, now that this kibbutz is fifty years old, family needs trump kibbutz policies and even kibbutz financial straits. This was not the case in the past.

6. Assistance—both physical and financial—in traveling to visit one's adult children. This means that if a single elderly person is about to travel, he or she might need to be accompanied by a younger person. Also, if she or he cannot manage traveling by bus, she or he might request that the kibbutz provide car transportation and compensate her or him in the same manner as someone traveling by bus. The values conflict between supporting one's adult child and supporting one's kibbutz is a variant of the perpetual tug between satisfying the needs of the self and of the group to which one belongs.

Approximately eight months after I delivered my report to the *mazkirim* at the end of my stay, the kibbutz took a survey of its members' attitudes.[10] Ninety-five members participated and listed their satisfactions and dissatisfactions with the kibbutz. The five most frequently cited sources of dissatisfaction were (1) the "general social situation," (2) inequality among members, (3) the lack of demographic growth because of the departure of kibbutz-born youth, (4) the way the

---

[9] Josef Shatil, "Kibbutz Changes in the 60's and 70's," *Israel Horizons* 20(3–4), 1972.

[10] One kibbutz member whom I befriended sent me newsletters on a regular basis after I returned home.

kibbutz has resorted to hiring labor rather than relying on self-labor,[11] and (5) lack of communication among the generations.[12]

The kibbutz created a standing committee with the title "Committee on the Elderly," composed of middle-aged women who attempted to improve the quality of life of the elderly and to advocate on their behalf. I attended most of the committee's meetings during the year I spent on Emek. The committee was active and understood that many older people whose children have left the kibbutz face psychological hardships. To deal with this situation, they encouraged "adoption," a system that is used to make Ulpan members and volunteers feel more at home on the kibbutz. Thus, the committee reported approvingly that there was at least one case of a middle-aged member who has informally "adopted" an older couple without (adult) children on the kibbutz. These people are considered to be "alone," again reinforcing the fact that the intergenerational family—not the single individual—has become the essential institution for feeling at home on the kibbutz. Similarly, this issue in modified form was at the heart of the striking mothers whose *beit yeladim* abutted that in which Yali was living.

---

[11] Kibbutz ideology generally opposes the idea of hiring nonkibbutz members because a hired laborer by definition is exploited so that the business (in this case the kibbutz) can make a profit.

[12] Internal newsletter of Kibbutz Emek, March 27, 1981.

CHAPTER 6

Being a Woman, a Wife, 33 years old,
a Jew and a Potential Member

My husband fulfilling his kitchen duties.

At the time of this study (1979–1980), I was concerned with women's rights and called myself a feminist, but my consciousness about these issues was much less informed than it is now. In addition, at that time there was little, if any, discussion in the fieldwork literature about the impact of gender on research methods. In the last two decades, however, this topic has received much attention.

"... Gender differences in fieldwork are not simply a source of difficulty for male and female researchers, which lead to exclusion from particular social situations. Rather, these differences constitute a source of knowledge within a specific situation. It is not a matter of trying to 'overcome' the effects which the gender of the researcher has on a particular field situation, but to explore how the participant observer's gender identity becomes intertwined with the process of knowing."[1]

Now gender awareness is strong in the fieldwork literature, particularly in reports written by women researchers.

I came into the kibbutz as a woman, one of my personal selves. My gender had a decisive role in my job assignments[2] and relationships. Similarly, my gender identity was strongly *reinforced* by my entry into the world of women's work. The settings I chose to work in—a division of the factory, a branch of the laundry, the greenhouse, and the chicken coop—were attractive to me as a sociologist because elderly people predominated there or ran those branches.[3] The women's labor organizer in the kibbutz (*sadranit avodah*) asked me to work, however, where the kibbutz always has a labor shortage. Those are the branches that women are supposed to fill—the kitchen and children's houses.[4] The women's branches were always seeking workers because these work areas had little appeal and low prestige. Their pool of workers was all women, rather than all people. As a woman, I was part of the "female labor force" managed by the *sadranit avodah*.[5] Carrying out the work that the *sadranit avodah* wanted me to do reinforced the notion that I was a "typical, normal, or natural" woman. Essentialism was in full swing on the kibbutz.[6] The men brought in the money; the women contributed babies. Both were necessary and valued,[7] but the men's work had greater prestige and freedom of movement.[8] If I had declined women's work, I believe the women of the kibbutz would have resented me, particularly because I had a child using the kibbutz's child-care services. I may have been seen as thinking I was "too good" for these jobs, that I was a snob. I would also have been making a political statement

---

[1] Les Back, "Gendered Participation: Masculinity and Fieldwork in a South London Adolescent Community," in Diane Bell, Pat Caplan, and Wazir Jahan Karim (eds.), *Gendered Fields: Women, Men & Ethnography*, pp. 215–233 (London: Routledge & Kegan Paul, 1993).

[2] Calvin Goldscheider wrote that there is "greater gender occupational segregation in the kibbutz than in Israel as a whole . . . the occupational status of women in the kibbutz is simply inferior to that of women in the rest of Israel." *Israel's Changing Society: Population, Ethnicity and Development*, p. 163 (Boulder, CO: Westview Press, 1996).

[3] I did not work in settings that required skills I did not have, for example, physician, bookkeeper, organizer of the factory, mechanic.

[4] Women on the kibbutz may have a harder time eliminating class differences in labor than do men.

[5] Kibbutz member who organizes the female labor force. This is a rotating position.

[6] "Essentialism is the view that there is an essential, innate human nature based on biological reality . . . Essentialist thinking was often couched in universals, forcing all women into a single grouping because the paramount characteristic of 'woman' was seen as her difference from 'man.'" Hunter College Women's Studies Collective, *Women's Realities, Women's Choices*, p. 71 (New York: Oxford University Press, 2005).

[7] For example, on the holiday of Shavuot, all the mothers who had given birth during the previous year rode with their babies on a hay-covered flatbed truck drawn by a tractor. The fathers did not ride in this way.

[8] See also Susan Sered, *What Makes Women Sick? Maternity, Modesty and Militarism in Israeli Society* (Hanover, NH, and London: Brandeis University Press, 2000).

about the desirability of women entering nontraditional work and avoiding women's work.

> 289:5: [At the mechanic's (N) house, elderly couple] I thanked him for fixing Yali's stroller. "Maybe I should work in the metal shop," I said, just to tease. "No women worked there," N replied, "there has never been a woman working there. In the beginning (of Emek's existence), the women wanted to drive the tractors, but they stopped. No one forced them out." He thinks people are doing their "natural work." He read in the kibbutz publications that men were going to start working as kindergarten teachers, but he thinks that it's always going to be only one or two (men who do this). On the other hand, M, his wife, thought men *should* go into it. "They have the right and the responsibility to do so," she said. I believe this difference of opinion represents the fact that social change is in the making, but isn't here yet. There may be a "cultural lag" here, as Mirra Komorovsky wrote.[9]

During the year of my fieldwork, not a single man worked in child care.[10] Toward the end of the year, my sponsor arranged that the enthusiastic but inexperienced and untrained seventeen-year-old son (B) of one of his American friends could volunteer on the kibbutz as a child-care worker!

> 323:7: My sponsor talks to U, the coordinator of the education committee. It is being arranged! Whom will B work with? He wants to work with the older kids. But perhaps he'll work with Yali's *metapelet* X since no one wants to work with her or perhaps with Z since she is "leaving" to study physical care of children at the hospital. This means he would work with L. I can't even begin to picture it, and yet they are open to considering it probably because he's an outsider. Since no one wants to work in child care, everyone is welcome to work in child care. Barriers to entry into that line of work here are very low. But having a boy work in child care is an innovation from the outside, not from inside the kibbutz.[11]

Men were the opinion setters in the kibbutz, and generally they perceived work branches such as the kitchen, *batei yeladim*, and laundry as nonproductive and therefore worth less than branches such as agriculture and industry, which brought in income. The issue of job placement was one example of the fact that I was always perceived as a woman.

Being a woman was an asset at times and an obstacle at others, to my getting to know certain aspects of kibbutz life. With younger women, I shared the roles of mother, night guard of the *batei yeladim,* worker in the *beit yeladim*, and kitchen worker. I became acquainted with the younger men because of these women's roles. They were the husbands of the women with whom I worked, the fathers of the children in my daughter's group, the sons of the older people I was

---

[9] See Mirra Komarovsky, "Cultural Contradictions and Sex Roles," *The American Journal of Sociology*, vol 52, no. 3 (November 1946): 184–89.

[10] See Rae Lesser Blumberg, "As You Sow, So Shall You Reap: Updating a Structural Analysis of Sexual Stratification in the Kibbutz," *Gender & Society* 1(3), 1987.

[11] In general, Israel is not an insular society and is open to many ideas from other cultures. Those who don't like these innovations blame the outside cultures rather than understand that some Israeli insiders are adopting them. An example is feminism, which frequently is "blamed" on Americans by its Israeli critics.

interviewing, the co-workers in a labor branch, or the occupants of important roles in the kibbutz that led me to interview them. It was logically impossible to be part of all-male groups to learn what kinds of topics arose among them. For this kind of information, my husband's occasional visits were very helpful to me.

> 81:1: Yom Kippur. Almost everyone is eating.[12] Another political statement! My husband went to the dining room to wash dishes. [Yali and I went to join him for breakfast later, something I would never do on Yom Kippur back in the States. He had just sat down to eat with the men who had been working with him. Later he told me that they had been gossiping about what people were doing, i.e. eating or fasting. I was interested because obviously I have never been in an all-male conversation on the kibbutz.[13]

Being part of a group of conversing men was not taboo for a woman but merely unusual. There needed to be a reason to be part of the group.

> 313:8: Picked up Yali, took her swimming, O was there, I asked him about the car; V (male) overheard us and said that no one wants the job of organizing the cars ever since D died in a car crash. But V is annoyed that there are only 3 cars at the kibbutz members' disposal. B, who was there, slid his beach chair over to V and got into a long conversation about this problem. Then Y joined the group. As in a cocktail party, conversation partners are constantly changing. This was a rare opportunity for me to sit next to a group of guys talking among themselves.

I had no difficulties in setting up one-on-one *formal* interviews with men, but it felt awkward for me to socialize *informally* with male groups.[14]

Old men had lost the prestige that younger men had on the kibbutz, the prestige that inhered in the "cult of masculinity"[15] that was part of the country's founding ideology and persists to this day.[16] With aging, masculinity diminished, and therefore my access to older men increased.[17] In general, gerontologists have found that gender distinctions diminish greatly in old age. In the kibbutz this was true as well. The gender distinctions among old people seemed less significant than among younger people. I was almost as likely to "hang out" with a group of old men as I was with a group of old women. In addition, the older people—men and women—were generally defined as "Shula's customers."

---

[12] The Jewish religion instructs Jews to fast on Yom Kippur, the Day of Atonement. There are religious kibbutzim where all members fast on Yom Kippur.

[13] When male-female couples go into the field together, it is typical for the man to study the men or male institutions and for the woman to study the women and their concerns.

[14] For a discussion of this problem, see "Appendix: Methodology," in Jacqueline P. Wiseman, *Stations of the Lost: The Treatment of Skid Row Alcoholics* (Chicago: University of Chicago Press, 1970/1979).

[15] See Tamar Mayer, "From Zero to Hero: Masculinity in Jewish Nationalism," in Esther Fuchs (ed.), *Israeli Women's Studies* (New Brunswick, NJ: Rutgers University Press, 2005). See also Liora R. Halperin, "Is It Really Fate? The 'Women's Question' on the Kibbutz in the Midst of the 1936 Arab Revolt," unpublished ms., 2003.

[16] Selma Koss Brown, "Illusion of Equality: Kibbutz Women and the Ideology of the 'New Jew,'" *International Journal of Women's Studies* 2(3):268–286, 1979.

[17] See Barbara Myerhoff, *Number Our Days* (New York: Touchstone Books, 1978).

I believe there were numerous occasions in which I was seen not as a "regular woman," but as androgynous because I was a researcher, a temporary resident, and a person from America. Thus, men were comfortable making sexist remarks in front of me because I was "not a kibbutz woman."

> 285:7: He was talking about accents and said that Chaim Herzog is the radio announcer during wars even though he is not militarily accurate, because his voice is a comfort to housewives. [What a putdown!]

Some elderly men disparaged the work and workers of the collective laundry[18] where I worked even though their own wives worked there: "It's really a waste of your time working in the laundry, there are only old women there, and you won't learn anything." And he knew I'm studying aging!

In most respects, being a woman was an enormous asset for developing rapport with the older members, many of whom may have seen me as a surrogate daughter or a social worker, a typically female role.[19] It was easy for me to sit and talk with old men and women, particularly those who were interested in taking on the role of my teacher or of the surrogate grandparent of my daughter. With them, I was easily able to establish a friendship that I could draw on while doing research and while resting from that role. They also were available to me as potential friends because they had free time, something less available to younger people.

In addition to being perceived as a "woman," I was also a "heterosexual woman," although the significance of that identity is apparent to me only now. There was one lesbian couple on the kibbutz, and there were possibly other women who were not "out" as lesbians.[20] Although nonmembers, the two women of the lesbian couple were socially accepted, in my opinion, because they were good workers and had lived on the kibbutz for a long time. Had I been a lesbian, I probably would have spent more time with them than I did. As a heterosexual woman, wife, and mother, I interacted with this couple as friends and neighbors and never discussed their relationship. The whole topic of "homosexuality" remained largely invisible except for the following conversation:

> 284:3: S talked about her three children with me. The three of them are completely different from one another. N is an uncomplicated guy. A, on the other hand, is very complicated and "talks to her about things." She gave as an example the fact that he had invited a volunteer to his room [i.e. initiated a potential sexual encounter]. The volunteer "was difficult" at first and explained to him that she was "sort of a lesbian." She has been here for a year and lives with a woman in the volunteer quarters. "But after that things were ok," S told me. She explained to her son that sometimes people like both sexes. [I couldn't figure out what she meant by "ok." Did her son have sex with the volunteer or did he understand why the

---

[18] Collective laundry where clean clothes are folded, ironed, repaired, and sorted.

[19] Lois Easterday, Diana Papdemas, Laura Schorr, and Catherine Valentine, "The Making of a Female Researcher: Role Problems in Fieldwork," *Urban Life* 6(3):333–348, 1977.

[20] See Nurit Barkai, "To Re-construct the Community: Lesbians on a Kibbutz," in Chava Frankfort-Nachmias and Erella Shadmi (eds.), *Sappho in the Holy Land: Lesbian Existence and Dilemmas in Contemporary Israel*, pp. 65–72 (Albany: SUNY Press, 2005).

volunteer was not interested?] We talked about the naturalness of homosexuality and that we repress ourselves.

As a young woman whose husband was not present on the kibbutz most of the time, I was the object of a certain amount of sexual attention, some of which was disguised by one individual as "trying to be helpful to me in my research." He visited me late at night, brought me gifts, and talked about his sexual prowess with other women. He told me that "free love" was an honored kibbutz tradition. It took enormous effort and tact to discourage his sexual attention while retaining his willingness to be helpful to me in my research.[21] I truly wanted him as a friend. Ruth Horowitz writes briefly about how she managed a related situation:

> My lack of care with appearance, which both males and females continually remarked upon, allowed me to play down my sexual identity. However, I was very careful not to spend too much time alone with any one male and not to dance with them at the many parties and dances I attended. . . . The first dimension of my identity that I discovered they were constructing was as 'a lady,' which placed me in a respected but somewhat distant position from them. A 'lady' implied that a woman was unobtainable sexually.[22]

One of the strategies I used to dampen this kibbutz member's sexual interest in me was to try to befriend other people in his family, thereby making our relation one between his family and me rather than simply between the two of us. In addition to my own disinterest in a sexual relation, I learned that it is not the kibbutz norm to have affairs. To allow such a relation to develop would, I believe, have cast me in the role of "sexually available volunteer" or "neurotic American" who is easily exploited, in other words, a fool.

> 283:1: I slept later than usual; straightened up my room; feeling wonderful after having danced last night. P is probably right when he told me that I have excess libido, which is why I love the excitement of dancing! But is he saying that as a come-on as well?

I may not have been the object of sexual harassment from others (except one elderly man, discussed later) because I am an average-looking woman who, although slim, is not exotic. Tall blondes from Scandinavia who volunteer on the kibbutz usually have a different experience.

Having a husband in a community that places a high value on marriage and monogamy meant that men would be unlikely to hassle me and that kibbutz women would not feel threatened, as they might be if a single woman lived among them for a year. Having a husband who was not around much of the time, however, meant that I was subject to a certain amount of mild flirtation and teasing.

> 175:2: E was teasing me about trying to get into my apartment instead of his son's since the apartments look the same. He told me a joke about a man who makes this mistake while a woman is showering and hangs around to apologize.

---

[21] Lenore Manderson, "Taboo: Sex, Identity and Erotic Subjectivity in Anthropological Fieldwork," *Oceania* 67, 1997. See also Amanda Coffey, *The Ethnographic Self: Fieldwork and the Representation of Identity* (Beverly Hills, CA: Sage, 1999).

[22] Ruth Horowitz, "Getting In," in Carolyn D. Smith and William Kornblum (eds.), *In the Field*, p. 49 (New York: Praeger, 1989).

Another instance of mild flirtation and teasing lasted over several days at the start of my project. It could be that several kibbutz men were testing me to see what kind of a woman I was and what my "real" reason was for spending a year on a kibbutz without my husband. In addition, in the beginning of the project, before I knew many people, and while I was trying to establish myself as "worth talking to," I would impulsively just sit next to someone and introduce myself so that I could get to know him. It is possible that some men saw this behavior as sexually provocative. I then had to extricate myself.

> 27:2: I told him (M, an older man) what I was doing here at Emek, my method of interviewing people, etc. I first thought he was someone else. I didn't even know his name.
>
> 27:2: He told me that everyday he walks to the nearby town and back, just for the exercise. He does that at 5:00 in the afternoon. Innocently, I asked him what he sees along the way. And he said, 'young women.'
>
> 31:3: I'm beginning to feel a little uncomfortable around him. He seemed to try to hold my hand, or am I mistaken? He showed me his office. He says he has two jobs and gets two salaries. I have to find out about him from someone.
>
> 33:1: I had lunch with someone whose name I think is E. I could be completely wrong. Plopped myself down opposite her. Didn't eat with M even though he was hanging around as if I would do so. I was rejecting him.

After a while, I decided to sit down next to him again so that he would not define my *not* doing so as evidence of any sexual ambivalence on my part. I thought having lunch with him would demonstrate that we could have a "normal" relationship. I think, though, that he took it to mean something else.

> 111:6: He told me he had just read a book about the Eskimos who have a custom—when a guest comes, you let him sleep with your wife. If he doesn't do so, you are insulted. "I finished reading another book by a journalist who walked from Nepal to Tibet and on the way saw strange things. In one isolated area there was no town but just a few families living together consisting of several brothers and one woman who was wife to all of them. When a child was born, they didn't know whose it was. When this man visited the aristocracy he was led, as a guest, to the bedroom of the host's wife. I think that is a great custom," he concluded.

I said, "It is always interesting to talk to you, that's why I joined you for lunch."

He said, "Oh, I'm disappointed that that's why. This week my wife has been in the city visiting someone, so I've been alone a lot, watching a lot of TV. I've been freer than usual."

> 131:3: He sat down to tell me about his fall today or yesterday. He slipped down the steps of the office building because of his slick sandals. He told me the details of what happened since then. He has pain whenever he changes movements. The doctor took a look but didn't say a thing about what he should do, including whether to put heat or cold on it. I suggested massage. He said it would definitely help him to be massaged by a young woman. I felt I had fallen into a trap.

After this encounter, I realized that what this man wanted to do was have a harmless, joking relation with me. His goal was to see me squirm. I allowed that kind of a relation to continue and also tried to develop a relationship with his wife.

Months later, while I interviewed a young female kibbutz member about the place of volunteers on the kibbutz, she said

> 120: In the last three years something happened to the old people.

> Me: Which old people?
> She: People like M. I think they haven't spoken to anyone in their lives except the volunteers. [Laughter]

I recognized that what I had experienced with this man was part of a pattern for him. He had very strained relations with other members of the kibbutz, and so outsiders (i.e., female volunteers and researchers) played a useful role in his life. This woman's remark also reminded me that everyone knew who was talking to whom and constructed an image of them based on these observations.

Being a woman meant that I utilized some of the cosmetic services on the kibbutz. To the best of my knowledge, men did not do this. The beauty parlor was a gossip mill.

> 60:3: C pointed out S from whom I could get a haircut. S is an attractive young woman who had just returned from Paris where she visited her mother. M told the story that S had told her: "When the clerk at Ben Gurion airport saw that she came from the kibbutz, he called his supervisor over to see what kibbutz women could look like." C said this wasn't a compliment to herself as a kibbutz woman, and also that S didn't look Parisian, but rather *South* Parisian, which is where immigrants from North Africa live (which means she is *Mizrachi* and not *Ashkenazi*). C stressed that S actually was born in Morocco (low prestige country of origin).

Even though getting a haircut is not an intimate experience, my choosing to have S cut my hair allowed for a certain closeness that helped us establish a relationship.

BEING A WIFE

Among the variety of personal selves that was significant for doing my research, the roles of mother and woman ranked high and complemented, but were not the same as, the role of wife. After spending the first week with us on the kibbutz, helping us settle in, my husband, then a professor of history at the University of Michigan, moved to Jerusalem to carry out his own research projects. Because I wore a wedding ring, and perhaps because I had a child, I believe that most people on the kibbutz knew I was married, even though my husband was not with me most of the time.

> 327:3: H says that he knows that J from Los Angeles is married. He was informed that everyone should stay away from her even though she doesn't wear a wedding ring. He himself doesn't wear a ring for three reasons: his friend had his finger ripped off because of a ring, it will get lost in the orchard. And why advertise you're married, it will just turn people off! Clearly, he was flirting with me. "Your own ring made your position crystal clear," he said.

Nearly every subsequent Thursday afternoon my husband drove to Emek from Jerusalem, and every Sunday morning he left Emek to return to Jerusalem.

On Fridays while I was at work, he went to the kibbutz archive to do research of his own.

In addition, my husband spent one week at Emek during the winter and visited us during holidays whenever he could. He also traveled abroad occasionally. Because of his travel both in the country and abroad, my family life was similar to that of several kibbutz women whose husbands served in the army or were involved in some other work outside the kibbutz that necessitated their residing away from their families. Sometimes people interpreted this absence as bad for children.

> 22:2: R is O's grandmother; O's father is her son. He is a dancer and travels a lot, so "O has the same problem as Yali, not seeing his father very much," R said.
>
> 322:3: S brought an Egged bus driver[23] from town to look into the possibility of buying our car when we leave the country. The two of them and my husband sat at one table, while Yali and I sat at another. R came up to me and said I should join the three men since Yali doesn't see her father very much! (I was so taken aback by being told what to do, that I couldn't even come up with a quick retort!)

In the eyes of some, I was thus not only a mother but also a mother who might be endangering her child by allowing the child's father to be absent a lot. Thus, I was grouped with the mothers of children with relatively absent fathers.

This idea of family members not fulfilling their obligations was not limited to mothers and fathers of children but had serious repercussions for the care of the elderly kibbutz members. As many kibbutz members told me sarcastically, young people who leave the kibbutz receive the greatest gift imaginable—care of their parents free of charge. In other words, because the kibbutz is responsible for all its members, that obligation stays in place even when family members leave. I, too, was benefiting from this philosophy—the kibbutz replaced the tasks that my husband might have assumed. Kibbutz tasks are specified; family obligations are less so and are more difficult to enforce.

Another unintended consequence of my husband's living elsewhere was that people related to me as a person whose husband has a car and drives back and forth from Jerusalem—a definite asset!

> 302:3: From the next table, N [who almost never initiates conversation with me] came over to ask for a ride *from* Jerusalem in the middle of the week for someone *else* who wants to come to the kibbutz wedding.

Because making a request clearly has nothing to do with having a relationship, I presume that fulfilling a request also has no or little impact on relationship building. The underlying principle of the kibbutz—that everyone is responsible for each other—means that favors are traded as a matter of course and inherent obligation, not as a consequence of special relationships. Thus, the elderly can expect to receive excellent care regardless of any negative reputation they may have had in the past.

---

[23] The leading public transport operator in Israel.

I was also perceived as the wife of someone who traveled to the United States:

> 217:2: [My husband] just arrived from the States. Everybody is asking him about what's going on there. "Politically, Israel is losing support," he announced, as if he had his finger on the pulse of America. His knowledge and opinions are an asset to my standing in the kibbutz.

Having a husband and child meant that we constituted "a family" and could participate as "a family" in the numerous kibbutz rituals that occurred on holidays and Friday evenings. Being in a family made one normal. Couples without children are "couples" (not families) if they are older or "potential families" if they are younger. Single individuals are "adopted" by families, so that everyone can see himself or herself being part of a family. Had I been on the kibbutz as a single woman or a single parent, I would likely have been "adopted" by a couple.

> 142:1: Experiencing the "sanctity of the family," i.e. when the three of us sit together in the dining room, it is rare that someone will join us.

Functioning as a family was the "normal" way to exist as an adult on a kibbutz. It was what one was supposed to do (i.e., be together) from 4:00 p.m. each day until one went to sleep each night and then again all day on Saturdays. From the time one arose until 4:00 p.m. approximately was "kibbutz time." B is always telling me that "family" is winning out over "kibbutz."

Elderly widows and widowers who are good friends constitute families among themselves. They try very hard to continue working so as to adhere to the sunrise-to-4:00 kibbutz work schedule. After that, they socialize with friends, neighbors, or biological family members. For some widows or widowers, losing their spouse was as much of a disaster as it would be in a noncommunal environment because they needed to reconstitute some sort of a family.

> 295:4: E sees D as "someone who wants to die, ever since her husband died. D's husband was a wonderful person. He worked in the archives. She used to accompany him and do everything for him. Then, after he died, she refused to do what she used to be able to do; and now she really cannot do anything any more. No one can convince her, no one can help her overcome her depression."

My husband and I constituted both a family (with our daughter) and a "couple," and as a couple we could visit other couples, which we frequently did when invited, from early on in my stay until the end of my stay. These get-togethers were defined as "not research," although because I was a participant observer, everything was grist for my mill. Some people used my research role as the basis for informal visiting; others resented the fact that the informal visiting was "not pure" if I asked a pointed question related to aging. In part, this awkwardness came about because post-four o'clock was not supposed to be work time for kibbutz members, but it was research work time for me.

> 315:3: L thinks the kibbutz has not received good newcomers. *Klita* (absorption/integration of new immigrants) has been a failure, she says, particularly when you think about Y who is an *effes* (a zero). L repeated all the stories about the kibbutz bailing Y out of the debts he had incurred before he joined

the kibbutz. [My husband] presented another point of view, i.e. that Y was prevented from introducing innovations into his kibbutz workplace. S said to him that he must have been talking to Y (a put-down of [my husband], since he was seen as just repeating Y's point of view). L also said that [my husband] appears to speak exclusively to academics (another put-down). How much is my status affected by people's attitudes toward [my husband]? Probably a lot.

As a recognized family, we took family outings, just like other families were expected to do, both on the kibbutz and off. For example, on Saturdays (the day of rest) we took Yali to visit the kibbutz horses, to climb trees, to slide down the huge cottonseed stacks, and to visit the cows, just as other couples did with their young children. We took her to the swimming pool nearly every Saturday and taught her to swim. We also took her on outings in the vicinity:

> 245:2: On a walk [back at the kibbutz], when I was looking for Yali, I started talking with R. I told him I had been to the hill area today . . . Then he talked about the *tiyul* (trip) he had made in the morning with his family to the reservoir that is on land (beyond the next kibbutz) owned by Emek. Clearly, my family is engaging in appropriate, normative behavior. I am a mother and wife, not "just a researcher."

Having a family meant that my situation paralleled that of most kibbutz members. One important difference, however, was that I had no other relatives on the kibbutz such as parents or siblings, nor did I have parents or siblings in the rest of the country. Ours was an "isolated family." Many kibbutz members are part of multi-generational extended kibbutz families and thus have numerous people to whom they can turn for help. Young couples frequently entrust their children to the grandparents for care. Sometimes a nonkibbutz member of a kibbutz family will come to the kibbutz to receive care. This is particularly true for elderly parents of kibbutz members. In my case, however, all the "family" care my daughter could receive came from my husband and me.

Personal care in the kibbutz was conceptualized as being the responsibility both of "the family" and of "the kibbutz." For example, a seventy-eight-year-old woman who used an oxygen tank said to me, "from 3:00 on, my husband takes care of me. Then the kibbutz doesn't have to take care any more." In my case, too, my child was taken care of by "the kibbutz" (meaning her *metapelet*) and by her "family"—the difference with the rest of the kibbutz members was that her "family" was limited to two people and actually to only one person (me) most of the time.

Another form of assistance that my husband provided me with concerned the reading of research materials. Because he is a native Hebrew speaker, he translated some written Hebrew materials for me until I became skilled enough to read and understand them on my own. As an academic, he was sought out by other academics on the kibbutz:

> 207:1: My husband and I spent the evening with S and M. S and my husband got into a discussion about academics, whereas M and I talked about kibbutz life. This felt very much like an old-fashioned sex-differentiated dinner party. I think it is difficult for people to see me as an academic when I am a wife, particularly when [my husband] is around. In fact, when he is around, it is hard to be seen as anything but "a wife."

My husband also met with some people I didn't have a chance to talk to and then told me what they said.[24]

> 57:1: At the swimming pool [my husband] spoke with a Polish professor of literature from Warsaw who has family in Emek named Z. As a person who has been to Poland, [my husband] was of interest to the visitor. Apparently Z had taught this Polish man Hebrew and he now he speaks it perfectly. This person considers himself a Pole first and a Jew second. He had some harsh things to say about one of the kibbutz members. After their conversation, [my husband] told me about what had been said. I could not have participated in that conversation, so this was beneficial.

My husband volunteered for one of the harvest call-ups in part so that I could understand what that activity consisted of, although I knew that I couldn't participate given that I had to take care of Yali that day.

> 217:1: [My husband] decided to participate in the grapefruit harvest. Other volunteer youth had come. People departed from the dining room at 9:00 a.m. and returned at noon. He reported that none of the founders or members of the next age group participated except for S and S. Thus, the call-up must be defined as something for the young and for those who want to demonstrate that although old chronologically, they are young physically—a kind of macho performance. The work was very demanding.

Occasionally my husband hung around with the men and reported back to me informally. For example, he occasionally helped out with the dishwashing and told me what was discussed there.

> 182:1: [My husband] woke early to do rotation with Y who expressed disappointment in the ability of 'young people' (i.e. recently released from the army) to stand up and state their point of view clearly. He attributes this problem to the kibbutz educational system. This was in reference to the program last night (which I missed given my attempt at recuperation) on youth who return to the kibbutz. I wonder if this pattern makes any sense. Perhaps the older people dominate and thus intimidate younger people.

My husband developed his own friendships on the kibbutz and did favors for members. He took care of Yali so that I could do some interviewing of people who came to the kibbutz only on weekends. Because he was not around on a daily basis, I was able to interview people only at night after I had gotten Yali to sleep. For this reason I did not experience one important aspect of kibbutz life—leisure time.

> 129:1: A day when I have *any* time for myself is a good day.

Given the importance of family life on a kibbutz, if my husband had been around more of the time, I might have felt pressure from kibbutz members to spend more time with him. Conversely, I would have been pressured to spend less time with "the kibbutz" as a whole, a process that would have made it difficult to carry out

---

[24] Les Back, "Gendered Participation: Masculinity and Fieldwork in a South London Adolescent Community," in Diane Bell, Pat Caplan, and Wazir Jahan Karim (eds.), *Gendered Fields: Women, Men & Ethnography*, pp. 215–233 (London: Routledge & Kegan Paul, 1993).

my research. As a participant observer, I needed to be free to associate and mingle as much as possible with whatever time was available to me after my responsibilities with work and with my daughter were taken care of. As a young woman with a child and an absent husband, I was in an ideal position to be adopted by the elderly. They were happy to do this, as long as it did not incur any real obligations on their part.

BEING THIRTY-THREE YEARS OLD

Like most societies, the kibbutz strongly differentiates into age and gender groups. Each age group (cohort) of people born on the kibbutz has its own name, which it is given when a group of six infants enters a particular *beit yeladim*.[25] As the group of six grows older, it is supposed to develop into a tightly knit peer group. The group members are supposed to be each other's friends for life. Some age groups are composed of people who *joined* the kibbutz together as a unit.

Even though I was not part of a group whose members were born and raised together on the kibbutz or a member of a group whose members joined together, I was made part—in a very loose way—of an approximate age group, just as I was of my gender group. Thus, it would have been strange to "hang out" with teenagers just as it would have been unconventional to be seen with groups of men on a regular basis because I was not a born member of these groups. My special purpose for being on the kibbutz, however, made it possible for me to "hang out" with old people, even though doing so would have seemed strange under other circumstances.

> 60:5: M asked me why I was interested in old people (with an expression on her face indicating it was a strange interest). I told her that old people living on a kibbutz are a new phenomenon, and that I'm interested in communities, and this is a fascinating one. [Clearly, I did not say that I enjoyed the company of older people, which is the truth.]

It was an anomaly in kibbutz life that even though I was thirty-three years old, I voluntarily spent much of my time with people over the age of sixty-five who were not my relatives. My special research role allowed me to cross the boundaries of my age group and socialize with older members. I learned that the anomalous positions of other nonmembers (i.e., people who were not raised on the kibbutz and did not join in a group) also freed them from restrictive age-group memberships.

> 18:3: N said that as an outsider she has relationships with *all* the generations, whereas those born here are only with their peer group.

The elderly people became my cohort and friends because I spent so much time with them. I liked them a great deal, and we frequently did favors for one another. Nevertheless, one older member said that even though I was only a temporary kibbutz resident, I should have friends my own age.[26] He said, "All you need is one or

---

[25] These names frequently come from the world of flowers and nature in general.

[26] A group of such friends is called a *chevra*.

two friends." I insisted that my outsider status freed me from the conventional concept of having friends in one's age group.

One age group I did *not* get to know well was children older than my daughter. If she had had older siblings, I would have gotten to know children that age because they would have been part of the children's houses of different age groups. This knowledge is, of course, characteristic of kibbutz members because they tend to have families with more than one child. I did try to learn which children belonged to which families so that I could identify the children and help them when I was a night watchperson. But I did not really get to know them well.

As a wife, mother, and thirty-three-year-old woman, I was also too old for the kibbutz teenagers and got to know them only superficially. The high school youth went to school in a different kibbutz, and thus I hardly got to know them at all. Nor did I interact much with the soldiers who returned to the kibbutz occasionally. I did not meet those people "on leave" from the kibbutz for whatever purpose [study, travel, etc.]. Only one or two high school-aged girls worked in one of my work places (the greenhouse). Young men who had completed their army service either were on the kibbutz very temporarily because they were preparing to go on long trips abroad or were engaged in agriculture or the dairy, where I did not work.

Being a foreigner and English speaker allowed me to develop good relations with volunteers and other English speakers, regardless of age. Although older than most volunteers, I did get to know them more than many kibbutz members my age might have because we shared the bond of a common language—English.

> 55:1: L (a volunteer engaged to a kibbutz member) and I cleaned onions for a long time. She told me all about the sexual liaisons between the volunteers and the young kibbutz members. Specifically, which kibbutz young person was sleeping with which volunteer.

Many volunteers wanted to share their insights about Israel and the kibbutz with me. Generally I was amazed at how little the volunteers knew about their surroundings. One of them with whom I spoke did not understand exactly where Israel was located geographically. I was also impressed with how little this mattered because all she had to do was work, and the kibbutz would take care of the rest.

Being relatively young did not seem to create any barriers between elderly people and me. All except two agreed to be interviewed in depth, and even these two women I got to know somewhat because I attended the club for elderly affairs and participated in hikes and parties designed for older people. (When I gave my feedback report to the old age club, people were fascinated by the fact that two women did not cooperate in being interviewed and wanted to guess who they were.)

In a few instances, an older person told me that I could not understand older people because I was relatively young. However, these people used this criticism of me as an opportunity to give me extensive instruction.

> Y (79 years) is a forceful, remarkable woman, just as everyone had told me I would find her to be, if I interviewed her. At the start of our interview, I could

see that she was fully prepared to give me a lecture on old age in the kibbutz by reading out loud two articles she had written on the topic. Y was particularly interesting to interview because she told me she was *opposed* to my project. She doesn't believe that young "experts" can understand aging. In addition, she believes the kibbutz is doing an optimal job with the elderly and needs no consultation. She completely rejects the idea of having social workers on the kibbutz. Yet she spoke enthusiastically to me. I think the key is that I waited a long time to speak with her, didn't pressure her, and let her invite me. I presented myself as someone who wanted to learn from her, and she is used to that role, since she gives private lessons in languages to kibbutz members.

96:4: M says she's sorry that I'm not older and therefore able to understand certain things. For example, her grandmother used to say that people are like wine. As they age, the dirt sinks to the bottom and the wine becomes clear.

6/24/80: Suicide seems to fascinate Z. She said that a young person couldn't understand the issue of suicide among the elderly. She accepts suicide as a right of older people, and considers it a reasonable choice.

Interviewing older people on topics such as death and sickness can be frightening or enlightening and reassuring, depending on one's maturity and current state of mind, as I learned.

One of the challenges of doing research on the elderly is the definition of when old age begins. To simplify the matter, I used the conventional definition of sixty-five years of age to mark when individuals receive retirement benefits in the United States, an age that is also used in much gerontological research. Material inviting a person to join AARP, however, arrives much earlier in U.S. homes—at age fifty-five! In the kibbutz, as elsewhere, people used both chronological and subjective definitions of old age in describing both others and themselves. For example:

P is 77 years old. He told me that he became quite ill when he was 75, and it is only since then that he considers himself old. Self-definition as old seems to take an event that represents a subjective change in one's self-concept, rather than the passing of a birthday. Also, old age is equated with illness.

"Being old" and "feeling old" were frequently differentiated for me. "You're as old as you feel," many people told me. The opposite also holds. A person can be chronologically young and act "old."

M: (72 years old): "Sometimes people are old when they are 55!"

There is also the fluctuating subjective reality, depending on changing events.

M: "I feel old when I'm sick, but not when I'm not."

Another indicator of feeling old is the desire to write about the past, to review one's life.

77:6: S is thinking about writing her memoirs now because she believes they are an integral part of Jewish history. She feels a certain urgency about doing it because her mother had planned to do so and had even purchased a tape recorder for the purpose, but then lost interest and died.

Many people wanted to talk to me about "who is old" or "when old age starts" and how it is misperceived depending on one's own age and shifts depending on what year we are talking about. The relative nature of "old" was stressed.

> 82:4: At the teachers' staff meeting there were about 12 teachers, *metaplot* and special teachers plus the principal, sitting around waiting for latecomers to arrive. There was some joking about old age (probably brought on by my presence). The women told stories about how young people define "old" as people who are slightly older than they. C said that in the past 35 was considered old because people who were about 19 or 20 years old founded the kibbutz.
>
> 320:3: Sitting with a group of people who are members of the second cohort to join the kibbutz. They talked about the fact that they didn't feel old at the time because there were "old people" here when they arrived who were only 35 at the time. They won't feel old until the founders are dead, they said. I believe that is because only when they are the "oldest" will be they old. Until then, they are always younger than another group.

At times I had to take the initiative to meet with an older person because he or she assumed I would not want to meet him or her socially even though it was my research interest. These are people with low self-esteem who think they have nothing to say.

> J interview: She had thought of inviting me, she said, but didn't think I would be interested since I am young and she is an old lady.

In general, my being younger gave older people more of a task to make sure I understood what being older meant. Because youth is valued on the kibbutz, older people may have liked talking to me because of my relative youth. I also feel that there may be a pattern: Young people can have access to social relations with the elderly, whereas the reverse is not true. This pattern reflects the relatively lower prestige of older people.

BEING A JEW

I am a Jew in the technical legal sense (born of a Jewish mother) and also in the sociological sense because I was socialized by my family to internalize having a Jewish identity. Israel is a Jewish state, and thus going to Israel to conduct a study meant that I was doing research in a place connected to my identity (regardless of the fact that I had not previously lived on a kibbutz). It is common for fieldworkers to study places or phenomena that relate to their birthplaces or birth identities. For example, having done fieldwork in a Palestinian refugee camp in Lebanon, Suad Joseph[27] wrote, "Having been born in Lebanon, I was in the 1970s in many ways more like my Lebanese friends and family than my American friends in my sense of self." Barbara Myerhoff studied the people of her own culture, albeit a different age group.[28] Edmundo Morales "decided to return to his native region in the Andes

---

[27] Suad Joseph, "Relationality and Ethnographic Subjectivity: Key Informants and the Construction of Personhood in Fieldwork," in Diane L. Wolf (ed.), *Feminist Dilemmas in Fieldwork*, p. 108 (Boulder, CO: Westview Press, 1996).

[28] Barbara Myerhoff, *Number Our Days* (New York: Dutton, 1978).

Mountains to explore the changes that had occurred there as a result of the shift of the local economy toward the production and processing of cocaine for export."[29] Hans Buechler wrote,

> I was not a complete stranger to Bolivian culture when I conducted my first field-work there. Born of Swiss parents, I grew up in La Paz, Bolivia, went to a Bolivian school until the fifth grade, and spent most of my vacations in a peasant community near Compi. So I was familiar with the Bolivian national culture in which Aymara migrants participate to a large extent.[30]
>
> And yet, knowing who you are does not mean that others will recognize that identity.

I thought it was self-evident to everyone on the kibbutz that I was Jewish, given the fact that I spoke Hebrew, have a Hebrew name, gave my daughter a Hebrew name, and am married to a former Israeli. But because there is so much "people traffic" through the kibbutz, it is understandable that some people were unsure. For instance, Yali's *metapelet* asked me after a few days if I was Jewish (9:2). I was astounded that she did not assume I was but said "yes" without showing any emotion. When people who thought I was *not* Jewish learned that I was, they seemed relieved and much more interested in me than they formerly had been.

Jewishness was a contested category on the kibbutz. For example, some "born Jewish" kibbutz members perceived kibbutz members who had converted to Judaism as nevertheless "not Jewish." The "pseudo-Jewishness" of converts was part of the rationale by some (who considered their status as Jews to be questionable) for not liking, respecting, or understanding them. These attempts to separate oneself from the "not real Jews" did not draw on the technicalities of conversion but rather on differentiating behavior.

> 64:1: R told me that the children of one of the new members are not bright because they are *goyim* (i.e. people who are not Jewish) [even tough they are converts]. "They've got a hole in their head, so they can't learn. An example is D who couldn't get through her nursing course although she received a lot of help."
>
> 139:3: L told me that C (who says she is not Jewish) must be Jewish in her roots since her coloring and temperament are so different from non-Jewish Swedes. "Also, she's so aggressive."

Recognizing the ambivalence toward non-Jews, I was somewhat concerned if it was thought that I was not Jewish.

> 155:12: M asked me what I was doing, making doughnuts in the kitchen for Chanukah [a Jewish holiday]. I was on edge, so I said, "Ask the *sadranit avodah*." I also said, "Why not? I'm also Jewish!"

Few people talked about Judaism itself; they just categorized people as Jewish or not. Exceptions to this generalization are the converts to Judaism and the people

---

[29] Edmundo Morales, "Researching Peasants and Drug Producers," in Carolyn D. Smith and William Kornblum (eds.), *In the Field*, p. 115 (New York: Praeger, 1989).

[30] Hans Buechler in Frances Henry and Satish Saberwal (eds.), *Stress and Response in Fieldwork*, p. 8 (New York: Holt, Rinehart and Winston, 1969).

who had been more religious in their countries of origin than they had become on the kibbutz. These people liked to talk about Judaism:

> 327:1: E (an American immigrant and convert) wants to follow up my questions with a personal question of me. "How do I feel as a non-orthodox Jew in Israel?" I steer the conversation back to her. She converted to Judaism after having lifelong doubts about Catholicism, being interested in history, etc. She had negative physical stereotypes about Jews and was surprised to find them 'typical' in appearance. She came to Israel once on a tour from the air force base in England where her husband was serving as a 'lay rabbi.' She was impressed with the beauty of this area, went back to the States, read up on kibbutz. The office that places immigrants sent her and her husband here because this particular kibbutz fit the formal criteria they were looking for. "But the office didn't know the actual character of this kibbutz." She and her husband are disappointed. She came for ideological reasons and then found that the kibbutz she came to was not ideologically oriented.

When I told her I had to end the conversation because I had to go, she was upset. She needs to talk to someone at breakfast because she doesn't talk to anyone at work. She needs to fill her "talk quotient" or she'll "go nuts," she said. Clearly kibbutz members have not accepted her.

Some people thought the kibbutz had gone overboard in its rejection of religion:

> 221:1: H married an Emek kibbutz member about 2½ years ago. She thinks Emek is too extreme in its rejection of religion. "The marriage ceremony and the bar mitzvah are stripped of all religious reference," she said. I also noted this at the four funerals I attended of Emek members. "Some people make a religion out of rejecting religion!" she said.

Nevertheless, the question of what makes the kibbutz "Jewish" if the members do not participate in rabbi-led life cycle events did crop up. When an outsider asked the question, the member felt insulted.

> 8:4: When C went to the dentist today, someone in the waiting room said to her, "If the kibbutz is not religious, how can you know that you're Jewish?"

Although the answer to this question continues to evolve, the kibbutz members have developed a lifestyle that answers it, consisting of a particular set of attitudes and experiences concerning religion. Its original ideology considered religion in political terms, as Marx did. "Religion is the opiate of the masses." Religion was the identifying characteristic of the founders' parents' generation; and they, the founding kibbutz members, wanted to create change, to throw off the yoke of traditional ways. They wanted to be outdoors in the fields and sun, bent over the plow, not indoors in the religious study hall, bent over books. Thus, the youth movement on which this kibbutz was founded rejected religious observance and belief altogether, although through the substitute ideology of Zionism, its members retained a strong sense of identification as Jews and saw their immigration to Palestine as a means of expressing their Jewishness and saving their lives and the lives of other Jews. For example, they did not eliminate holidays but rather redefined them or returned them to their biblical roots rather than their later manifestations. As Calvin Goldscheider wrote, "The long Jewish Diaspora of 2,000 years is viewed simply as an empty interlude between the origin of a Jewish nation in the land of Israel and the return of Jews to their land of origin."[31] Rather than reject Passover, Yom Kippur, or marriage, they wrote a new Hagaddah,[32] created a new set of Yom Kippur rituals, established a new way of getting married, and more.. There was a sense that being religious in the old-fashioned way was inimical to physical survival and that Jews had to take matters into their own hands rather than passively await the Messiah the way religious Jews did.

Nowadays there is renewed antipathy toward religion among secular Israeli Jews in part because of the intense politicization of this issue in Israeli society. In general, Emek members are opposed to the extensive power that religious parties have acquired within Israel, power that they use to impose their beliefs on others. The power of the religious establishment far exceeds its demographic share in the overall population. In various studies, only 22 percent of Israelis declare themselves as committed religiously.[33] Goldscheider writes, "only one Judaism, Orthodoxy, is legitimate in Israeli society . . . Israel and its leaders are not committed to ethnic or religious pluralism in the same way that is characteristic of American Jewry."[34] According to state law, weddings must be performed by Orthodox rabbis, although this ceremony is not considered the binding one in the kibbutz. I witnessed the rabbi-led marriage ceremony of one couple in the kibbutz, which only about twenty people attended. After the rabbi completed his role, the kibbutz members and guests launched into the "real" wedding, the one defined by kibbutz customs. Hundreds of people attended this. An analogy in the United States might be the role of civil law in the marriage ceremony—it's there but not significant.

The kibbutz members are opposed to proselytizing by religious Jews. For instance, at the funeral of a young kibbutz woman who had died in a car accident, a group of Orthodox religious women who lived in a nearby town claimed that just before she died, the young woman asked that religious prayers be said at her graveside. This was patently a lie because the woman had been killed instantaneously. It was dubious that these religious women even knew the woman who had died. Yet, they made this claim in order to influence the crowd gathered around her graveside. This act was considered to be distasteful in the extreme.

Yet, some kibbutz members in Emek recognize that religion can have a meaningful role in some people's lives and that it should not be dismissed altogether. Ironically, one of the kibbutz artists, a decidedly secular man, uses religious themes in most of his paintings. He sees these themes as constituting Jewish culture, not

---

[31] Calvin Goldscheider, *Israel's Changing Society: Population, Ethnicity, and Development*, p. 24 (Boulder, CO: Westview Press, 1996).

[32] Book read as a group at the festive Seder meal at Passover.

[33] See Nira Yuval-Davis, "Bearers of the Collective: Women and Religious Legislation in Israel," in Esther Fuchs (ed.), *Israeli Women's Studies*, pp. 121–132 (New Brunswick, NJ: Rutgers University Press, 2005).

[34] Goldscheider, p. 236.

exclusively Jewish religion. Some kibbutz members told me that becoming religious and practicing some of the traditional religious behaviors are common phenomena connected with aging and signify fear of death.

The Sabbath defines the weekly cycle in the kibbutz, particularly in contrast
to countries that have a two-day workweek break. Not only do people work less on
the Sabbath, but also they partake in ceremonies—as a kibbutz—to mark the day
as special (sacred). Learning these ceremonies begins at a very young age.

> 23:1: In the children's houses, the Kabalat Shabbat[35] ceremony occurs shortly
> before lunch on Fridays because they are at "home" after 4:00. The children are
> cleaned from their morning play and sit at the table adorned with a white table-
> cloth and flowers that the parents and *metapelet* have brought. There are two
> small lit candles [which is actually a religious ritual]. The *metapelet* sings a few
> Sabbath songs and any other songs that the children request, e.g. *aviron* (about an
> airplane), *rakevet* (about a choo-choo train), etc. Then they receive sweets and
> the *metapelet* reads them a story as they sit around the table. I find this ritual
> interesting given that Emek is not a religious kibbutz. I should ask if the Sabbath
> is celebrated like this in all the toddler houses or just in this one. I'd be interested
> to know which families light Sabbath candles here. D said her parents do (hers is
> a converted family).

Most Jewish holidays in the annual cycle are celebrated on Emek, even though
Emek defines itself as a defiantly secular, in contrast to a religious, kibbutz. Many
members believe that Emek celebrates the Jewish holidays in ways that reflect
the experience of the ancient Hebrews and thus has produced a more authentic
Judaism.

> 70:1: At lunch E said, "You can feel the holiday in the air." What does that
> mean? It is certainly not like the US, where holidays are commercialized to such
> an extent that you can't escape it. Here there are little messages from kids posted
> in various work-branches like the kitchen and the laundry sorting room. There
> are little "Happy New Year" signs posted all around. We received fruit in large
> quantity and presents from the *Kolbo* (general store). Today I received a gift from
> "the kitchen" (a cake server and chocolate); children sent messages. Today a copy
> of the kibbutz newspaper came out and the kibbutz movement distributed songs/
> poems. There is a big sign posted on the bulletin board—Shana Tova to *our*
> kibbutz (Happy New Year)—which is warmer than to *the* kibbutz, I suppose.
> There are lots of preparations for the big meal tomorrow night and extra workers
> in the kitchen. G is washing the chairs down. Are the lawns being cut for this
> purpose, too? There is a big posting of who has what work duties during the party
> and clean up. I am not doing anything in particular and wonder if I should be.
> C brought a honey cake to her father. There will be guests, a slide show and a day
> of rest, but it will be Shabbat anyhow. I have a new question: I have *received* some
> gifts. To whom should I *give* gifts on Rosh Hashanah? I'll ask.
>
> 70:3: P and T said that you don't give a *metapelet* a present for Rosh
> Hashanah. Rather, someone who is talented puts up a drawing with a greeting.
> You might bring a flower from your garden if you have one, which T does every
> week. There are a lot of Rosh Hashanah signs up in the beit yeladim, plus a chart
> of birthdays and a picture of Y.

---

[35] Ceremony to mark the start of the Sabbath, it takes place on Friday at sunset.

My sponsor's family gave gifts to my husband and me:

> 71:3: From my sponsor, my husband received a three-volume set of the encyclopedic *Hashomer*. Yali received a tape of Israeli songs, a pin, a card and a handkerchief. We brought them flowers.
>
> My neighbor brought Yali candies as well.

Being a Jew enabled me to understand much of kibbutz culture but not all of it. The average child on a kibbutz receives a much more thorough education in Bible than I have had, for example. They know the place names mentioned throughout the Bible and where these places can be found in contemporary Israel. During one evening in which the kibbutz members got together and played a kind of Jeopardy quiz show, I was able to answer very few questions. I felt that I had received an inadequate Jewish education and that perhaps I was more of an outsider than I had previously recognized.

Thus, I was tied to the kibbutz members in many ways as a Jew but separated from them as well because I am an American Jew and not an Israeli Jew. On the kibbutz, I became much more of a secular Jew than I was in the United States[36], while at the same time I was probably more observant (i.e., I carried out certain rituals) than most people on the kibbutz. I ate on Yom Kippur with nearly everyone else (the influence of kibbutz secularism), for example, but I lit the Friday night candles privately in my little house, unlike most kibbutz members, who celebrated the Sabbath in other ways (the influence of my Conservative socialization). I learned that the ties that bind could serve to separate when the ties are only similar, not identical.

> 78:3: "I have two daughters-in-law who don't observe anything on the Sabbath," she said, " except that they light the Friday night candles (without blessing them) for their beauty. I approve of this."

This ambivalence surrounding religion is intensified on Yom Kippur, the holiest day of the year for religious Jews.

> 80:2: On the way back from the pool I saw K dressed for Yom Kippur. She said she was going to the next city, since to not do anything (on the holiday) was not cultured . . .
>
> Another kibbutz mother was taking her child to a nearby village "to show her" the customs some people practice, much to her husband's chagrin.

The ambivalence that people feel about religion was also apparent in the extent to which people had asked each other and me whether they would fast on Yom Kippur.

> 80:3: One pair of "permanent volunteer" women was in a peculiarly difficult position. They wanted to fast on Yom Kippur, but their job was to cook for people who need a special diet (e.g. diabetics), a job that had to be performed regardless of any other considerations. They couldn't find anyone who would switch jobs

---

[36] I was raised as a Conservative Jew (in contrast to Reform or Orthodox). At the time, Reconstructionism had not yet developed in the United States. In Israel at the time (and still to a large extent), there are two overall categories of Jews: religious and secular. The Jews of Emek were secular.

with them for the day. They resented the fact that people were taking their hostility concerning religion out on them in this indirect way, i.e. by assigning them this job.

It seems that many people knew about this ironic situation and commented on it.

> 78:3: "It doesn't seem fair to have people who are fasting cook for those who are not."

When Yom Kippur began, I went into the dining room for dinner, as everyone did. People seemed to be particularly hearty in wishing me and each other "good appetite" as if to underscore the point that we were eating despite its being Yom Kippur.

> 78:4: In the past, as an act of defiance, a movie was shown on the eve of Yom Kippur. One family of converts to Judaism objected vigorously. For a few years it was cancelled. Now the movie is back again, but the decision was to have a movie with Jewish content, as a form of compromise or creativity. This year the movie is about the Dreyfus affair.

Members of one family invited me to their home to listen to good (i.e. classical) music—another way of making it a special, important, but not God-centered evening. Finally, an intimate kibbutz meeting was called for the evening by the *mazkirim,* an opportunity for people to discuss openly their feelings about how life was going for the kibbutz as a whole. It was to be a meeting of reflection and review, just as Yom Kippur is intended to be. The focus of religious Yom Kippur is the individual and his or her atonement. By contrast, the focus of this secular kibbutz's Yom Kippur meeting was the group or society and how it could be improved. The review concerned "how we were living up to our ideals as a kibbutz." God was not involved. The meeting was to be a short retreat, an attempt to create an "other" place from which to reflect on everyday life, a time when people could feel free to say what they might not have been able to say ordinarily. People were invited to gather for a frank assessment of what they feel, where they think Emek is going, and what is wrong. It was to be a stock taking with no pressure to make policy or decisions. A meeting of this sort on Erev Yom Kippur is a strong tradition on Emek because the holiday coincides with the anniversary of the kibbutz's founding.

About fifty people attended in the small, uncomfortable room beneath the dining hall. Because it was so crowded, many couldn't hear, and most were extremely hot. It reminded me very much of the crowded, uncomfortable, hot synagogues on Yom Kippur in the United States whose services I have attended. Some of the elderly walked out early to get relief from the physical conditions. People of all ages attended, but the young apparently came to listen. They didn't speak at all. Surprisingly, people did not interrupt each other. Three people took notes—one person who was going to write a summary for the internal newsletter, one who was going to send a summary to the soldiers from Emek, and me. Interestingly, many who spoke were the founders, the old-timers: T, M, S K, Y, and U. They considered themselves significant commentators on the current state of affairs. Perhaps they used this opportunity to speak philosophically because they were not involved in actual practical decision making.

The *mazkir* opened the meeting by saying there was discontent in the kibbutz, discontent that should be discussed openly at the meeting. The first person to speak, T, announced that he was disheartened by four problems: the existence of hired labor,[37] the fact that some kibbutz members work outside the kibbutz, the ratio of young people to old,[38] and the quality of the food. From his perspective the first two issues negate the very ideology on which the kibbutz was founded.

This founder's unwillingness to see that original ideology should change is thought by many younger members to characterize the thinking of all the founders. These younger people and a minority of the older ones believe that in order to survive, the kibbutz has to be flexible with regard to its original principles and that the very flexibility has allowed the kibbutz to accommodate to the times and to prosper.

The second person to speak was M, who asked that Y, a fellow member of the founding group, tell the history of the kibbutz. Y declined. The third to speak was a young man, father of four children, and son of a founder. He asked everyone to live by the *essence* of the principles, not by the way they happen to be institutionalized. He asked people to *participate* in the community rather than simply be *dependent* on it. He was disturbed by several incidents of cruelty among the children and felt that in general there was need for more open communication.

The fourth to speak was S, an older woman who was not a founder but joined at a later date. She was disturbed by the fact that applicants for membership in Emek were not required to have an ideological commitment to kibbutz values. Instead of asking what their beliefs were, the application system consisted primarily of psychological testing, a fact she considered appalling. If the kibbutz uses such tests as admission criteria, then the kibbutz cannot claim to represent an ideology. She said that the disregard of political affiliation among applicants mirrors the weakening of political consciousness within the kibbutz. There are no political committees, no reading rooms, no formal affiliation with the political parties, and no feedback from the people working in the parties, she complained.

Y asked if a young person would speak to this issue, but no one responded. Next came K, a founder who had become an educator. He was concerned with the relation between the individual and the community, an issue that had never been fully discussed or resolved in his view. The community should determine what the individual will do, he insisted. If that could be implemented, then there would be no thefts or destruction of property. Instead, the kibbutz has become too liberal, too tolerant of individual deviation and of the erosion of principles, a prime example of which is the fact that kibbutz members work outside the kibbutz.

Y then used his former invitation to speak. It was remarkable, he commented, that there should be a sense of crisis, even though individual needs were met.

---

[37] Hired labor is now commonplace in kibbutzim but at that time was a new phenomenon. Ideologically, the kibbutz community strove to be self-sufficient and to exist on the basis of the labor of its members. See also Marjorie Strom, "The Thai Revolution: The Changes in Agriculture in the Kibbutzim and Moshavim of the Arava in the 1990s," in Michal Palgi and Shulamit Reinharz (eds.) *One Hundred Years of Kibbutz Life: A Century of the Arts, Ideas and Reinvention* (in process)

[38] The problem here is the small number of young people.

It certainly wasn't a material crisis. What was needed was a "community of values," but this depended on identification between the individual and the community.

> He said, "We should recognize that even in the past it was never the case that 100% of kibbutz members fully identified with the kibbutz. Rather at best 70% identified, and 30% were on the periphery. The trouble is that now 20% identify and 80% feel that they are on the periphery. Because so many people are marginal, because there is so little "we-feeling," there is a sense of anarchy. The kibbutz has become an amorphous body that people do not feel they can rely on. It is never clear that a decision made today will be followed tomorrow, or that a decision made by the group will be considered binding by the individual. [The mothers' strike was a prime example.] Y concluded by saying that it was imperative that the current situation change, and that the key to change was education. Thus his idea of change was to revert to the past.

Y had the negative reputation of being a "preacher" and of being stuck on the single theme of education. I could see by his speech how that reputation was reinforced by his behavior. In addition, his "sermon," like the others that preceded his, was reminiscent ironically of what one is likely to hear on Yom Kippur from a rabbi. The principles the rabbi might refer to would be Jewish; the principles this group urged were socialist.

R, a middle-aged woman, was annoyed by what she was hearing, particularly the differentiation by age groups. True, there was a major problem of disinterest in other people's welfare and general impatience, but many good things about the kibbutz were being overlooked. She said kibbutz members needed to have open hearts and open minds rather than to think that some members were "extraneous."

U, a young woman, argued passionately that communication had broken down among members. People didn't agree even on the meaning of each other's words and had long ago stopped listening to one another. One way to begin to break through this barrier is to use the word *I* when speaking, she suggested (reflecting her recent interest in the human potential movement). She explained the current anomie in terms I had heard from many members: The kibbutz is too heterogeneous in the sense that some people who came from "the city" and married into the kibbutz (i.e., married a kibbutz member) have no background in kibbutz life. Indirectly referring to Y, she said it is useless to live in the past or future, which is what we do. We must deal with the problems of the present. It is also useless to compare life inside and outside the kibbutz. While we are here, we have to express commitment to our kibbutz. We should try to feel and express our natural attachment to this place rather than saying, "I gave twenty years, now it's your turn to put out."

Others suffer from an inability to delay gratification, U observed. They want material goods, and they want them now. "We have to understand our priorities," she said. "If it's materialism, then you can be certain that you will never be satisfied," again mirroring an old Jewish phrase.

E, an old-timer, was getting discouraged at this point. He said that the problems were numerous and there were no solutions. M, a middle-aged *mazkir*, said that wasn't true. All we need to do is smile at each other and smile at ourselves.

If everyone were ready to say what he or she would be willing to do for the kibbutz, we would be in good shape. We have solved all the big things. What's left are the little things.

U, an old-timer, began to feel inspired by the openness of the members but said that age groups should organize this type of discussion. "It's unnatural for grandchildren and grandparents to open up in the same place. The kibbutz can't learn from the elderly anymore. We've already taught you all we know. We believe that a shared basis of values is needed. It is only because of these special values that we have a right to exist. We live well. What we need is internal ideals. Parents need to teach them to their children."

The meeting ended when the hour was late. Because people don't usually talk in this self-reflective way, I had had a unique opportunity to hear what was on their minds. I came away recognizing, as usual, that there was discontent in the midst of commitment and commitment in the midst of discontent. Was there resolve to change and do better, as there was supposed to be at the end of a Yom Kippur service? People had given speeches. Had everyone really been listening? Were they willing to consider other points of view? Did it mean anything that only fifty people had attended and that such a small room had been set aside for this purpose?

The next day at lunch G analyzed the discussion by saying that people really self-disclosed and revealed what was deep in their hearts. While G and I were eating, one of the women who had spoken up at the meeting joined us. I told her I really respected what she had said. No sooner was this said than the two women began to criticize the meeting. They felt that it could have been more productive if there had been a plan to discuss specific topics, but I suggested that spontaneity was also useful.

People had the day off on Yom Kippur. Some used it to do their laundry, which seemed ostentatiously hung to dry in front of their houses, once again defying the ban on working that religious people observe on Yom Kippur. Joining in the general tenor of events and demonstrating the power of kibbutz norms, I sat outside my own home eating ice cream after lunch. Some people were building Succot[39] in preparation for the next holiday. Others were off to a rehearsal for an elaborate celebration that would take place in a week.

That evening when I was putting my tray on the dishwasher carousel, a *mazkir* and an older member asked me for my impressions of the previous evening's meeting. I think I was asked because the meeting was significant to them, and they saw me as a kind of outside judge. In addition, it is clear that one of the major tasks of kibbutz life (as of most institutions) is to continuously reevaluate in informal conversation people's behavior, everyday activities, and the meaning of the kibbutz (institution) in general. Thus, the meeting, which had been a kind of stock taking soon became itself something to take stock of. The elderly were as involved with this as anyone else. Not only was the Erev Yom Kippur meeting a creative

---

[39] Succot is the name of the fall holiday in which Jews are commanded to build small structures (also called succot) in which they eat (and sometimes sleep) for eight days, to commemorate the way Jews lived in the desert after their escape from Egypt.

transformation of the customs of religious Jews, but also it symbolized the most important activity of kibbutz interaction—continuous mutual criticism as part of a more general search for an understanding of what they had created.

Most of the cycle of Jewish holidays is celebrated on this kibbutz even though it is defiantly secular in contrast to a religious kibbutz.[40]

> 2:2: My sponsor spoke about problems the kibbutz is working on. First was the topic of holidays—specifically, how to celebrate them. It is obvious that the community needs holidays, but they should have meaning. They do celebrate Succot, Shavuot,[41] Chanukah, Pesach and Rosh Hashanah. Probably others too. Pesach he called the Holiday of Freedom.[42] Yom Kippur is not celebrated because it is religious only and people of Emek are not believers. Some people choose to fast, as is their privilege. Ironically, I think he said that the kitchen coordinator fasted. In the past people worked, now they don't work but rather clean their own houses. So it's really meaningless, but they try not to offend others in the vicinity, which would occur if they had their tractor going, etc. Of course, there are three jobs that are always necessary, no matter what—the cowshed, the children's houses and the kitchen. There was no committee at the time of the Shavuot holiday, so preparations fell on the *mazkirut*, who had a couple of helpers and did a terrible job.

As on all kibbutzim, the Jewish holidays rooted in agriculture are given special forms of expression. The Jewish holidays are celebrated as part of the history of the Jewish people and as a continuation with biblical events and agricultural phenomena rather than as an opportunity to worship or give thanks to God. There is no synagogue on this kibbutz, and yet every Friday evening there is a special celebration and ceremony to "welcome the Sabbath" in which individual kibbutz members read poems for the whole kibbutz or a small choir sings special songs.

My attention was not on the question of religion per se but rather on the attitudes and behaviors of the elderly with regard to religion. Their behavior at holiday time made it possible for me to see if religion was meaningful to the elderly on this militantly secular kibbutz.

> 85:6: Pointing to 75-year-old C who was sitting alone during a Succot party for the whole kibbutz in the *hadar haochel,* my sponsor said, "She used to be a very radical woman. But now she has turned to religion again from her childhood. She even fasted on Yom Kippur."

---

[40] There are sixteen religious kibbutzim in Israel, with a total of approximately nineteen thousand members. Aryei Fishman has conducted research on these kibbutzim, providing explanations for their lower mortality rates and higher economic productivity in comparison with secular kibbutzim. See "The Religious Kibbutz: A Note on the Theories of Marx, Sombart and Weber on Judaism and Economic Success," *Sociological Analysis* 50(3):281–290, 1989.

[41] A spring-time holiday to celebrate the Jewish people's receipt of the Ten Commandments at Mount Sinai. Shavuot is also connected to the grain harvest in Israel and thus has both religious and agricultural meanings.

[42] There are also completely secular holidays such as Israel Independence Day.

Some people (not my sponsor) believed that as you age, you should try to express more tolerance of individual kibbutz members' differences, including tolerance of their religiosity.

> 78:3: "One older woman on the kibbutz is becoming religious in her old age, wanting to go to services, etc. I won't tell you her name, but you'll find it on the list posted downstairs of the people who plan to fast on Yom Kippur." These people wrote their names on a list posted on the bulletin board so that the kitchen organizer could modify the quantities of food cooked that day. This list was a rather public declaration of one's degree of religious observance and the subject of much joking, gossip, and interpretation. One other function of the list was to clarify that some guests or volunteers were, in fact, Jewish, although, of course, one could fast without being Jewish.

The kibbutz celebrated Israeli and Jewish holidays as a community, and every Friday night the membership gathered to eat special food in a formally organized multigenerational fixed family-based seating plan. It was the only meal during the week that members serve members sitting at tables. All other meals were self-service from large carts. Also unlike all other meals, a short cultural program was offered before the Friday night meal. During the afternoon, candles were lit (again, without blessings) in some of the children's houses, and flowers and treats were incorporated into a special celebration in all of them. These are examples of the numerous ways kibbutz members have transformed traditional Jewish holidays and rituals into forms acceptable to people who do not consider themselves religious. These transformed rituals were also practiced in individual homes on the kibbutz. Sometimes these rituals involved family members coming together and watching TV, listening to music, and chatting; in other instances ceremonies using symbolic objects were created. Israel is the only country established as a homeland for the Jewish people, derived from the concept that it was the Jewish people's former home and that Jews are therefore returning home. Because Israel is a Jewish state, being Jewish was a significant factor in my identity while studying the kibbutz, although it probably would not be significant in many sociological research settings. Being Jewish was the aspect of my identity that some people found the easiest to understand. In the eyes of kibbutz members, being Jewish was more of a legitimizing element for my doing the study than was being a sociologist.

> 323:4: D wanted to know—again—why I was interested in studying the kibbutz. So I started, 'I'm Jewish, etc.' I knew that for her, the idea of research was foreign. But the idea that Jews would be interested in what a kibbutz was, made sense.

Kibbutz members told me that being a Jew tied me to the kibbutz in ways that transcended the manifest reason I was there—to do my study. But being a Jew also separated me from them because I am an American Jew and not an Israeli Jew.

Just as I was continuously asked why *I* came to the kibbutz, so, too, I asked all the people I interviewed why *they* came. The story that most older people told me about how and why they came to the kibbutz started with the story of their having endured harsh anti-Semitism in whatever town they lived in, in eastern Europe. Coming to Israel (or Palestine, as it was called before 1948) saved their lives. Almost all of those who did not come were murdered in the Holocaust. The homes from which these kibbutz members came in Europe were traditional in their practice of the Jewish religion. Many older people liked to reminisce about their origins and the beliefs their parents held dear.

> 8:3: In the swimming pool, a grandmother of a child I had met, her husband and another man were discussing *kashrut* (keeping kosher). "You can eat milk 6 hours after meat; you can eat meat 3 hours after milk, and chicken is considered to be a little calf," the grandmother said. "Why?," someone asked. Because "meat sticks more to the teeth than chicken does." That's what this woman learned in her parents' home!

These people, like almost all the others in the kibbutz, are not only Israelis—they are Jews, and some are Holocaust survivors.

> 77:2: I noticed that the woman getting food in front of me has a concentration camp number on her arm.

As it turns out, I am not only a Jew but also a daughter of Holocaust survivors and a granddaughter of people who were killed during the Holocaust. I was born in Amsterdam, Holland, because my parents escaped to the Netherlands from Germany and were hidden in various parts of the country throughout the war. Questions about my personal history came up frequently during this study. People routinely asked me where I was born and wanted an explanation of why I, as an American, was born in Amsterdam. (It may be considered rude to not ask visitors to the kibbutz where they were born. Lack of investigation signifies disinterest.) My explanation, no matter how brief, always included a mention of the Holocaust and thus reinforced our shared identities as Jews and as related to survivors. One bond I had with older members was my understanding of this shared history. Younger kibbutz members, born in Israel, did not necessarily feel connected to this past and had to learn about it in school.

Being questioned about one's origins is probably more common for foreigners visiting Israel than for visitors to many other places because of the interest that many Israelis have in the dispersion of the Jewish people and the paths that people took to "return" even if only for a visit. There is also a folk notion that if one examined each case carefully, one would discover how each Jew is related to another Jew. This type of questioning has become labeled "playing Jewish geography."[43] Extracting information about my origins was a mixed blessing. Some members criticized me for not living in Israel *because* I am Jewish. They explained how important it was for Jews to strengthen Israel with their very presence, given the overwhelming losses the Jewish people had suffered during the Holocaust. The people who said this to me were Holocaust survivors or their offspring. One woman told me her story in a way that was so chilling that I reexperience it frequently.

> z: I stood in line with my mother in Auschwitz. She was told to go to the left, and I to the right. She was holding onto my arm. When we were separated, she squeezed

---

[43] Thus, I found out that one of the kibbutz members is related to sociologist and colleague Nancy Chodorow.

my arm a little bit. I didn't look at her. I couldn't. I can feel that squeeze on my arm
to this day, over here, right above my elbow. I think you should come here and be
with us. It's the only rational thing to do.

Her narrative leap from the story of Auschwitz to my responsibility to live in Israel
was quite common.

BEING A POTENTIAL MEMBER

Even though I was defined in advance as someone who would leave the kibbutz
after a year, there was, in some people's minds, a possibility that I would stay and
thus some questioning about my potential for staying. The kibbutz is a proselytizing society in the sense that it wants people to join. My reading of the participant
observation literature shows that this phenomenon of inviting the researcher to
become a permanent member of a community is quite common. A few kibbutz
members asked me explicitly to consider joining the kibbutz. In their eyes, being a
researcher was not my "master status." Rather, being a Jew was.[44] And being a Jew
created a connection to the kibbutz that transcended the manifest reason I was
there—to do my study. Lynn Davidman found the same subtle pressure in her
study of Jewish women in the United States who were in training to become
Orthodox.[45] While this low-key recruitment activity was going on by some members based on their view that my identity as a Jew was my master status, others
seemed unaware that I was Jewish because they saw me primarily as an outsider.
So many outsiders (i.e., volunteers) were gentiles that they probably simply put me
in that category.

Thus, although being Jewish was an asset in my ability to understand the
background and life of the kibbutz members, it also created a bind for me because
it made me a potential member. Thus, my not joining, even though I was Jewish,
had to be explained.

> 13:4: I told S (my elderly neighbor) and T (her sister, a member) that I have
> the status of a temporary member. S asked if I would join.
> 248:1: C (elderly man) sits with us on day of Pesach. His attitude: we should
> stay.

Although I did toy fleetingly with the idea of joining, I never seriously considered
it despite repeated explanations by kibbutz members as to why I should join. To
compensate for my "errant ways," I redoubled my efforts to establish an identity as
a helpful "temporary member" who conducted her research in a way compatible
with their wishes. I did not want my research to fail simply because I was not joining the kibbutz. My identity as a Jew transformed me into a "potential joiner" and

---

[44] The sociological term *master status* refers to the primary identifying characteristic of an individual, an achieved or ascribed status that overshadows all other social positions. In Israel, religion
functions as a master status.

[45] Lynn Davidman, *Tradition in a Rootless World: Women Turn to Orthodox Judaism* (Berkeley
and Los Angeles: University of California Press, 1991). See p. 54 for a full discussion in her own
research and in that of other researchers.

thus an "actual rejecter" of the kibbutz in many kibbutz members' eyes. There was no neutral territory.

> 151:1: Z (elderly) asked me if I wanted to join the kibbutz because "you have a suitable personality." He said I could be active in the kibbutz, by which he meant, take a role in shaping things.
>
> 221:2: S asked me if I wouldn't consider living in this country on a kibbutz and suggested an Anglo-Saxon kibbutz, probably of the Ichud (a less ideological kibbutz movement) that has good experience in absorbing newcomers.

By not responding to this suggestion I was also in the uncomfortable position of having to reject the very person who was talking to me.

> 221:2: A (elderly man) was talking about the fact that I should move to this country, that conditions aren't important, and conditions are bad, but the will to live here is the important thing. He said that when he arrived in Palestine, he was given three British pounds, which he had to return, and a metal bed frame. Now, *olim* (i.e. immigrants) make all sorts of demands. So conditions would be easy for me.
>
> 285:1: This got us [G and me] onto the topic of the difficulty of people deciding to move here and this, in turn, got us to the topic of my staying on the kibbutz. She said there would be plenty of work in my field. I talked [lamely] about [my husband]'s difficulty, e.g. Where would he put his personal library and how could he keep it? She said, "Have you seen your sponsor's library?" (Meaning there won't be a problem in finding room for lots of books.) Then she said she doesn't think people should be convinced to join a kibbutz. You have to want to do it. She gave as an example the teacher, N, who is a hired worker, not a member, although she lives as if she were a member.

I was not ready to "go native" and become a member of the phenomenon I was studying, knowing full well that many researchers struggle with this problem. Nor was I willing to deceive kibbutz members into thinking I was seriously considering the option. Instead I tried to answer people's questions honestly and with respect, offering an answer that was honest rather than dissembling with an answer they wanted to hear.

CHAPTER 7

Being an American, an Academic, a Sociologist/Anthropologist/ Gerontologist, Dancer and Daughter

Members of my daughter's group playing.

Even though I spoke Hebrew, I don't think I was ever mistaken for an Israeli because my accent was distinctly and perhaps heavily "American English." It did not take long for me to realize that for some people I represented "America" on the kibbutz.[1] The United States was not an obscure, unfamiliar country to the

---

[1] One of the families on the kibbutz had emigrated from the United States. Because it was the lone American family and because of some of the wife's personal characteristics, the family was poorly integrated, perhaps giving the impression that Americans don't make good kibbutz members.

123

kibbutz members. Many of them had traveled to the United States or had relatives who lived there, including their own children who had married Americans. American women were a major "problem" in that they lured away kibbutz "sons."

> 68:4: When I told her I had been ill, she said she hadn't been ill for 22 years, and then 4 months ago the doctors took one look at her and said she needed her hernia repaired. She suffered terribly from the operation and to this day feels weak. She "didn't know how to lie in bed" since she was never sick. She didn't even write to her son in America until the operation was over and he came to see her. He married a girl from San Francisco, and they are there now so the wife can be near her parents and he can study. They have one child. Her son will finish his studies in one and a half years, at which point his mother is certain he will return to the kibbutz but she can't speak for the daughter-in-law(!)

America is a threat because it serves as a magnet, drawing people out of the kibbutz and out of Israel. From this perspective, even though I was an American woman, I was not a true problem because I was already married. Given that I was married, the danger was small that I would lure one of the men away to America, as sometimes happened with the young volunteers and kibbutz youth.

> 62:1: E was going to a wedding that night. She had a friend who is going to America because she married an American. E tried to convince me that I should come to Israel to even things out numerically.

To my surprise, a few young female members wanted to try living in the United States and spoke to me about it surreptitiously. One of them, a recently divorced woman, for instance, asked me to help her write an ad for a "friend" in the personal column of *The Village Voice*. "America" is typically connected with finding a mate or going there because that's what one's partner wants or just going there to seek one's fortune or enhanced educational opportunities. Obviously, some of these relationships do not work out.

> 27:1: She told me about E who works in the children's kitchen and who married a volunteer. They went to America. Didn't work out there. Then came back here. Divorced. She went to Tel Aviv. Remarried. Divorced. Sent the kids here to the kibbutz. She has now returned. It's rather chaotic.

Aside from the threat posed by marriage to Americans, kibbutz members thought America was a good place. And to that extent, they projected positive feelings onto me.

> 74:2: Read the newspaper special issue for Rosh Hashanah, as T suggested I do. It contained a story of a young woman about to go into the army saying she's doing it because she has to. And since when she gets out "there will only be TV awaiting her in Israel," she's seriously considering immigrating to the US.
>
> 131:4: Y (young woman), G's mother, keeps on saying to everyone that everything is better in the U.S., cleaner, etc.

On the other hand, American groups have founded numerous kibbutzim, for example, Kibbutz Gesher Haziv, Kibbutz Kfar Blum, Kibbutz Gezer, and Kibbutz Ketura.

315:2: L asked lots of questions about what Israelis in America feel toward Israel and American politics, etc. He is interested in American developments and has a lot of admiration for America's absorption of refugees and the intermixing of populations, which he sees as similar to Israel.

America did not have an entirely positive reputation, however. Kibbutz members talked in somewhat stereotypical terms about the dangers of urban life (e.g., the high murder rates in Detroit and New York City) and the unavailability of medical care.

22:3: She said that the poet Bialik hoped the Jewish people would be so normal that there would be Jewish thieves. "Bialik would be happy now! There is so much crime in Israel, embezzlement, etc. that it's like Chicago, which used to be the symbol of crime!"

67:5: She said, "We are spoiled on this kibbutz in terms of medical care. There are doctors, nurses, ambulance, infirmary, and a hospital close by." She told about how scared she had been in Boston. And about the night she had a rapid heartbeat and had relied on her friend's connections to get medical care.

For some people, my being an American could have been an obstacle to establishing rapport because it was a symbol that could provoke intense negative feelings.

132:2: Z (old man) at work with quiet bitterness. "The kibbutz young don't care about politics. They want to leave this Garden of Eden that has been created for them and go to America where they can work 20 hours a day and fill their pockets with money."

Another woman asked me to keep the secret that she and her husband were thinking of emigrating and asked me what I thought her chances were of finding work in the United States. The topic of emigration is a sore one in Israel because it contradicts the basic Zionist idea of *aliyah*, that is, the *opportunity/right* of every Jew to live in Israel, which sometimes is translated into his or her *responsibility* to do so. Israeli Jews who immigrate to America violate the rationale for the creation of the Jewish state, represent a "brain drain,"[2] and may be precipitating a demographic crisis in terms of the proportion of Arabs and Jews in Israel, which could undermine the balance of being a Jewish yet democratic state. Thus, American Jews are asked to stay in Israel, and Israeli Jews are shamed if they leave.

131:4: Z said she had heard I like it here very much. I asked her who told her but she couldn't remember. She wishes I would write my book, then come and stay.

The fact that some women spoke with me in a clandestine way about emigrating underscores the sensitivity of these issues. It was particularly difficult for me to deal with these secrets given that I had been interviewing older people on precisely what such decisions on the part of their children meant to them.

For those kibbutz members who were fervently Zionist, it made no sense to them that a Jew would live anywhere other than in Israel. They did not accept the validity of the very concept of American Jewry; they could not understand how anyone could have a meaningful Jewish life there or speak Hebrew or do anything

---

[2] Dina Kraft, "Israel struggles with brain drain," JTA (Jewish Telegraph Agency), p. 1., March 30, 2008

other than perpetuate the negative stereotypes that had developed about Jews in the Diaspora. This attitude was made clear when my parents came to visit.

> 285:6: H (an elderly member) spoke to me and asked if those people were my parents. "How come they speak Hebrew?"
> Later my father got annoyed at the *mazkir* who asked him, incredulously, how he happened to know Hebrew. My father said, "You know, you're not the only people who speak Hebrew." It's as if the Israelis own the language; as if American Jews are illegitimate, not really Jews.

Sometimes my being an American made me the butt of political jokes concerning Israeli-American relations.

> Lunch with K and G: G doesn't want to talk in front of me since I'm an American. K thinks I'll tell Carter!

The few *American* members of this particular kibbutz particularly welcomed my presence in part because it gave them the opportunity to speak English with me. One of them, a woman who had been a member for approximately eight years and was quite unhappy because she had not found suitable work, spoke with me at length about what it was like to be a marginal kibbutz member. Being able to express her frustrations in English allowed her to clarify her feelings, she claimed. Being an English-speaking person gave me a skill that many of the members made use of frequently.

> 49:5: R had an English speaker with her and asked me to sit with her to help her understand what's going on.
> 197:2: M didn't work today since she went to see a psychologist about her son who doesn't concentrate on things that don't interest him. She is really not concerned since he does seem to concentrate on things that do interest him. She asked me to speak English with him, to help him with his language skills.

All year long I had requests to type, edit, explain, read, or comment on something in English.

Despite the fact that my accent always reminded people that I was an American, my acceptance as a researcher closely parallels that described by an *Israeli* researcher who studied the kibbutz, Amia Lieblich.[3] She found that key aspects of her success were being an outsider and doing work with potential to help the kibbutz. In my case, my fluency in Hebrew even though I was an American, my willingness to listen to people, my extended length of stay, my taking on jobs in the kibbutz, including *shmira* (night watch), and my daughter were pointed out to me repeatedly as factors that people appreciated.

> 27:3: He asked me where I learned Hebrew and whether I had learned grammar. He corrected one mistake I made, and I thanked him for it. Can't remember what it was. Throughout the meal, he could not have been more charming. He even complimented me on my Hebrew. He did ask me some grammar questions, which I did not know. He taught me the expression *be'eruv*

---

[3] Amia Lieblich, *Kibbutz Makom: Report from an Israeli Kibbutz* (New York: Random House, Pantheon, 1981).

chaiai, meaning "in the evening of my life," or "in my old age." He hoped my Hebrew would become more elegant or poetic.

54:2: He also asked me a few times if I knew a Hebrew word and challenged me about what it meant. He would like me to speak Hebrew better so he could speak to me more freely. He told me he likes to interject phrases, aphorisms, etc., into his speech.

Altogether, I never felt that my less-than-perfect Hebrew was an obstacle, and I did feel that my being a native English speaker was a plus. Being an American meant that I continuously compared what I was learning about old age on a kibbutz with what I knew about old age in various U.S. environments.

BEING AN ACADEMIC

As in the case of "being an American," having an academic education and "being a professor" were phenomena that provoked ambivalent feelings in the kibbutz at the time of my study. As mentioned earlier, the initiative that young Jews took to come to Palestine from eastern Europe frequently meant forsaking the possibility of obtaining higher education. Those who preferred to remain behind in Europe in order to study were "traitors to the Zionist cause," even though, ironically, education itself had always been exalted in Jewish cultures. This was another arena in which Zionism turned Judaism on its head.

> K [elderly woman]: "So from the time that I left the cowshed (meaning stopped working there), I continued to work in other places. I believe in physical work. To this day, there are too many white-collar workers among Jews; too many artists and professors. We had to create a healthy nation that would also have agriculture and crafts, and we had to have Jews who could work with their hands.
>
> "I was very talented—I could have been anything. On the other hand, I was weak and thin, but I said to myself, 'I will go for physical work and I will go to the kibbutz. I'm going to help create a settlement. I'll go to the cowshed and to the kitchen and to the laundry.' I didn't really like it very much, but my conscience told me that that's how it should be. Others will be professors, but not me. Nevertheless, even in those manual jobs, I found something of interest. Particularly in the cowshed."

After their arrival in Palestine, there certainly was no time for the young farmers to get a formal education. Instead they developed an ideology that life in the kibbutz is an education in and of itself and that people should educate each other. Preferring academic study was grounds for being thrown out of the youth movement that was preparing the young founders (and currently elderly) for life in Palestine.

> 7:5: My sponsor: "There is an issue about what the founders gave up in order to create a kibbutz. Like higher education. And now they want their children to have what they deprived themselves of. What should the younger generation get? What should the boys get when they return from the army? This is called the debate between 'self-realization and collective commitment.' But of course this raises a question: Is the purpose of self-realization to build a non-alienated society, or is self-realization ego-centrism and selfishness?"

To try to develop a career and to be career-oriented represent negative values because they are perceived to be self-oriented. One man, quite opposed to self-realization, even wrote a book about its dangers for society.[4] Thus, few of the oldest kibbutz members (i.e., the founders) had a university education, although many had trade school training abroad in preparation for immigration to Palestine, where they expected to be engaged in physical labor. The ideology of their youth movement was to study only those fields that were practical for obtaining employment in Palestine. Many current young and middle-aged kibbutz members, on the other hand, had some college education or had earned advanced degrees, and the older members were ambivalent about this.

> 22:3: He told me, "There is always a need for teachers, and so we should train teachers. And besides which, young women want to study. Just study. That's a prime value nowadays. When I came to the kibbutz, people gave up their studies including a person studying medicine, just to work in agriculture.[5] Now work isn't so important. In addition when the kibbutz sends people to study, they don't supplement the funds the kibbutz gives them by *working* to pay for their education. They don't get a job. Rather, they simply live 'the good life.'"
>
> 132:2: At work an old member said to me with scorn, "We wanted a kibbutz; the young want degrees."
>
> 304:4: L said that the situation was not good in Holland either. Farms that were "in the family" for generations now have no takers among the young. Everyone wants to study.

Among the middle-aged members were numerous academics. Many kibbutz members had intense negative feelings about these academics, perceiving them as "lazy."

> 114: I saw graffiti on the sign-up list for people to serve as guides for guests (from outside the kibbutz) during the kibbutz anniversary celebration. Someone had listed all the academics, but next to each one wrote, "abroad" as a way of ridiculing them for not staying home and doing their fair share of work for the community.
>
> 186:X: "I take pride in doing physical work, and will harvest the grapefruit, unlike the professors here who disdain this kind of work."

Kibbutz members who wanted to study in a university had to present a request to the education committee. This request was granted only if it did not represent a drain on the kibbutz economy and labor supply. People who were afforded an education were supposed to study something that would be useful to the kibbutz. Members thought that people who received an education in a field that was not usable would likely be attracted to working off the kibbutz and would be lured away. On the other hand, many of the people who were attracted to the kibbutz

---

[4] Ironically, his son studied the oboe in the United States and then returned to join the Jerusalem Symphony Orchestra. Another son left the kibbutz to pursue his career/talent in the city. His daughter is also an artist.

[5] Kibbutz members concerned about the lure of study realized that this problem was not unique to the kibbutz but rather occurs throughout the world. The shift from agrarian to industrial society and ultimately to the information society was painful to some kibbutz members.

were extremely intelligent people who were responding to a complex ideology. Over time, some of them became writers, poets, and scholars. Several such people were members of the kibbutz I studied.

> 10:1: I told D [an old man] about my book [*On Becoming a Social Scientist*] and he said he'd like to see it. The title reminded him of Margaret Mead's *Coming of Age in Samoa,* which he thought was an interesting book. He told me that he was in the midst of publishing his third book.
>
> 151:2: With regard to the four kibbutz members who are professors, he approves of their work, thinks the kibbutz should have all different kinds of people. He agrees, though, that not everyone thinks this way. He believes it was good that they 'worked' first (meaning that these people did regular kibbutz work for years and only later became professors).
>
> 296:5: This noon I was at the archives getting material from the journals when B beckoned to me from his office across the yard. He was cleaning it up after 3 or 4 years of its collecting dirt and paper. We had a wide-ranging conversation, plus he gave me many books and pamphlets. He told me that he had started working on an encyclopedia in 1954 at the beginning of the "Stalinist disillusionment."[6] He had never been a true believer like some (don't tell my wife, he said) in the "false messiah," and therefore he was more acceptable to all the people who he wanted to contribute to the encyclopedia. In the course of those years preparing the encyclopedia, he corresponded with hundreds of people. And he now wants to put the correspondence together and give it to the archive. Many of them started as unknowns and now are recognized as great intellects. He has lately gotten a little out of touch with the academic world. The people who have moved into positions of influence were studying for their MA's when he knew them in [the city]. He has not taught now for several years. His encyclopedia work is finished now. It was supposed to be one volume, but turned out to be six. Currently he is working on a book on Jewish art and has written 200 pages already.
>
> Another reason he succeeded was that he was from an elite youth group, and that opened doors for him all the time, "as if you would say you are a Shaker or a Quaker in the States," he said. He was thought of as respectable, honest, etc. He had the reputation of being a pioneer, although now you would never say that people in Emek are living the pioneering life. He said the issue of Stalinism was so important to the kibbutz that when people began to speak againstStalin, there really was a danger the kibbutz would break up.

This man told me he has not worked exclusively on his books. Between volumes he taught, studied in another country, was *mazkir* several times (refers to this period frequently), and had grandchildren, which keep him busy.

Some of the numerous kibbutz members who had a low opinion of higher education saw it as a "parasitic" form of life, an existence that lives off the manual

---

[6] Several founders of one of the kibbutz movements, Kibbutz Artzi, created the political party Mapam, which espoused communism and identified with the Soviet Union. At first (from 1948 through the late 1950s), Kibbutz Artzi leaders overlooked Stalin's hostile attitude toward Zionism or attributed it to misunderstanding. In 1952, one such leader, Hazan, went so far as to label the Soviet Union as the "Jewish people's second homeland." When they learned, however, about Stalin's fabrication of the Jewish Doctors' Plot against Soviet leadership, previous enthusiasts of Stalin became disillusioned and changed positions.

labor of others. Being a "parasite" was the worst, and most common, epithet hurled by kibbutz members at one another, not always behind their backs. I do not think they despised higher education per se but rather were afraid of it because it would lure people off the kibbutz and endanger the Jewish people because they would not know how to do nonacademic work and would become dependent on the labor of others.

I believe that gaining the trust of potential critics of my being an academic came through demonstrating my own commitment to regular kibbutz work. Sometimes I was teased about my lack of background in rural living—I was "an urban thinker," not someone who knew what "living close to nature" was all about. For instance, I complained mildly about how muddy it was during the rainy season and how the mud confined Yali and me to our room during the afternoons, which was problematic for me because she had no TV to watch.

> 183:1: He said that I "am not an 'agriculturalist,' and therefore I don't know that the rainfall is good."

One surprising aspect of the kibbutz's reaction to my being an academic was that people continuously asked me what I was studying. No matter how often I told them, they could not understand that I was not writing my dissertation. When I told them I already had my doctorate, they sometimes became more enthusiastic about what I was doing, as if conducting research beyond the dissertation represented more of a commitment than "having to get the data for your dissertation." Somehow I became "a real researcher" rather than "a student."

Other academics and students among the kibbutz members frequently related to me as an academic. They gave me requests for literature, translation, editing, or citations. One painter asked me to translate and perhaps edit his resume so that it would be appropriate for an academic audience.

> 320:5: After J decided that I was an 'anthropologist,' she told me she is taking a course at the university in anthropology. The teacher has asked her to make a presentation on 'the heart patient as a culture.' Could I help her? What is culture? How should she do the paper? I gave her some ideas. She wanted me to do the whole thing practically. She said I should come over, but then said it was not right to invite me over to do this. She would invite me afterwards. I told her to work on it and then I'd give her feedback. What chutzpah![7]

Many people who wanted to help me in my research suggested things I should read or told me I should read a lot. They offered to instruct me on what I should know.

> 75:1: T is a very talkative man. Right away he wanted to lecture me . . .
>
> 137:6: E said I must read literature, just as his students should read, he wants me to understand deeply, not superficially.
>
> 245:2: My sponsor suggested I read an important ideological article written by a kibbutz member and published in an important kibbutz journal. He also said that that particular issue contained many articles about a particular concept that I had been asking about.

---

[7] Means "gall, nerve."

Late at night, keyed up by so much activity during the day, I usually read for hours or pored over archival records because I couldn't fall asleep and typing would be disturbing to my neighbors. The academics who had published books gave me their own writings and asked me to give them an opinion. The kibbutz archivist showed me the section of the archive devoted to all the publications of kibbutz members. Many of the academics clipped articles and lent me books they thought would be interesting to me. My interaction around them reinforced their roles and mine. My interaction with these people also helped me understand that the kibbutz is constantly doing research on itself and that my work would be only an additional attempt, not the single effort in articulating its culture of aging.

Nonacademic kibbutz members who appreciated higher education frequently engaged me in discussions of books they had read or theories they found interesting, such as comparative analyses of Erik Erikson, Sigmund Freud, and Jean Piaget. They enjoyed having an academic around as a resource for such discussions.

> 183:6: S said I had *protektzia* (meaning an "in") with V because I have a Ph.D.—something she admires.

But being an academic also meant that I had numerous tasks from my "previous life" to complete—articles to finish, galleys to read, correspondence to keep up with. This set of tasks, in combination with everything else I was doing, added to my level of exhaustion.

> 1:5: Typed a letter to [journal] with regard to the review.
> 172:6: Worked on the paper that will be included in the British collection.
> 174:1: Worked at home in the morning on the outline for my article.
> 181:4: Between 2:00–4:00 read K's dissertation draft (my student) and fell asleep.
> 183:1: Picked up the newspaper, then went to my room to work on the chapter I had been invited to write.
> 219:1: Worked on letters of recommendation.
> 302:1: Mailed letters. Decided not to eat breakfast. Didn't approach P and M for interview since they were sitting with L. Went back to room. Typed chapter for anthology. Made progress.

I also got a lot of pleasure from the academic work:

> 181:4: Had a wonderful time reading M's 'book.' It reminds me of the outside world and my former self.

My being an academic (not simply a researcher) was sometimes visible to kibbutz members. For instance, when I went to the university and participated in a day-long conference on "aging in the kibbutz," I traveled in a big kibbutz truck. Most of the people in the truck wanted to know where I was going. When I returned to the kibbutz, wearing a skirt and blouse rather than work clothes, my outfit also provoked questions. Where had I been? I had given a ten-minute response in Hebrew to a panel of Israeli researchers in front of a large audience. Coming home to the kibbutz, I felt elated at having been able to do this. I didn't tell many kibbutz members about it because I thought it might make them feel like objects of my research rather than the friends they had become.

Although on the kibbutz I did not hide the fact that I was a researcher, I did not like to talk about the lectures I gave outside the kibbutz or the writing I planned to do. In a sense this was a hidden identity, just as, I am sure, kibbutz members had identities that they kept hidden from me. The reason I minimized talking about my academic work was that no matter how cooperative people were with me, I could not help but feel that they would consider anything I wrote to be a judgment of them. I wanted them to see me as a person who was interested in them—interested in understanding and perhaps assisting and not judgmental at all.

> 307:3: "For old people the conditions are great!" she said. "But, of course, some people are never satisfied; they always want more; that's what the standard of living does to you." I told her I wasn't the kind of person who always wanted more. She said it's because I've already achieved my degrees! But I said it also has to do with my parents' Holocaust background and told her my story. I don't know why I got into it. Perhaps it wasn't relevant.

I now know why I "got into it." I was trying to be the kind of person she admired while still being the person I was—an academic.

At the time of doing this study, computers were a new phenomenon. The factory purchased the first computer on the kibbutz, and with its arrival a tour was arranged for the old age club. One of the members said, "As a sociologist you don't need this tour." There was an assumption about what I knew and didn't know. Although people interacted with me intensively, there was also probably some uneasiness about having a researcher in their midst who was studying them. This discomfort was expressed continuously in friendly jokes:

> On Friday I was having breakfast with Z and S, the soup cook. In a light manner, I asked S how she was doing and she said "excellent!" Then she joked and said, "If I had told you anything else, you would have written it down." Later I went home, and wrote that down.
>
> 4:1: My husband told me there was a joke going around about me (already?). First there were 50 dentists; next there will be 50 manicurists, and then 50 sociologists will arrive to study the condition of the elderly. [I guess they think what I'm doing is absurd.]
>
> 6:5: My sponsor's wife asked what pseudonym I will use for Emek? *Kibbutz Hakshishim? Kshishiland?*[8]
>
> 233:2: Y (about 45 years old): Will you talk to me only if I am 70?
>
> 281:2: U stopped by where I was dancing and asked if I came to see the old people dance! [He probably couldn't figure out what I was doing there since it was not designed specifically for older people.]
>
> 302:2: D teased me about the fact that I make two people old every time I sit down. Miriam, with whom I was sitting and who is an old woman, disagreed. So did I.

When people joked with me about my being a researcher, I tried to banter in return, as in the following example, which also illustrates the affectionate relations that we developed over time:

> 54:1: Breakfast. D moved over from his table to where I was sitting, in order to talk to me. He asked me whom I have interviewed so far and how things are going.

---

[8] *Kashish* means "old person"; *kshishi* is the adjective; and *keshishim* is the plural.

With pseudo-sadness he said that for me, he is not a man but only a case. To keep up the joke, I said, 'less than a case, you are simply a number.'

He then asked if he will appear in my book as an x.

I said 'a small x' . . .

As we parted I said I wouldn't tell him it was good to talk to him as usual because I have already told him that. But he said I could tell him anyhow.

I took notes frequently and publicly, including writing while sitting on a chair on the tiny lawn outside my little house. I did this from the beginning of my stay.

> 19:4: Tonight a movie was shown on the kibbutz. Seemed like about 100 people attended in the old dining room. People were strolling back from the movies using the path in front of my house. I was sitting outside since it was so hot and they saw me writing.
>
> 292:3: S is eating dinner with us and tells us she is the *shomeret laila* (woman who watches over the children at night). A asked me if I wrote that down.

Of course, some members must have felt that my very presence was an invasion of their privacy, even though the kibbutz as a whole (or at least those present at the initial meeting) had approved my project:

> 66:2: At lunch O told me about a girl who had hurt herself and was recovering in bed. She had a tape deck on one side of her bed, and a TV on the other. The same arrangement existed in A's room (very old man). I said I had seen it in his room. And O said, "About this you also take notes?" She seemed aggressive to me. Perhaps continuous observation means that I am never out of role, and that if they have something they don't want observed, they are never safe from me. They can escape an interview by refusing me, but can they escape being observed? Probably not. This might be uncomfortable for some people. I will try to give them, or at least O, more room.
>
> 133:1: N saw me looking at the rain chart and asked jokingly if even that is within my research domain. I said, "I'm interested in everything." I've said this so often. May be that's the hardest thing for people to grasp about participant observation.
>
> N: I will talk to you only if you don't tape me and don't take notes.
> Me: Fine with me. [This writing is from memory.]

Gradually, however, people began to seek me out to tell me *their* interpretations of life on the kibbutz in every aspect, just as I had tried to communicate that I was interested in "everything."

> 281:2: After dancing I was sitting around with the person who had been leading the dancing (F) and those who had come to the session. F said that I should interview him because he has completely different theories and will force me to start my work all over again. Everyone tells me that they themselves are the exception to whatever rules I come up with for explaining the kibbutz. On the last day on the kibbutz, I went around to the houses of people with whom I feel particularly close and gave them my address in the States. On the path, a young woman stopped me to tell me that there is one thing I should know about the kibbutz that bothers her—everyone knows everything about everyone at all times, except one thing—what goes on between a husband and wife in bed. "No, that's not true, people probably know that too," she added. I was amazed. Here it was the *last* day I was on the kibbutz and people were still coming up to me to make sure

I got it right. This felt like the last minute of a therapy session when the patient finally is willing to say what is most important, because s/he is about to leave.

I think it became valuable for people to believe that someone knew exactly what they think and how they feel. I believe I played that role for people and perhaps helped redefine what an academic is. I accepted what people wanted to tell me rather than defining in advance what I wanted to hear from them.

BEING A SOCIOLOGIST/ANTHROPOLOGIST/ GERONTOLOGIST

The attitude that people had toward what I was doing seems to have hinged not only on research in and of itself or how I was doing it but also on the specific subject matter of *old age*. I was associated with "old age." This association evoked an ambivalent response from the start. Here are some blatant examples:

> S: I think you should not be a gerontologist. It is a depressing topic. You can't help but become part of the thing you are studying.
> Me: I like the topic!

> 61:7: The kibbutz treasurer invited [my husband] and me to come to his home on Friday evening after dinner in order to discuss the pension system and 'to get me away from the elderly.'

Members of all ages respected old people for what they had accomplished in the past, but they also began to perceive them as people who need services rather than people who can contribute to the kibbutz. The very act of studying old age on the kibbutz, then, was further proof of the costs of this age group, that is, they needed to be studied and were being studied at the expense of other, more pressing, topics. They were becoming a service division of the kibbutz economy, like child care, the kitchen, or the laundry—a division that absorbed rather than created resources.

> 6:1: My sponsor introduced me to D in the dining room. When told I was studying the old-timers, he said it wasn't worth doing, but then said he was joking. I'm not sure he was.

During the year I lived in the kibbutz, an overwhelming amount of activity and information concerning aging was evident. Kibbutz members took courses on gerontology at the local community college, and television programs on the topic were aired. Some of the off-kibbutz events I attended were the following:

1. An all-day workshop on aging based on a large-scale research project conducted at the university;

2. An all-day workshop on aging conducted by the Inter-Kibbutz Consortium on Aging;

3. An all-day workshop on aging and health; and

4. A meeting for *mazkirim* on issues of aging.

On the kibbutz itself, numerous activities also were related to learning about the elderly:

1. A lecture at Kibbutz Emek by David Atar, the coordinator of the Inter-Kibbutz Movement's Committee on Aging;

2. A day-long consultation by a kibbutz expert on aging and leisure activities, conducted at Kibbutz Emek;

3. A report to the old age club of Kibbutz Emek by a kibbutz member concerning one of the day-long workshops he had attended; and

4. Continuous meetings of Kibbutz Emek's elderly committee concerning phone installations and the creation of health care and workshop settings.

Kibbutz members were probably feeling inundated with information. At meetings of the elderly committee, I sometimes was given materials such as a translation into Hebrew of an interview by famed American gerontologist Robert N. Butler around the theme that aging is not an illness. All of this activity contributed to some people feeling annoyed at the disproportionate attention given aging:

> 115:9: I went to the home of my sponsor and his wife. They asked how the day had gone with the expert who had come to Kibbutz Emek. She and my sponsor think there is absolutely no need to create a sheltered workshop for the elderly in the unused building in the center of the kibbutz. "Why is there so much concern for the elderly? Why not for the young," etc.?

Toward the end of my study, I concurred:

> 239:2: F said the elderly are not *the* important research issue. I agreed. But then again, I had not chosen the topic because it was the most important one to study.

Some people felt this was all the more a waste of time and energy given that the subject of the condition of the elderly is simplistic, and there is no need to study anything about it.

> 147:2: Joined one of the *mazkirim* for a workshop on elderly designed specifically for *mazkirim* held at Kibbutz Ein Hashofet with David Atar. The *mazkir* didn't expect many people to attend today "because of the topic and the weather." About 20 *mazkirim* were present . . .
>
> The *mazkir* drove me back when the workshop was over. He said he had learned nothing. My interpretation of his comment is that 1) he's preoccupied with other problems; 2) he's saturated with news about the elderly including the tour this past Tuesday; 3) and he's not aware of what there is to know. He said he has no questions. Thinks all the other kibbutzim can learn from what Emek has done [I don't think so]. Thinks the kibbutz elderly are fussy and arrogant.

And even if the topic is important, it was not clear that an outside researcher—or any researcher—could accomplish much to "solve the problems."

> 48:5: Me: What are your expectations of me?
>
> MAZKIR: I am ambivalent since it is hard for a kibbutz to absorb things that are not organic. You can't overcome the indigenous processes. On the other hand, I am open to new ideas, things we haven't seen before. That "nothing will come of it—your project—is very close to my thought about it. It's my opinion that we've got it very good here; we just don't know it. I would like your conclusions to tell us how good we've got it. I think it would be helpful for our social relations. I am satisfied because the kibbutz is doing so much for the elderly. But it hurts me to see how people are acting, eating themselves up, and eating up others as well."

For many people, aging simply was not the key issue of concern in the kibbutz.

15:5: The key issue, she told me, is *azivat banim*, meaning the fact that children who are born on the kibbutz do not stay on to become members but leave when they become adults.

19:3: The key issue, he told me, is that the kibbutz is having trouble exerting its authority over individuals.

Part of my task as a researcher was to legitimize the very subject matter I was studying. Although some people appreciated the significance of the topic, others would have liked to steer me to other issues that they cared about even more.

On the other hand, studying the elderly was an asset because the elderly are probably the easiest of all the kibbutz age groups to study. Their schedules are more flexible than are those of the younger adults with children. This is as true on the kibbutz as it is elsewhere. O'Brien wrote of her study in Catalonia:

I spent a large proportion of my time with the retired members of the community, many of whom found time hanging heavily on their hands after so many years of work. Those who had no family were particularly happy to spend hours talking and were a mine of information, as well as being wonderful storytellers and therefore a pleasure to listen to.[9]

Because of my interest, people continuously fed me information that "I should know." The following example occurred early in my stay when I was taking care of Yali's needs and not even asking questions:

20:1: I spent some time in the children's clothing center today making a list of the clothes we brought with us so that we could be sure all the clothes would eventually came back to me after it had been in the laundry system all year. The coordinator is a woman in her 40's. She looked at some of the designs on Yali's clothes and said, 'Here is something you should know because of your work. It is very difficult to get the old ladies who work here making clothes for the children to change their ways. They still make clothes the way they used to a long time ago. I urge them to try something new but they are opposed.'

I was bombarded by information, saturated with ideas, deluged with hypotheses. I had successfully become a research sponge. Members began to stop me to give me information in reference to the elderly:

221:2: Friday at lunch spoke at length with A and then with F. B embarrassed me by coming by and saying that one of my 'patients' is sick. M. Now his wife, N, is sick too. And the health committee coordinator is going to see the couple at the suggestion of the health service provider. He didn't want me to do anything—just to know it.

As the year went on, the tables turned, and members began to ask me for information about the elderly:

221:2: She asked me how the research was coming along and asked me how many people there were over 65. She was shocked to hear that there are 87. "That's

⁹ Oonagh O'Brien, "Sisters, Parents, Neighbours, Friends: Reflections on Fieldwork in North Catalonia (France)," in *Gendered Fields: Women, Men & Ethnography*, ed. Diane Bell, Pat Caplan, and Wazir Jahan Karim (New York: Routledge, 1993), 236.

more than the number of young people!" [What does she mean by young? Under 30? Why is she shocked? Doesn't she know this? She lives here, after all.]

240:2: T came to me to ask for demographic material re the kibbutz. He is member of the committee concerned with members' housing needs. He wants the kibbutz to build temporary housing, not permanent housing, for new members. I said I would meet him at noon . . . back to room . . . and started working up the data for him.

240:3: Lunch. Approached T. Showed him [what I had done], and he asked me for more tables!

They also criticized me for my interpretations. I believe that such criticism is a sign of accepting me and showing me that they know I can take criticism.

222:2: F pointed out an article in today's newspaper about the Haifa research studies on aging. He said that I over-identify with the elderly when I say they are more active socially than the young are. May be he's right. I am not defensive. I present myself simply as a learner.

BEING A DANCER

A typical day on the kibbutz for an adult member consists of working, eating, resting, and taking care of one's children or grandchildren, perhaps studying or engaging in a hobby, gardening, watching television, and going to sleep. Sometimes people take a course in a local community college or in the educational center of the kibbutz movement. The weekend, or rest days, consists of a single day (Saturday or Sabbath), as it does in most of Israel, rather than two days, as it does in many other parts of the world, and many of those "rest days" are actually "work days" if one has a rotation duty (in child care, the cowshed, or the kitchen, etc.).

In my particular circumstance, because I was a temporarily single mother of a two- to three-year-old, worked on the kibbutz, and was conducting intensive interviewing, observing, and writing field notes, I had almost no leisure time.[10] I found this leisure deficit to be particularly difficult when I also had rotations on the Sabbath and thus had no break whatsoever. It was also tedious to not have some recreational activities in which I would simply "be myself" rather than be a researcher, mother, worker, and so forth. I was delighted, therefore, when I learned that a folk dance club met occasionally because dance has been one of my lifelong hobbies. As it turned out, even while I attended the dance sessions, I couldn't help but develop field notes in my head that I later recorded.

41:6: Brought Yali to bed. Went dancing. [They seem to organize sessions of the dance club after a wedding has taken place, since all the chairs are already out of the dining room.]

Recognizing that I was a person who needed some recreation, I came to appreciate the extent that recreation was essential to older people as well.

Taped interview with Y: "I'm sure you have come across the problem of leisure time. How to keep them (old people, of which she was one) occupied. Everybody

---

[10] Part of the problem was structural, that is, being a "single mother." But part is my personality. I tend to take on a lot of work and engage in many projects.

knocks their head against the wall, trying to keep them busy so they won't think about death, so they won't be bored, seeing as how they only work a few hours per day. For me, that problem doesn't exist. On the contrary, I don't have enough time, and I have to arrange things so I can finally find some time for myself. And I work fewer than three hours per day, difficult hours as they might be, and I work at night!

Occasionally I attended a kibbutz movie night, but my real enjoyment came from the periodic sessions of the dance club.

> 191:7: Went back to the *heder,* ate, brought Yali to bed, changed, went folk dancing. Who attends? M, T, Y, H, A, T, R, L, MU, the volunteer, and D, D's daughter, E, M, A, T came last night. C (E didn't come), S, J, and R. G didn't come and was asked after. There were also a few kids and some strangers.
>
> I started the dancing off since it was getting so late. The whole club lasts only one hour really. After doing some fast dances, G taught [a particular dance] with a mistake, which I got him to correct. Others noticed the error, too. Then we did a lot of exercise and movement to disco music before reviewing some other dances. Good evening. Wish there would be more of it . . . I told G it was a good session, and he agreed in typical fashion by saying, "It wasn't bad."

When a kibbutz member died, dancing was cancelled because the entire kibbutz (and not just the family or social group of the individual) honored the memory of the deceased by suspending entertainment.

The bulletin board in the hall on the floor level beneath the dining room was a nerve center of the kibbutz. Its contents shaped the mood of the kibbutz. Whenever I saw an announcement that dancing would take place, my spirits rose in anticipation, sometimes to have them dashed immediately.

> 302:1: Went to the dining room and before I had lunch, I checked out the bulletin board, and saw a notice for dancing tonight. [A short time later,] I saw the notice on the board that D had died [mother, age approximately 35]. All the other notices were taken down. M was standing nearby and explained what had happened: car accident, D had been speeding. I was shocked; I couldn't function. She had been so "alive." Others around me seemed fine, however. Perhaps they are so used to losses, that they handle them better than I do. I don't know the norms for reacting to this kind of sudden loss. I tried to be calm. It would certainly be ridiculous if I were more affected by the death of a person I knew only slightly than were those people who knew her well.

It is difficult for the kibbutz to determine the proper balance between the recreational needs of certain groups and the need to respect other groups who feel a great sense of loss. There were four deaths during the year I was on the kibbutz. I would have felt uncomfortable dancing in the aftermath of some of them but not all. I presume the kibbutz members felt the same way.

Aside from the dance club, folk dancing and folk dance performances were standard parts of wedding celebrations and holiday parties. These occasions were elaborate performances at which I shared the role of spectator with the rest of the kibbutz members. Dance was part of the original cathartic physical activity of kibbutz founders, something that some cynical young people are challenging today.

> T (a young woman) gave me an illustration of how annoying old people can be by telling me about a movie that had been shown here. The film concerned another kibbutz in which young members had complained about not having anything to do. After the movie an old woman stood up and said—"what do they mean they have nothing to do? They should get up and dance all night like we did." T said the elderly impose their old solutions on current problems.

Conversely, young people's desire to dance (not necessarily folk dance) is a way they differentiate themselves from the old:

> 304: T told of SH who worked in the *mashtela* (greenhouse) yesterday. When T told her how work was done with old tools in the past, she said, "Leave me alone with stories about the pioneers. I want to dance and live it up."

On some level, therefore, dance was a meaningful symbol in this kibbutz's culture. For this reason, it was also an aspect of members' lives that they criticized if it was not done correctly.

> 131:4: They mentioned a Dutch couple that taught folk dancing and played the accordion. The woman was criticized for not teaching correctly. She was then given the job of cleaning toilets, I was told. They left the kibbutz.

Dancing was so important to me as a release that I found myself taking the lead in keeping the evening going when dancing actually did take place. At the time I recognized that perhaps I should have been more passive, given my role as researcher.

> 305:1: I said I organized the dancing at the end, perhaps I shouldn't have shown off. I don't mean to, I just want to dance!

William Foote Whyte has written about a situation in *Street Corner Society* in which he adopted the behavior of the group he was studying by cursing.

> One evening as I was walking down the street with the Nortons . . . I cut loose with a string of obscenities and profanity. . . . Doc shook his head and said: "Bill, you're not supposed to talk like that" . . . I tried to explain that I was only using terms that were common on the street corner. Doc insisted, however, that I was different and that they wanted me to be that way.[11]

Whyte subsequently reports making "the most serious mistake of all my time in Cornerville." This occurred when he voted three times in a citywide election to support a particular candidate. "When I went in to vote the second time in my home precinct, I was challenged, and, for a few agonizing seconds, I thought I was going to be arrested." He concludes that "it is even more important for the field-worker to be able to live with himself than to live with other people." Whyte's mistake was in taking on group behavior that was inconsistent with his own values.

---

[11] William Foote Whyte, *Learning from the Field*, pp. 66–67 (Beverly Hills, CA: Sage, 1984).

My concern was different—I not only adopted their (completely legal) behavior (dance) but also took a leadership position in their activities. It was as if I was showing them how to perform their own culture.

I also had the sense that I should be passive during the four funerals in the course of the year. During the burials I felt the contradiction most acutely between being a member of a community and studying it. Although I felt sincere sorrow and pain at the death of these four members, it seemed inappropriate to express these emotions lest they seem to be morbid displays. I did not know all four of them intimately. The same was true at dance—I felt that I could participate but that I should hold myself back and not express their culture even more enthusiastically than they do.

Nevertheless, I was disappointed when people did not take advantage of the opportunity to dance when it was available.

> 81:2: G said jokingly after the dance that it would not exactly be characteristic of Emek that people rush 'to get rid of their children at night' so that they can be free and come to dance.
>
> 205:1: S stopped by where I was eating lunch to comment on my dancing. She asked me when I would make my debut. I asked her why she doesn't dance and she said she would lose her breath, and "besides, I'm fat." (Like R had said.) But dancing might prevent further fatness. Besides she's not fat. She said she feels like jumping in when standing on the sidelines. But she doesn't do it.
>
> 211:2: Tonight's folk dance performance was well attended by all age groups. Lots of old people present. G and Y were part of the troupe. Afterwards when the kibbutz was invited to dance, there was a poor response.

Dancing was my only hobby at the kibbutz other than swimming with Yali. There were other activities in which to partake, but I had no time. Occasionally, particularly when my husband was visiting, we took in movies shown on the kibbutz, but they were usually grade B or lower. The lack of other forms of entertainment and relaxation made dancing all the more important to me. Moreover, dancing allowed me to feel young and be among young people in contrast to the way I spent most of my time.

BEING A DAUGHTER

My parents live in the United States, but while I was doing my year of fieldwork, they came to visit their granddaughter and me in the field. In order to arrange for their visit, I made an appointment with the *mazkir*.

> 200:5: Went to Y's office. He was talking to M who gestured that I should take a chair. I made three points: first, about my parents coming, could they have an apartment? The room next to me would be ideal. I asked him to write it down since he didn't at first. When I said, "They would like to pay." M said, "This is not a hotel. On the other hand, there are no rules about how to deal with guests of guests. We will have to discuss it."
>
> He asked if my parents would work. I said, "I don't know. "
>
> I should have said "No," [my husband] later told me. "But they do speak Hebrew; they are 60 years old," I said. Clearly the currency is labor, not cash.

Questioned if they have been here before, etc. "They want to see what I'm doing."

285:6: E said my father was like one of the "old time Jews."[12] My parents are a curiosity to the kibbutz members. I think they make me appear more human, like I have other dimensions, a history.

My parents also helped me by taking Yali to Jerusalem for one week, giving me time to conduct interviews during the hours that I would have been taking care of her. Just as is true for kibbutz members, having parents is an asset for child care until they need care themselves.

In this chapter and the previous one, I provided information about a set of selves that was relevant to others while I conducted fieldwork. These were the selves that I brought to the field and, although somewhat subject to change, would be part of me wherever I went—a mother, a woman, a wife, a particular age (thirty-three at the time), a Jew, an American, an academic, a sociologist/anthropologist/gerontologist, a dancer, and a daughter, the latter two manifesting themselves only briefly. Each of these selves provided a window through which to see the other, to be seen, and in my case, to understand the elderly kibbutz member in his or her environment. This multiplicity of selves served the function of providing different members of the kibbutz with ways of connecting with me and me with them. I became the intersection of these parts, in conjunction with the other sets that I call "research selves" and "situational selves." It is to "situational selves" that I now turn.

---

[12] I don't know what aspect of my then-sixty-year-old father's appearance or behavior made him seem like an "old time Jew." But the reference includes a learned, European rather than a muscular Israeli. Historian Anita Shapira has written that the "diasporic Jew was cowardly, helpless, and submissive. In contrast, the community in Palestine was supposed to be brave, masculine, bold and uncompromising." See her *Land and Power: The Zionist Resort to Force, 1881–1948*, p. 219 (Stanford, CA: Stanford University Press, 1992).

CHAPTER 8

Situational Selves: Being a Worker, Being Temporary

Members of the old age club participating in a local trip.

In this final part of the book, I offer the third cluster of "selves." Unlike those selves—research and personal—discussed in earlier chapters, 8, 9 and 10 deal with selves that *emerged* in the fieldwork process. For this reason, I call them "situational." In my case, these selves are worker, stranger, or temporary person (which kibbutz members interpreted either positively—staying for a *full* year—or negatively—staying for *only* one year), volunteer (or "neither a volunteer nor a hired worker," that is, having a liminal status), a person who is sick, a hostess, a friend, a neighbor, a homemaker, and more. Some of these selves provided a steady stream of information (e.g. neighbor, homemaker, and hostess). Although I did not expect these roles to be relevant to my research, they became extremely meaningful and once again contributed to the array of lenses through which I learned about the kibbutz and its members. The emergence of selves helped me understand the fieldwork site itself, while the fieldwork site provoked understanding of my selves. I call the selves that arise out of, or rise to, the occasion "situational" because typically they do not last beyond the fieldwork situation ("friend" may last), although they are relevant at the time. My ultimate role was "leaver," a role that disappeared and was replaced by "the person who once lived among us."

BEING A WORKER

Other than the roles of researcher and mother, the role of worker was the most important I had on the kibbutz. Had I not been a worker, I would have been isolated within the kibbutz and would not have understood aging or any other phenomenon, I believe. Thus, I begin this **group of chapters** of *Observing the Observer* with a discussion of being a worker, the essential element of a person's life and reputation within the kibbutz community at the time of this study.

As a person who wanted to do research on a kibbutz, I could have lived either on-site or off-site. On-site, I might have been able to pay for the services I needed (e.g., housing, meals, laundry, child care) as I would anywhere else; or on-site, I could have *worked* on the kibbutz in exchange for those services. I chose to do the latter. I lived on the kibbutz and performed work to earn my keep[1] for two reasons. First, I wanted to participate in kibbutz life in a way similar to members so as to enhance my understanding of what a kibbutz is experientially.[2] In many other fieldwork experiences, researchers do not receive housing, meals, and other amenities from the officials of the site itself. In other cases, the fieldworker may pay a family in the setting for room and board. In most fieldwork reports, however, the researcher does not inform the reader of the way these matters were taken care of—a major deficiency in my view. In my case, because the kibbutz was a relatively cash-free community, I attempted to relate to the kibbutz in that way as well— work for service rather than cash for service. (To "pay" for my husband's visits, he did the same. He, too, worked occasionally.)

In addition, I wanted to find a convenient way of meeting people and having them observe me, so that I could form relationships to facilitate my research, especially with those people I hoped to interview. In other words, I wanted to see and be seen. Working in the kibbutz was an ideal way to attain these two objectives. Its

---

[1] The question of who was paying for my research arose many times. Because I came without a grant and worked in the kibbutz, one could say that there was a barter exchange between the kibbutz and me.

[2] *On Becoming a Social Scientist: From Survey Research to Participant Observation and Experiential Analysis* (New Brunswick, NJ: Transaction Books, 1984).

drawback, however, was the toll it took on my stamina and health because I took on this role in addition to my researcher and mother roles and so many others.

Because being a good worker bestows legitimacy as a member of a kibbutz, I believed that if I worked well, I would be accepted and assisted as a researcher. What is a good worker? Someone who shows up on time and devotes energy to working while on the job. Someone who is not a slacker or deadwood; someone who doesn't go along for the ride or get a free ride. The measure of work is effort and commitment, not necessarily efficiency. There are many jokes in kibbutz culture about work and people who do not work hard enough. There are also jokes about people who work too hard, as if they are trying to make a point about how good they are.

> 207:1: Arrived at Y's workplace at 6:30 a.m. and people were already busy at work in the offices. M and D at least, M saying she had been at work since 4:30 a.m.(!) in response to the request from the coordinator of women's work that she fill in somewhere in the afternoon.

> In other words, she came to work early so she could work additional hours at a different job in the afternoon! The following stories about grueling work, told to me by elderly women, were typical:

> 190:5: When I first got here (i.e. joined the kibbutz), I worked in the hospital in the nearby town doing laundry for them and earning money for the kibbutz. Since I was new to the work, I needed more time to finish. I worked 10, 12, 14 hours per day and got overtime pay which I gave the kibbutz treasurer. He said I had worked so hard, that I should take a day off. But I didn't take it, since they needed the work done.

> 100:2 P said that when she first came to the kibbutz, her job was to remove stones from the fields. She remembers that the work was so hard that she got nosebleeds. One of the members said that he was going to tell the work coordinator about this so P could have a different work assignment. But P was not about to let that happen, so she hid her face behind something whenever she got the nosebleed so no one would see. She ended her story by saying that the attitude toward work was different then from now.

By making the decision to work, I was taking on a familiar kibbutz community role—worker—and a burden of guilt if I did not live up to these extraordinary expectations.

There were three exceptions to this emphasis on work as the highest value. In one case, an extremely talented late middle-aged man disparaged the kibbutz community's definition of work as effort and time. He thought work should be evaluated by efficiency and profit, particularly now that there were labor-saving devices. Work should be rational and scientific, not backbreaking. A second qualification concerned what I discovered to be transcendent values. For example, the kibbutz honored the concept of the Sabbath, the day of rest, and minimized work on that day. No one became virtuous in the eyes of the kibbutz if he or she worked hard on the Sabbath. And in line with transcendent values, some kibbutz members went on strike—even abandoning the value of work—to show their displeasure when frustrated. While I was in the kibbutz, there were several actual strikes, threatened strikes, or talk about strikes. For example, a bulletin board notice announced that the *kabalat shabbat* committee (responsible for the ceremony and entertainment before Friday evening dinner) was on strike because there had been too much noise in the dining room the previous weeks. People had arrived late, and parents did not adequately control their children in the dining room. My friend told me that this was the committee's way of punishing the kibbutz. Much more common was the individual (rather than the group) strike, however.

> 78:1: The problem with the new children's house is that there is a sewage blockage in the new neighborhood, and the houses stink. That's why a *metapelet* went on strike today, but her co-workers aren't united with her.

In another instance,

> 86:1; 10/6/79: C came by . . . and we discussed Yali's move (from the infant house to the toddler house), i.e. the move of the children whom she serves as *metapelet*. She also told me about the discussion that will take place among the parents and the other *metaplot* (pl.) of her group tonight. She has given an ultimatum that she will quit working with the group if the parents don't abide by whatever is decided tonight. Perhaps she can get away with this since some of the mothers formerly were her students.

I also discovered that parallel to being on a "work strike," one can be on a "culture strike":

> 9/18/79: After dinner I sat around in the dining hall talking to M (an elderly man). I asked him casually if he was participating in the upcoming celebration. When he said, "No," I asked him why.
>
> "It's a personal issue. I've been angry with the kibbutz for a year or more and I don't want to get involved." At first he didn't want to tell me what the issue was, but then it came tumbling out.
>
> "I don't want you to have a negative impression of me. I have a daughter at another kibbutz and there the old people are treated with respect. Here they are not. The problem centers on the repair and improvement of housing. A plan was approved several years ago and every year I've been waiting for them to get around to fixing my house, but they don't do it. And I'm the oldest one here. Younger people get what they want because they've got power and don't care about the elderly. I want my house improved because I've got to make it more comfortable for my wife to clean. It now takes her a full day! I also want to make it larger so that my daughter [who does not live on the kibbutz] can sleep over with her family when she comes. She's never slept over! We just want to enjoy a better house in the few years we've got left, especially considering the fact that I've given 50 years of my life to the kibbutz. There was one couple here with two daughters and we got one of those daughters to leave after she made everyone miserable. Before leaving she said, 'Why should I stay here just to support these old people?' Then there was a youth group who came and one of the girls made a similar comment. She didn't even stay! There were about 18 kids in that group, and we gave them everything, but only 2 stayed."
>
> ME: "Do you really think that the young people are trying to take things before the elderly, given your experience on the secretariat?"
>
> He laughed cynically as if to agree. "I used to have the role of the enfant terrible, but my efforts were Quixotic. I wasn't able to stop the social processes.

They might get around to doing my apartment next year, but my wife is already 73 and she's not that interested in it anymore because it involves a lot of dirt, noise, and mess. Seven years ago it might have been nice."

This was the bitterest conversation I had heard yet on the kibbutz. It was impossible to continue talking because Yali was screaming. M took my tray back for me to the dishwashing rack. While he was gone, the treasurer stopped by my table and said, "If M is contributing to your research, the whole thing is invalidated."

The least frequently invoked reason not to work is that one has become elderly and "deserves a break." This idea is rarely heard, however, because the notion of earning your keep or working hard "for the kibbutz" is deeply engrained in the older kibbutz members, particularly the ones who created the kibbutz.

For them the notion of retirement smacks of taking advantage of those who are working, and thus the elderly want to work as long as they can, even if their doing so requires setting up special conditions so that they can work.

THE ELDERLY AND WORK

The elderly people of Kibbutz Emek continue to work outside their homes in a regular workplace. Of the eighty-two people age sixty-five and older, seventy-six (93%) were working. In the United States in 1972, only 16 percent of the population over the age of sixty-five were gainfully employed outside the home, although many others wanted to do so for two reasons. There is growing awareness worldwide that because the longevity is increasing, it is important to find meaningful activities as well as income in the last phase of life. At the time of my study, only three elderly people had no place of work in the kibbutz. Two of these people were almost completely bedridden. In addition, two women and one man worked less than two hours per day. They are completely satisfied with this arrangement because they have a place of work, a place to go. One of these women requires a great deal of assistance to get to work. She interprets receiving this assistance as her right, although it is economically irrational for an able-bodied worker to devote her time to enable a disabled person to go to work. A more economically rational approach would be to have an able-bodied person bring work of some sort to a group of disabled individuals. The fact that economically irrational activity goes on means that noneconomic normative needs are being met, as I learned from participating as a worker.

The two women who were not working at all were seventy-four and seventy-eight years old; the man was seventy-nine. The man is "out of work" because the kibbutz work branch in which he participated has closed. As the kibbutz continues to go through major economic shifts, it has to decide whether to retrain older workers to fit into the newer jobs. The barriers to work are the lack of a suitable place and ill health, not age itself. If people have worked hard their whole lives, as these people have, they are unlikely to have developed hobbies or alternative enjoyable, time-consuming activities. This lack may also propel them to stay "on the job" as long as possible. For elderly individuals with families on the kibbutz, their children and grandchildren can become their hobby. If all of the children have moved away, the challenge of how to fill one's time becomes more pressing. Television watching is only a partial remedy. The question arises as to whether the kibbutz itself has an obligation to teach people about hobbies to prepare them for the life stage beyond work. And if it does not, how can this phase of life be rewarding and meaningful?

Kibbutz members work in designated work branches *on* the kibbutz, or they work *off* the kibbutz. Each work branch has a manager. An elected kibbutz member (called a *merakez meshek*) is responsible for coordinating all the work branches. She or he carries out this responsibility with the assistance of a "works committee" composed of elected members. In the committees, the various work branch managers typically advocate for increased investments and personnel for their branches at the expense of other branches. Each tries to make her or his branch profitable. Just as some individuals complain that the kibbutz has not invested in their individual living quarters, so, too, they complain that the kibbutz has not invested sufficiently in their work branch. Service branches (e.g., education, dining services, health, medical care) are not geared to profit, but their representatives, too, advocate for more personnel and investment. Every branch perceives itself as understaffed in a way that sounds similar to discussions in an academic department.

Kibbutz members work in kibbutz factories, agricultural branches, education, the kitchen, and more. If one holds a job *outside* the kibbutz, the money earned must be given to the kibbutz. Members who work *inside* the kibbutz do not earn salaries. Both they and the outside workers receive payment in kind from the kibbutz in the form of services they ostensibly need (e.g., food, housing, clothing) and some cash to use as they wish. (At the time, kibbutzim were changing these policies to enhance personal rewards and choices. Now, 30 years later, there is much more privatization of income.[3]) Many individual kibbutz members at the time already had supplementary sources of income that they ketp for private use even though this violated official kibbutz ideology and policy that all resources should be shared. These private resources came from gifts, inheritances, and money earned abroad.

Every kibbutz member is expected to contribute his or her fair share of labor to the collective good and to do so without complaint. Kibbutz society attempts to be class free with all work valued equally. Again, the ideology does not always match reality. There are real differences among people in terms of intelligence, levels of responsibility of the work they do, and other assets such as charm, talent, and beauty. The standard joke, told to me repeatedly, was that the only way to make everyone equal is to cut everyone down to the same size—literally cut off everyone's head.

There are profound differences between the perceived value of the work deemed "productive" and the work deemed "services." Kibbutz economic organization does not include the idea of accumulated benefits related to work performance. Kibbutz labor assignments are organized by a *sadran avodah*

---

[3] Igal Charney and Michal Palgi, "Reinventing the kibbutz: the `community expansion' project," in Michal Palgi and Shulamit Reinharz (eds.), *One Hundred Years of Kibbutz Life* (in process).

(coordinator of men's work) and a *sadranit avodah* (coordinator of women's work), who try to match the labor supply (i.e., members and sometimes volunteers and Ulpanistim) with the needs for labor in the work branches. Most of the time these two people organize only certain branches of the kibbutz, primarily the service branches, because other branches are stable as a result of the high level of skill required by the workers to participate in them.

Work in a kibbutz has symbolic meaning different from the one that Westerners are used to—it is not completely a burden, a way of asserting oneself competitively or professionally, or a source of anxiety in the sense that another person could take one's job. Rather it is a form of participation in the round of community life. Thus, kibbutz members who work off the kibbutz are frequently perceived as outsiders because their work does not allow them to interact intensively with other members. (This holds true even for army officers whose work people respect but nevertheless work *off* the kibbutz.) On the other hand, these off-site workers bring in needed cash because the kibbutz does need cash in order to purchase items from the world outside the kibbutz. Most members who work off the kibbutz do undertake some work in the kibbutz. Having to work *on*, to compensate for having worked *off*, the kibbutz demonstrates the relative value of these two forms of work. After working *off* the kibbutz for a few years, for example, a kibbutz member might be asked to spend a year doing kitchen duty in the kibbutz. The reverse is never true. Strangely, working *on* the kibbutz is thus seen as a punishment or payment, like teaching might be seen in academia. People who work *off* the kibbutz are perceived as being free, unsupervised by communal observation. Recognizing this, a kibbutz member who does work outside may feel guilty about doing so while persisting in that work, as I discussed in the first chapter.

A kibbutz member who is a professor with a faculty appointment at an Israeli university and who spends a sabbatical year in another country doing sophisticated research might return for a year of dishwashing in a kibbutz before returning to his or her university duties. In a kibbutz, people's "work community" and their "residential community" overlap (except for those who work off the kibbutz). Coming home to the kibbutz after a day of hard work "on the outside" is like a man coming home to a wife who is tied to the kitchen and children. The degradations of gender, space, and the service economy are tightly linked.

The history of the kibbutz is tied intimately to the history of Jews coming to Palestine to seek employment and to learn how to do necessary but completely unfamiliar work in a foreign landscape. For example, in many of their countries of origin in eastern Europe, Jews were not allowed to own land. When they came to Palestine, however, they were expected to be farmers. In the first decades of the twentieth century, finding employment was one of the key concerns of the Jewish immigrants to Palestine. There was almost no industry, few farms, and little urban development. The economy was in its infancy, and the whole geographic area was known as the "backwater" of three great religions, rather than a land with economic development opportunities. The creation of the kibbutz idea was in part an answer to the need for work and income. At the time, people who could not find work or who could not physically carry out the work they were given considered themselves failures. They were so ashamed of this failing that they left the country or in some cases committed suicide.[4]

Even today, being thought of as a "good worker" practically assures one respect and prestige in a kibbutz. One should not work in a way that invites exploitation by others nor in a way that exploits anyone else. Being a "good worker" may even serve as social protection in a crisis, as is evident in the following example I was told:

> There was a case of a family who wanted to travel abroad. They made a request to the "travel committee," the *mazkir,* and the whole kibbutz community. They were turned down each time because they were needed as workers in their particular jobs.

Nevertheless, the family went abroad. The question then for the kibbutz to consider was whether to throw out the family (i.e., to rescind its membership in the kibbutz because it had violated kibbutz decisions). The family members were not thrown out because people liked them and because they were good workers. Conversely, to not be a good worker places you in jeopardy.

The issue of getting the work done was always complicated by the fact that the kibbutz could easily solve its need for labor by hiring outsiders. In contemporary kibbutzim, there is extensive employment not only of nonkibbutz Israelis and Israeli Arabs but also of agricultural workers from Thailand. In some kibbutzim, a whole section of the living area has become a Thai subcommunity. But among outside workers and potential new members, there is always the problem of how well they will work.

> 248:1: He said, "There is a need for more new members to replace the hired workers on the kibbutz, since hiring workers is not *kibbutzi* (i.e. what a kibbutz should be doing)."
>
> I asked, "Will these new members want to do the work that hired workers are now hired to do?" I was implying that simply having new members doesn't solve this particular problem. So he began to talk about the fact that the reason the new families aren't adjusting well is that they weren't part of the youth movement that prepares people to live on a kibbutz.
>
> I asked him to explain whether or not this was the case for a particular new member family. He said, "That man is worth nothing. In the city, he owned a printing press and didn't have to work" (meaning, he just hired people and lived on the profits). "Here he doesn't know how to work. He goes from workplace to workplace without becoming integrated."

Thus, I recognized that if I became a worker, I had to be a "good worker." I had to "know how to work." Only if I fulfilled that role would I be able to do research that relied on people talking to me. If I were a "bad worker," the benefits I would accrue as a result of being a worker in the first place would be undermined.

---

[4] See Deborah Bernstein, *Pioneers and Homemakers: Jewish Women in Pre-State Israel* (Albany, NY: SUNY Press, 1992) and Mark A. Raider and Miriam B. Raider-Roth (eds.), *The Plough Woman: Records of the Pioneer Women of Palestine* (A Critical Edition), (Hanover, NH: Brandeis University Press, 2002).

I had no experience, let alone training, in the work I performed: (1) cook in a kitchen that served hundreds of people at each meal, (2) day-care worker for six infants, (3) chicken coop worker, (4) worker in a large-scale laundry, (5) greenhouse worker, and (6) factory worker. These jobs were relatively low prestige but did enable me to meet many people. (If I had worked in factory management, the range would have been far smaller because the number of people qualified to work there is smaller.) My jobs gave me the opportunity to interact with kibbutz members of all ages, with members of both sexes, with nonmember hired workers (Arabs and Jews), with volunteers, guests, relatives, with parents and grandparents, sisters and brothers, work organizers, and branch members. It meant that I had access to the back stage and front stage of the kibbutz. It also meant that because I had no previous knowledge about how to do these jobs, I could ask many questions. These are ideal circumstances for a participant observer, if one is willing to do the work.

I believe the workplaces I selected and was steered to were appropriate for my research purposes. I agreed to work in two places that were requested of me and that are requested of nearly all women—the kitchen and a *beit yeladim*. I chose the other places—the chicken coop, greenhouse, factory, and the laundered-clothes sorting room—because these were places that were managed by older people or that had a lot of elderly workers. All of these workplaces were physically manageable.One day I tried my hand at work in the citrus groves. Under the general management of two young kibbutz men, I picked grapefruit with the volunteers who had come from all over the world. Much to my surprise, that outdoor work was simply beyond my physical abilities, given everything else I was doing. It was too exhausting to climb trees and ladders, fending off bees and then to crawl under the low prickly branches. If I had forced myself to pick grapefruits, I probably would not have been able to continue my research, and I would not have learned much about the elderly. Generally, fruit picking is work done by young male kibbutz members and by young volunteer men and women. In the past, however, kibbutz members did it even when they were not young. One seventy-two-year-old woman I interviewed *began* working in the orchard when she turned fifty, as did another man. My one-day experience in the fields at least enabled me to appreciate the sheer challenge of this type of work.

Another advantage of being a worker was that I could talk to other people about my work and find out what their attitudes were. For example, I had dinner with one woman who was on leave from the army and who was discussing with her parents which kibbutz work branch she would like to join when she got out of the army. When I said I worked in the greenhouse, she said:

> Well, I wouldn't want to work in the greenhouse with that old couple (the branch managers). They are extremely unappealing people, complaining all the time. That's why I just stay clear of them, because if I spend any time talking with them, they'll expect me to work with them.

Her comment taught me about the informal ways in which branch managers attract people to work in their branches. It also taught me that older people who are branch managers may have special problems attracting younger members.

Whereas an old person is not forced out of his or her position as work branch manager, the "works committee" can do things subtly that will make the worker angry enough to want to quit. Usually this means denying investments of money or workers because the "works committee" believes there is no future in the branch, particularly if young people are not moving into it. This, of course, is a catch-22. Thus, it is important for older branch managers to recruit young members but then also to pass on the power to them.

One elderly member who was a branch manager complained to me bitterly about this lack of investment. As a researcher, I stored his complaint as a question on the list I would inquire about when I interviewed the kibbutz treasurer: Were there special issues related to older people being work branch managers? The treasurer answered my question by telling me the point of view of "the rest of the kibbutz":

> The problem with that branch is how to get young people to work there. (This is the perennial problem in a voluntary society—how to motivate people to do what they do not want to do.)[5] Every kibbutz has its branch where young people don't want to work, he told me. In other kibbutzim it might be the chicken coops. Not here. In fact, just look at our coops. J works an incredibly hard day there. If there are no young workers to take over, there's no way the branch can continue.
>
> The dairy manager knows this, yet the kibbutz just invested 1 million pounds in the dairy just to keep him happy. As far as I'm concerned, that was 'thrown out money.' He had his little fit, and then he sent a letter of apology to the "works committee." In fact, what he really wants is for someone to tell him to shut it down so he can quit and then blame him or her. But no one will tell him that because they are afraid he will commit suicide as his wife did 7 years ago. His outbursts will continue because the situation cannot improve. It's really a shame because he is so well known outside the kibbutz for his work in dairies. And here, in his own kibbutz, his own dairy is not effective. He can't let it be shut down and move into something else. There's a real discrepancy between his esteem on the 'outside' and the 'inside.'

Because of my lack of labor experience, becoming a "good worker" was not easy. In addition, my many other tasks (i.e., being a researcher, a mother, and a house-keeper in addition to taking care of my health) left me little energy for regular kibbutz work. Nevertheless, I assumed that the same was true (if to a lesser extent) for other kibbutz members and that whatever my circumstances, I would have to try to be a "good worker." Like everyone else, I frequently worried if I was "good enough" and what my reputation was as a worker. There were no standardized performance reviews to clarify the situation. You had to intuit your reputation or just not care about it.

That aspect of my self-in-the-kibbutz that related to work enabled me to have role relationships with many kibbutz members and institutions, just as did the

---

[5] The kibbutz is a voluntary society in another way. People do nice things for one another because they choose to, not because they have to. Sometimes individuals write stories in the kibbutz internal newsletter about the nice things someone has done for them. An example is eighty-year-old R, who wrote about young people visiting her to inform her that they were making better housing available to her.

resident aspect. It also made me acceptable in some members' eyes, as evidenced in this example from a transcribed interview with an elderly female kibbutz member:

> Young people have their own world. I can't intrude. I don't want to criticize it. They live differently. We didn't have a State (i.e. State of Israel had not yet been created when she joined the kibbutz). . . . They have military reserves, they live in a different world, and I can't stand the old people who criticize and criticize. . . . I say, "It's the young people's world; it's their kibbutz." I have to respect that this is how they want things. Except for one thing—work. I always tell them that whatever you want to do, fine, but you have to earn your keep. I ask the young people if they work enough to make a living. They make children (have a high birthrate) and in the afternoon they're already off the job. They only work a few hours. They're great socialists, but in the meantime, the Arabs are working, the volunteers are working, and the kids who go to the Ulpan are working. What about the young kibbutz members? That's the one thing I can't tolerate. I could never forgive them for that. But anything else they want? Let them have it any way they want.

After hearing her speech, I was relieved that I was working. And I probably wouldn't have gotten an interview with her if I hadn't been. As a worker, I also felt entitled to visit people in the workplaces in which I did not work. I learned that the mothers of young children take an hour off in the middle of the morning just to visit with their children (*sha'at ahava*) and that this can be disruptive both to their workplaces and to the children. I learned about the physical spaces in which people worked and the attitudes they had toward work. The following is an example:

> 116:5: 80-year-old N is dissatisfied with her workplace, the arts and crafts workshop, which she manages. She adheres to the unconventional position that it is absurd for elderly people to work, although she herself holds another job in addition to managing the arts and crafts workshop. She makes boxes for the children's toys. N asked me if I noticed that the focus of the advice provided by the kibbutz consultant on aging concerned work, rather than hobbies. [Her workplace falls under the hobby category.] N complained that she does not have an adequate budget or space to run the workshop. In particular, she is trying to incorporate the last room in the building into her workshop, but is meeting with resistance from those who want the room for other purposes. She is open 3 afternoons a week. Served me tea and cookies. Told me how she acquired looms at bargain prices. Now she can't use them all because of the lack of space. She also has a potter's wheel standing outside the building for lack of space.

Numerous older people complained to me about the inadequacy of their work facilities. I understood this as a way of enhancing their workplace, that is, they were important enough to complain about, to feel aggrieved about.

On the thirtieth day I was in the kibbutz, the *sadranit avodah* asked my daughter's *metapelet* when she thought I would be ready to work because the *metapelet* would know when Yali was "ready to let me go." The *sadranit* wanted me in the kitchen, and I agreed, knowing that working in the kitchen would be perceived as extremely helpful to the kibbutz. I would be on my way to being a "good worker," an accommodator. I began as a kitchen worker because the *sadranit avodah* actually said the kitchen was not a popular place to work and therefore was always short-handed. As a "temp," I took the least-desirable job.

> 43:1: M (45 years old) said she is too old for kitchen work. Strangely, she is not too old for child-care work, which is just as physical. The reason, in my view, for her differentiation is that she is bound up in the politics of child care, and no one cares about the kitchen. Child care is a hot button. Age has nothing to do with her work preferences.

In fact, as soon as the rumor went around that I would soon be working, people began to ask me informally if I would work in the kitchen. The kitchen was a kind of ground-level entry job (for women), a "black hole" that continuously needed to be replenished with workers. No matter what, meals needed to be prepared; people had to eat. The kitchen was defined as primarily women's work, and women had to find a way of getting out of it if they didn't want to work there.

Working in the kitchen (6:30 A.M. to 2:30 P.M.) meant preparing the noon meal, the major meal of the day. Not only did I help to prepare/cook whatever was being served, but also I served it in the communal dining room.[6] The cooks stood behind a large food wagon distributing cooked food to members who walked by with their trays. Clean-up occurred after the meal and was also the kitchen-workers' responsibility. Because nearly every kibbutz member ate his or her noon meal in this way, as a cook I was able to interact with nearly everyone simply by preparing and serving this meal. The sheer visibility of this role—standing there in a somewhat dirty apron testifying to my having worked "hard"—was useful. My presence was being established. In addition, most people had a comment about the offerings, and thus I was privy to jokes, complaints, and commentary about the food, the kibbutz, life, and me in general. As I dished out the food, data were dished back.

Kibbutz members generally changed their clothes in the middle of the day. In the morning they wore dark blue kibbutz-issue work clothes generally consisting of loosely fitting heavy cotton shirts and pants for men and the same for women or a smock to wear over shorts or a skirt. These clothes can become dirty. After the midday rest, people dressed in individually chosen more attractive clothing. I always wore work clothes at work, and thus walking along the paths to and from work I was perceived as a worker not only while I was at work itself. In all my jobs, I got very dirty.

The second most-important place for me to work, in terms of the kibbutz's needs, was in the *beit yeladim* or children's house. I worked there in order to accommodate the *sadranit avodah*:

> Today I had lunch with V, her 8-year-old daughter, and the daughter's friend. They told me that Y is their *metapelet* right now since R, who formerly was their *metapelet,* is working in the infirmary replacing three nurses—T who just had a baby, H who just had an operation, and S who is off on a year of study. The new

---

[6] Many kibbutzim have since closed down the communal dining halls because people prefer to eat at home and the large structures were expensive to maintain. See Clyde Haberman,"Reluctantly, a Kibbutz Turns To (Gasp!) the Stock Market," *The New York Times,* July 8, 1993

metapelet organized a game for the day, but V's daughter and her friend decided they didn't want to play. According to V, the girls are protesting their loss of R and the fact that Y is not really competent to be a *metapelet*. They don't like all these substitutes. "Y really isn't good at it. She yells at us all the time."

The parents of the kids in this group are going to meet to figure out what to do. "But where can we take someone from?" [meaning which branch can afford to give up a worker?] People have even approached V to take over R's job, but V, at 48 is really too old for this task, she says (bragging a bit, since these jobs are intended typically for younger women who are thought to understand children better). And besides, V explains that she was just recruited to work with the infants even though she's got a degree in comparative literature and is really needed in the high school. "Things are very tight at the moment. And it's a problem without a solution," she says, "because everybody is right."

They can't approach the wife of the *mazkir* to take the job because she's already been hospitalized for some sort of a nervous disorder. They've put her on the switchboard where there's no pressure. The other *mazkir* is certainly not going to pressure his wife to do it, if the other isn't. The woman who runs the *kolbo* (small store), considered to be a "soft job," said "no" when asked to be a *metapelet*. The kibbutz is unable to force people to do jobs they don't want to do. This is a "real problem."

A *metapelet* takes the job for a year. With groups like that of V's daughter, the interim or substitute *metapelet* is unable to achieve any authority over the children. Then the parents have a double job. They do their regular work, and when they return home, they have to argue with their children to take a shower, change their clothes, and speak respectfully, the typical tasks of a *metapelet*.

"There just aren't enough people," V tells me. If there were 100 more people, things would be better. Women just keep on having babies, and there are lots of old people who don't want to leave their workplaces, so they need help, and then there are those who do leave their workplaces, and they need even more help. There are just not enough people around to take care of all the things that people who can't work should be doing.

Given all of this, I knew it would make a lot of people happy if I accepted the position of temporary *metapelet*. Of course, one person working for a short period of time does nothing to solve the structural problems, defined by one member in the following way:

173:7: H (a *metapelet*) is pissed that she has a high turnover of helpers. Thinks "women who give birth to children every year like cats" should work with children, rather than the kibbutz forcing it on single women, volunteers, etc. She, on the other hand, likes the work, but if she didn't, she wouldn't do it, because she's already put in her time and she has only one child.

The simple act of selecting the branches in which I would work paralleled the issue in which kibbutz members were frequently engaged—where should they work? Where do they want to work? Where does the kibbutz need them to work? How do I balance my needs with the needs of the community? How hard do I want to try? Do I want to be a "sucker" and just serve the group? Do I want to be selfish and care about just myself? After working in two places where the kibbutz needed an extra pair of hands, I went on to request assignments where I thought I could benefit, that is, branches with many older people. I had paid my dues.

As a researcher focusing on issues of aging, I knew that older kibbutz members generally do not retire from work unless they become utterly disabled. Rather, they reduce their hours and/or change their workplace to accommodate their physical needs. As a worker in branches with older people, I could observe these phenomena first-hand and see what they meant in practice, not just theory.

> 108:2: Today I started my new job in the handwork section of the factory. There are several older workers there: T, Z, A, B, E and L. B talks a great deal while he works, and L is willing to listen. I spent some time talking with T about this work section. He said the work is not hard but requires concentration. He works daily from 6 a.m. to 10 a.m. in a separate corner of the room where his machine is set up. He likes working "alone" although formerly he worked with other people in the kibbutz garage. He is proud of the innovations he made on his machine.

I noticed that everyone arrives at a different time and goes to breakfast at a time that's good for him or her.

> L is the earliest to arrive and opens the place. She eats no breakfast. L in fact came outside to where I was working in a particular section to tell me to go to eat! She recently threatened to go on strike since not enough work was set up for her. (Oh no! May be my work is perceived as a problem since I could be seen as taking work away from this section.)

Instead of her having to go on strike, the coordinator of this section taught her how to use an additional machine.

> Each workplace has its own psychology and presents me with its own challenges. My reputation as a worker will most likely be the sum total of my performance in all of them.

Old women and men worked in the handwork section of the factory, but only old women worked in the *communa,* my next work place. Basically, the *communa* was a large room containing a cubby for each member, to which he or she would go to pick up clothes that had been laundered, ironed, folded, repaired, and stacked. A colored number labeled each item of clothing that went into the collective laundry, and the women of the *communa* sorted and organized all the laundry. Although each *communa* worker was responsible for a separate part of the "laundry chain," they worked in close enough proximity, sometimes face to face, that they could talk the whole time, as in a quilting bee. Thus, the *communa* was a hotbed of gossip and was ridiculed by others, perhaps because they feared the extent to which their character was being assassinated there.

> 269:1: Arrived at work—the *communa*—around 7:00 a.m. to find M and the two S's already there. [There's a competition here to see who can get to work earlier, just as I have heard that there is competition in some law firms in the U.S. as to who will stay latest.] One of the S's had been called out of work already to go to the pedicurist . . . So the other S got me started on folding sweaters. Then P came in. I hesitate to tell her to take my growing pile of folded sweaters and put them in the cubbies, although the pile is growing dangerously high. People seem

not to want to be interfered with in their work. H does this in the kitchen and is condemned . . . When (middle-aged) R arrived to pick up her large family's clothes, she began talking about the singing last night. She said U liked to do it, but she's the only one who leads singing. "It is too much for her to do it alone, and thus for the last few years they have not been singing much on the kibbutz (meaning community sing-alongs)." But R agreed that there is a "dialectic process" in place, and probably singing will start again. Usually they sing to guitars, not accordions. Knowing about another talented person on the kibbutz, I asked, "How about Z's son doing it?" She said, "No, he's a high school student!" [I guess this is not the appropriate age to lead the whole kibbutz in song.]

We also talked about the movie on Zionist history shown on TV last night. [Because I had been invited to watch TV at someone's house, I could participate in the discussion of a TV show for once!] Referring to the movie contents, S said that her husband had been in the labor battalion that had been portrayed in the show and had participated in the long-ago discussion about whether or not the group should go to Russia. He didn't go, but others did. She thinks he is a "prototypical kibbutznik." She now thinks of herself as an old woman particularly since she had a hard winter; she and her husband were sick a lot. She said spontaneously that people refer to ages like 70 as "not old" but she thinks of it as old. She has talked to her children about what kind of funeral she wants, but they say they would like the privilege of worrying about that. She was one of the first members of the committee on elderly affairs and said it was an offshoot of the health committee. She and P were continuing members of this committee. [All of this was simply said "into the air" rather than to anyone in particular. I tried to memorize all of it and think I succeeded.]

Having finished folding sweaters, I started sprinkling sheets in preparation for their being ironed on the big ironing machine. A and B didn't like the way I sprinkled, so I folded, and B sprinkled. A asked then if I wasn't going to eat, so I went and had lunch. [Then follow two pages of notes about my conversations at lunch.]

Walking back to the *communa,* I saw people winking about whether or not H is back at work on time. I started to fold the pre-sprinkled jeans. M got into a little tiff with V about whether or not a particular undershirt should be converted into a rag. She said she could make a "dream rag" out of it.

Someone commented on how many jeans M had managed to iron, and she said that she did the whole pile in 5 minutes less than a certain hour [do people clock their work?]. S talked about N who had come in [to pick up his clothes] and talked with her saying that she had been his *metapelet* from age 1 to 5, and his parents are still indebted to her for raising him well. And he still related to her well. [*Communa* gossip involves bragging; one brag worthy of respect is having good relations with young people.]

M bouncing in and out of the *communa,* getting things for her daughter who had just given birth. *Communa* workers were commenting about M being a young grandmother. "The baby is a girl; is she pretty?" If the baby is pretty, then it is the G family's influence, but whose—P or D (i.e. which person in the family?)? "Yes, even the oldest son was good-looking till he had an eye accident."

L came in and asked me to work on her side of the *communa,* which was what N apparently told her I would do. So I told her to straighten it out with R and then I went over to L's side to iron.

> I started talking to Z. I asked her what kind of work her son would do. 269: 5: She said, Probably work in the garage since he studied that work, although he didn't finish his studies." She would like him to be able to work with T, A and E since they would know how to relate to him as a human being, whereas if he worked with R, it would be no good. And she doesn't think any new person should be put into the factory. . She hopes that the manpower committee takes this into consideration and not just the manpower issue. With my inquiries about her family in place, I asked her what she thinks of the life of the elderly . . .

In the kitchen I learned that when people leave a job that they had worked in for a significant period of time, the co-workers in the branch host a departure party. Thus, the opportunity arises for people to express appreciation for one another, as might be true in an office in the United States.

> 92:4: The woman who peels vegetables asked me how the peppers were that I was using and that she had cleaned. She takes pride in her work. It turned out that today was the last day of her work on this job because she is shifting over to the factory. She is 69 years old. The kitchen coordinator threw her a party, including a wonderful cake baked by R, who will not give out the recipe since she did so once and that had "bad repercussions, so her husband suggested she not do it anymore."

The vegetable peeler asked me to translate into English her words of gratitude to the volunteers who had been working with her and to communicate her hopes that they continue working well with H, an older woman who would be replacing her. She said that she was touched by the party and would see all of us all the time (although everyone knew that once she moved to a different job, we would see less of her).

Shortly after that party there was an ice cream party to celebrate a birthday of one of the kitchen workers. I was astonished that anyone could eat so many sweets, given that we had just finished eating sweets to celebrate the "retirement from the kitchen." When I mentioned this to R, she explained that these parties were simply an opportunity for more gossip. "You can never have enough of that!" When I gave my interim report to the kibbutz secretariat, I talked about the meaningfulness of these work-site parties. Being a kibbutz worker allowed me to hear (and occasionally offer) gossip, the major way that information was transmitted in the kibbutz.

Some work sites allowed me to interact with young people, an opportunity that would have been much harder to come by otherwise:

> 313:6: H, T and R (three high school girls) working in the greenhouse with me, asked me to go to breakfast with them. H mentioned that the *mashtela* (meaning the head of the greenhouse) wanted a plant from a certain kibbutz member, but he didn't agree to have them cut it out of his garden, even though he has many of that kind. H mentioned that this man is not well liked. . . . His wife, however, is very sweet and smart. She is a physiotherapist. H went to her for a bit of

physiotherapy when her back hurt. "And of course, she has to deal with the old people who must drive her crazy."

They asked me what I did, and I told them I am trying to describe the conditions of the elderly and make recommendations. They said they don't know the elderly too well, nor where they live, but they did believe that they don't get along well with one another.

L said she has no grandparents and now she would like to have them, although when she was little she didn't think about it. She would enjoy meeting with the old people and having discussions with them.

H said that G (the head of the greenhouse) is not well liked. H mentioned that on the day that the elderly went on a tour of the Golan Heights, she stayed on the kibbutz and at one point, came to get flowers from the greenhouse. H asked her why she didn't go on the tour. She said her son had died there and she has been many times. But Y, G's husband, said later that it is because she doesn't associate much with the older people.

Trying to help me to understand older kibbutz members, L offered the following:

> 313:7: The elderly are small-minded, meaning they get all upset about minor things, like problems with their garden, who is throwing the trash onto whose garden, etc. They also bear grudges. [She also told me that young people share the problems I hear from old people, so I shouldn't think of them as the problems uniquely of the elderly. Y told me the same thing.]

Working allowed me to have a place in the dining room because one eats both breakfast and lunch with one's work group and only dinner with one's family. Thus, if I had not worked, I wouldn't have had an appropriate place to sit during two meals per day. I would have had to find people like myself to eat with, and there weren't any. Unlike being a mother and researcher, being a worker was not an aspect of myself that I brought to the kibbutz. It was an aspect of myself that was created in the kibbutz. Being a worker exposed my capabilities and my weaknesses to others and to me, while at the same time it allowed me access to numerous essential aspects of kibbutz life. I learned about my character, and the kibbutz members learned about it as well. This is an essential aspect of life in a kibbutz. Even though there were many advantages to being a worker, it was still hard work, and it is not surprising that I wrote in my field notes:

> I love my research days (i.e. days off from other work)!

BEING A TEMPORARY PERSON (STAYING FOR A FULL YEAR OR STAYING FOR ONLY ONE YEAR)

To the officers of the kibbutz it was important to work out an agreement of conditions between us that was acceptable to all of us. It was also important to them that I had no hidden problems that would cause them extra work or expense. Finally, it was important to nonoffice-holding kibbutz members that I would reside (i.e., use a dwelling) on the kibbutz temporarily (as opposed to permanently). I also learned that the community considered it important that I stay for a full year as opposed to a shorter period. Thus, one of the initial categories I was put into by kibbutz members was "a temporary person," visitor, or nonapplicant for permanent membership. In this community, the temporary/permanent dimension was highly significant. I was a *zmanit,* a temp.

> 18:3: M [i.e. a long-term resident, not a member] said about herself: I'm unimportant on the kibbutz. Everyone says I've got good ideas, but they aren't implemented.

As a temporary person, I was like a faculty member who had an appointment at one university but was working at another. I had specific responsibilities to the community, as it did to me. But the rest would be worked out on the basis of initiative and compatibility.

Sociologically, in such situations the question arises as to how much a host community will invest in a "temporary affiliate." In university settings, for example, turnover is expected—students come and students go. An interview with an older person showed me what "temporary" means in kibbutz life:

> SR: You prefer the people who live here, in contrast with the volunteers.
> T: It's not really a preference; it's knowing that the volunteers will be leaving soon. So, I should invite them? Every 3 months to start all over again, the same story.
> SR: So slowly, you turn away from doing that.
> T: The volunteers are not really connected, they are "as if"; they are "next to" the society. We don't have the strength to take care of them all the time. B gets involved because it's her work. That's what it's like for the old people like B; what they do becomes the most important thing for them. [She explained that volunteers are distributed among the members to be hosted, and she didn't know what to do with the last one since he spoke no Hebrew and she speaks almost no English.]
> M (another volunteer) is known from work, speaks Hebrew, and has a kibbutz boyfriend, so T has gotten to know her. Also L who is going to marry a "kibbutz son," is well known.

A "temporary affiliate" is a person who, by definition, usually has limited social value because a community's investment in him or her cannot pay off in terms of future interaction. An example might be staff investment in elderly people in nursing homes. These are relationships with no, or a limited, future. In a world in which temporary affiliation is the norm, however, as on college campuses, investment is worthwhile because the relationship will last over time if the graduate assumes the role of alumnus or alumna.

On the other hand, in most societies, the temporary person has value as a stranger —a person who is exotic and "other," a person who can hear secrets, and a person who provides a new perspective.

> 222:2: F said he just realized he was "old" when a young woman stood up on a bus to give him her seat. He wanted to say to her he would agree to sit if she would sit on his lap! He rushed off after telling me this anecdote, saying, "Now I've told you all!"

A "temporary affiliate" is someone whom the community knows it will lose as a future member. This issue is salient in the kibbutz because there are so many temporary people. So many people pass through. I would suggest that the two major social categories of people present at any one moment on a kibbutz are, in fact, members and temporary people (ranging from one day to several years). Or members and everyone else. I immediately was part of the second category in contrast to the first. For some people, that was the only thing that was salient about me for the entire year I was there—the fact that I would not stay. I automatically had diminished value—there was no reason for anyone to get to know me because I was not going to be around next year.

The "temporary" category contains many gradations, however. Some "temporaries" lived on the kibbutz for a few years and for that reason alone, if not for others, probably had higher social value than I. Some "temporaries" stayed for a summer or six months and most likely had less social value than I did because I would be on the kibbutz for one year. Some "temporaries" had permanent relations with kibbutz members (e.g., parent of a member). Thus, I found myself constantly being asked how long I would stay and reiterating endlessly that I would be staying for a year. This question expressed more than the kibbutz member's desire for information about me—it was, I believe, a way of placing me in the hierarchy of value within a community. In a way, this was like asking an academic what her or his rank is—tenured or not.

From a methodological point of view, my one-year stay made me normal among ethnographers, even if it gave me an ambiguous status among the kibbutz members. A few foreign researchers have attempted to get an overall picture of the "condition of" elderly kibbutz members on the basis of a short visit, ranging from a weekend to a few weeks. Although an overview of certain issues may be obtained from a short visit, and thus its brevity may be justified in the scientific community, a brief visit is most likely unable to deal with social processes, interpersonal relationships, and the members' ways of creating meaning. Moreover, the certainty that an outsider might feel about an aspect of kibbutz life based on observing during a brief encounter is almost sure to be undermined if she or he stays longer.

Kibbutz life consists of nearly imperceptible change on the one hand and dramatic events on the other. Opinions grind against each other until a reputation becomes rigid or a policy firm. Stories unfold; problems emerge; relationships change; children are born; people die. Had I stopped at one point in the process, I might mistakenly have prejudged the outcome. Thus, a major factor in the study was my presence for a year, which allowed me to experience change. But, of course, it was only one year and only that particular year. Although I stayed a full year, I always wonder what I would have learned if I had stayed longer.

One calendar year allowed me to participate in the cycle of seasons that constitutes the agricultural, school, holiday, and fiscal years. Understanding this cycle generated ideas about years to come and years that had passed. It enabled me to check whether my emergent interpretations and analyses had predictive power. As the year went on, I could anticipate situations and no longer had to ask so many questions, giving me confidence that I understood aspects of the setting. Staying a year also enabled me to wait and reschedule an interview if someone who had agreed to an interview became unexpectedly busy or had to cancel. Staying for a year enabled me to experience the cycle of moods as the kibbutz went through all

the weather changes of the year. Hot weather, or the hot season, was held responsible for many kibbutz problems.

> My sponsor said: "It's so hot, people don't visit each other."
> 38:6: She said, "People are a little edgy in August anyhow, since it's so hot.
> Things will get better soon."
> 48:2: He said, "Things are a little difficult right now in the kibbutz, with the
> weather being so hot, so many people on vacation. There really are pressures."

The mere fact of living in and working on the kibbutz for a year made it possible
for me to get to know a broad range of people on the kibbutz, just as they got to
know a lot of people because so many people pass through.

> 179:1: He said that there is a lot of [human] traffic through Emek, like a train
> station. He and his wife have gotten to know a lot of the passersby.

Staying for a year showed me that the kibbutz constantly deals with separation—
some old people separated from their parents during the Holocaust, which is com-
memorated each year and still felt intensely. The adults separated from their
children when the children were in the *batei yeladim*. Everyone deals with separation repeatedly as the young adults go to the army or decide to leave the kibbutz.
The community deals with the death of members.

Not all the "passengers" stay for a year. Some stay much longer. The fact that
I stayed for an entire year made me feel I was getting to know people well. I knew
different people's tastes in food, who would sit next to whom, and how they
responded to each other. I soon could predict what would happen next.

> 92:2: Breakfast. I joined O. E was at another table. Sitting there with O,
> everything was quiet . . . I knew it wouldn't take long for things to get very heated.
> There is a certain rhythm to most of our breakfasts. Today's blow-up came when
> the *mazkir* approached the table where the flower-arranging staff was eating and
> announced to them that he was going to present some flowers in the name of the
> *mazkirut* to R and perhaps to some of the actors in the kibbutz play. E was furious
> and said, 'Why shouldn't the electricians get flowers too?' We didn't know if she
> was arguing for the electricians or against the actors.

However, in the eyes of some members of the kibbutz, the continuous change
of kibbutz life was so important that a year was insufficient for understanding a
kibbutz. My plan to stay (only) a year illustrated to them that my study would be
superficial.

> 85:4: I told her that my goal was to examine the situation of the elderly
> members and to give the kibbutz some suggestions. *She said I wouldn't be able to
> do that* because the situation changes all the time. What is not happening today
> might occur tomorrow. The elderly are an "unstable population," in her view.

Although the methodological community might say that a single year is adequate
for the kind of study I was doing, some people in the kibbutz disagreed. I found
that people I defined as psychologically insecure (e.g., relative newcomers who
were kibbutz members) used their greater length of stay on the kibbutz relative to
mine as a way of pulling rank and undermining my right to claim I understood the
kibbutz.

101:1: C: "The social worker and you will learn different things because you are here for *such a short time,* but live here. Your beliefs probably reflect the fact that you are here such a short time. She's [the social worker] been here 4½ years, so she knows!" Does that mean that being an outsider will leave me forever ignorant in the insiders' eyes? What about the objectivity they wanted? Or is it just C's way of pulling rank?

Some stressed the brevity, rather than the length, of a year. Even people who were involved with me and helpful occasionally said more time was necessary:

198:3: Z grabbed me and asked me how things were going. I told him 'Well,' and he wished me good luck. But he said it would take at least 2 or 3 years for me to learn about the kibbutz. [A *mazkir* told me it takes people half a year.] What does it take? Nevertheless, he thinks my topic is an interesting one since every old person is a world unto himself.

Others stressed that the kibbutz was essentially unknowable.

6:5: H: "People who write about kibbutz are people who don't know about it."

It was unknown even by esteemed researchers who have lived on a kibbutz most of their lives:

57:1: S thinks that Menahem Rosner [one of the major sociologists of kib-butz life] doesn't understand the kibbutz.

If the kibbutz was unknowable or required enormous time before one could say that she or he knows it, then it was completely inappropriate for me to make rec-ommendations to the kibbutz. My recommendations would be based on incom-plete or misguided knowledge. I believe that the constant reminders of the near impossibility of understanding the kibbutz served to motivate me to study it as well as I could and to be cautious about what I claimed to know. These reminders were the way that some kibbutz members expressed the "otherness" and special quality of kibbutz life. After all, the kibbutz was founded, in part, to provide an alternative to nonsocialist living. Could I, as an inhabitant of the capitalist world, understand what it is like to live in a socialist society? Would I be arrogant and assume I could take the ideas from "my world" and use them to improve "their world"? What about the fact that "their world" was utopian?

252:1: [My husband] had dishwashing rotation this morning (Shabbat) with the *mazkir* to do last night's dishes. Yesterday the *mazkir* came by to say they could start at 7:00 a.m. this morning [a bit later than usual] since the meal had been self-service. We don't know why self-service means fewer dishes, although it does mean fewer serving pieces. [My husband] said that the *mazkir* is very sensi-tive about what [my husband] says since [my husband] had once suggested that instead of taking a one-hour breakfast break, they start earlier, and the *mazkir* had felt that [my husband] 'was already making suggestions for changing things.'

Clearly some members considered it arrogant when outsiders claimed to know what was going on and to know how to do things better. Conversely, I began to suspect that there is also a kind of arrogance in social science's assumption that we can quickly and definitively understand worlds that people spend their whole lives trying to understand. This reciprocal problem became a crisis for me at the end of the study. I am not alone. In fact, there is a term for this internalized dilemma: "the crisis of ethnographic authority." G. Thomas Couser, drawing on Deborah Reed-Danahay, implicitly recommends two ways out of this crisis—auto/ethnography, that is, "the writing of ethnography by 'natives' who were once its subjects" and "autobiographical (i.e., confessional) ethnography—texts in which trained observers explicitly address and analyze their personal relations with the natives they are writing about."[7]

Some kibbutz members pointed out the significance of my temporary status, not in terms of having adequate or inadequate knowledge for research but rather in terms of how I was more fortunate than permanent kibbutz members because my stay was shorter:

> 282:2: M explained to me that I was happy here since I'm temporary. Although this comment was said with ironic intention, I think it is actually quite important. After all, "many a truth is said in jest." Moreover, being temporary might have allowed me to experience more of the pleasures and fewer of the pains of membership. If I experienced the kibbutz from the vantage point of knowing I would be leaving, then my experience of it would be utterly different from that of kibbutz members who knew they were staying. If I was engaged in conflicts, for instance, I would know that I didn't have to live with them. Not sharing in long-term social obligations—one of the essences of kibbutz life—is something that radically separated my experiential understanding of the kibbutz from that of others.

Living on the kibbutz day and night for a year meant that I was always "bumping into" people. If I sensed that an individual would be hard to approach for formal interviews, I could interview her or him informally as I happened upon him or her. I called this "sidewalk interviewing."

> 305:3: On the way to the dining room, I bumped into G, we asked each other *ma nishma* [how are things?], which was an invitation to talk. G is completely bitter . . . she would like to leave.

Business and leisure hours are completely intermingled on the kibbutz. For certain needs, appointments are set, for example, when long discussions are needed or when material things are needed, such as to see the doctor or to sign up for insurance, but other matters are continuously settled and checked informally when passing. The fact that I would be there for a year might have provided some people with flexibility in relating to me and might even have provided a convenient cover for their delay in allowing me to interview them.

> 16:3: When I said I'd like to invite her to talk sometime, she seemed pleased but said, 'We have lots of time.'
> 60:2: I asked her if I could talk with her husband, the son of Z, but she said he works in the dairy nights and he is an actor in the play, plus they're preparing for the holidays. So I should wait until after the holidays.
> 60:6: S cancelled our interview appointment for today, too busy.

---

[7] *Journal of Contemporary Ethnography* 34(2):121–142, April 2005.

And I did the same:

> 45:4: S asked me if I had read his book and I said, "No, I was too busy." He said, "There's no rush."

Thus, my temporary status became salient to kibbutz members and to me and was loaded with meaning about whether the community was knowable, what my rank was in the kibbutz, and what my/their knowledge of the kibbutz actually meant.

Others, however, felt that whether I could be said to know the kibbutz was unrelated to the length of my stay. Rather, it had to do with whether people were willing to speak with me and whether I worked (i.e., took a job on the kibbutz). It was not the length of stay but rather whether I was "integrated." Thus, there was a difference in members' eyes between being a member and being a fully integrated and accepted member, let alone a difference between being a member and being a temp.

> 305:3: T claims it took her 15 years to be integrated here. B tried "to go to her husband's kibbutz" (i.e. tried to marry into the kibbutz in which her husband was born), realized she could never be integrated there, and "fled" within a week.

Being a resident, even if only a temporary resident, meant that I could experience the physical surroundings just as the members did. To them and to me, this was important. I could look out at the striking views, experience how far or close it was to the nearest town, and know what it felt like to walk up and down the path inclines, rest at the pool, enjoy the flowers, or wander off into the hidden corners of the kibbutz. Unlike many kibbutz members, however, who stuck to their own neighborhoods, I spent time in all the kibbutz neighborhoods because I interviewed people from all the age groups. Also unlike kibbutz residents, I sometimes got lost on the kibbutz. Because I was never given a directory of who lived where (I'm not sure that one existed), I sometimes had trouble finding the house in which the particular person I sought lived. This was particularly irksome at night when there was no one walking on the paths, it was dark, all the houses looked the same, and large dogs were roaming around.

Because I didn't know where everything was located, I had to find out by experience:

> 61:5: I went to the dining room and found A who had a few people waiting to talk to him. He said I could bring Yali's stroller to him to be repaired, which I later did. His shed has a big sign on it that says "POISON" so at first I didn't know that it was small repair shop.

By being a newcomer and yet part of the physical space, I could learn a great deal about the kibbutz by asking what different physical objects or areas meant.

> We talked about the horses. It turns out that T's son V had built the objects in the middle of the corral for his daughter. I understand by that, that through the expression of your individual interests, the kibbutz is built and developed, and not [only] by sacrifice.

For me personally, the volume of data I was able to gather in a year using in-depth interviewing, experiential analysis, participant observation, and the analysis of documents was probably the maximum I could analyze efficiently and meaningfully. And practically speaking, one year was all I had. I tried to reconcile myself to the fact that staying for one year had multiple meanings, assets, and deficits. Clearly people were telling me that despite the kibbutz having formally approved of my project, I would have to pass additional tests of acceptance based on the way I did my work and who I was as a human being. In a sense, I was treated like all new "members"—although they had "voted me in," I had yet to prove myself. The running joke in the kibbutz was that if people had to be voted in again (after having been members for years), most would not be accepted. In this way, kibbutz membership was different from being a member of a family.

Being a temporary person and a researcher did not stand in the way of my identifying deeply and completely with the kibbutz, as if I were a member. I realize I was doing that by examining interview transcripts and field notes:

> 305:2: Several other customers (from outside the kibbutz) came to the greenhouse needing our attention and wanting to pay by check although *our* treasurer does not want to accept checks. Later N told me where this tree, that they wanted to purchase, was planted on *our* kibbutz.

Identification in this case was mutual—I saw the kibbutz as ours, as did N. But as we have seen, people might belong to a kibbutz for quite a while without others feeling that they are truly members. The tension between belonging and not belonging can last a lifetime.

᭟

CHAPTER 9

Being a "Volunteer" (Neither a Volunteer nor a Hired Worker) and Being Sick

Women of all ages preparing donuts for Hanukah.

As is true of all social groups, a kibbutz, particularly a sizable kibbutz, is composed of people with many roles. Although the founding ideology was that all members would be equal in worth and would enjoy the same social status, it has become impossible to achieve that radical redefinition of a social group.[1] In a sense, the kibbutz is a failed sociological experiment if its founders had hoped

---

[1] Barbara Swirsky and Marilyn Safir (eds.), *Calling the Equality Bluff: Women in Israel* (NY: Teachers College Press, 1993).

to achieve total equality, uniformization, or dedifferentiation where age, gender and other human characteristic would be irrelevant.[2] It is also a failed experiment in the sense that it has attracted so few people – currently approximately 2% of the Israeli Jewish population. On the other hand, it is a successful sociological experiment because it has lasted one hundred years! And because it has not become authoritarian.[3]

The kibbutz soon became a differentiated society where people have different roles, worth, prestige, talent, appeal and luck. Aside from the social-psychological underpinnings for differentiation, economic forces are also at work—not that these two are so distinct. Basically, the members' desire for a continuous rise in the standard of living and the need to compete in the international marketplace necessitated the implementation of modern, efficient work practices and the employment of cheap labor.

Cheap labor in the kibbutz context are people who work in the kibbutz and receive less than the full benefits of members. These workers are called "hired laborers" (who could be anyone from a farm hand to a teacher) and "volunteers." "Hired workers" may be long-term or temporary. Temporary workers include volunteers who come from all over the world to experience kibbutz life, to make a stop on their global travels, to learn Hebrew, and to fulfill many other motivations. There are two types of volunteers—non-Jewish world travelers and Jewish people who want to learn Hebrew while living/working on a kibbutz. The latter type is called "Ulpanist" or "Ulpanistim" (plural) with the word referring to the Ulpan, a well-known intensive way of learning Hebrew.[4] Henry Near, one of the most prominent kibbutz historians, has provided useful information on this topic. He explains that by the end of the 1960s the percentage of hired workers in the fields and factories of individual kibbutzim was more or less steady, although there were marked differences between the kibbutz movements, ranging from 6.5 to 15 percent of the labor force. If the workers in the regional enterprises are included (economic institutions owned by a group of kibbutzim), these numbers must be increased by about half. These are not negligible numbers. In my experience, some of the hired laborers had worked for such a long period on the kibbutz that I inadvertently paid more attention to them than I should have as a researcher who was studying elderly members. From the perspective of kibbutz ideology, hired laborers are a necessary but unfortunate fact of kibbutz life. The idea is that if a kibbutz had all the members it needed, it would not need to hire people; and if all kibbutz members would be willing to do the full range of work required on a kibbutz, there would be no need to hire outsiders. A hired laborer, in a sense, is a

---

[2] See Rosabeth Moss Kanter, *Commitment and Community: Communes and Utopias in Sociological Perspective* (Cambridge, MA: Harvard University Press, 1972), for the best analysis of the sources of success and failure of communes.

[3] See Martin Buber, "Kibbutz: An Experiment that Did Not Fail," in Martin Buber *Paths in Utopia* (Routledge & Kegan Paul, 1949).

[4] There are ulpan programs on about 20 kibbutzim throughout Israel with variations in size, location, climate, agriculture, types of industry and general character. The ulpan program and general framework, however, are uniform. The duration of the ulpan kibbutz is 5 months. See http://www.kibbutzulpan.org/page.asp?ln=eng

symbol of kibbutz failure. A kibbutz was intended to be a community of worker/
members, but it has become a community of many types of workers.

> 334:3: Saw R at the clothing store, since I wanted to buy a bra. I asked for
> Susan, knowing that she worked there. R was irritated that the clothing store was
> considered "Susan's place" and not hers. "Susan is the hired worker," she told me.
> R then went on to tell the other workers of my mistake.

The presence of volunteer labor, in contrast to hired labor, is a function of the
uniqueness of Israeli history.

> The problem of temporary labor for seasonal work was eased in the wake of the
> Six-Day War, as large numbers of volunteers from abroad arrived in the country
> and were sent to work in the kibbutzim, filling in for the members who had been
> mobilized during the emergency. From that time on, voluntary workers from
> abroad—usually high school pupils, university students, or recent graduates—be-
> came an accepted component of the workforce of every kibbutz. Each of the kib-
> butz (political) movements opened an office to recruit, select, and allocate their
> working visitors, and most kibbutzim built special accommodation for them.[5]

Kibbutz members had mixed feelings about volunteers. Some attitudes were
sharply negative. For one thing, the volunteers' presence demonstrated vividly that
the kibbutz was unable to supply its need for labor from among its own membership. Moreover, young kibbutz members frequently formed sexual liaisons with
the volunteers, who typically were not Jewish and certainly were not Israelis. Thus,
the potential for marriages and departures arises when these foreign non-Jewish
people live right in the kibbutz. On the other hand, volunteers were new people,
people with whom members could interact, particularly when they were tired of
interacting with one another only.

> 285:6: I saw A [very elderly, outgoing kibbutz member] hugging the volun-
> teer K spontaneously, not a farewell or anything, just a sign of friendship.
> 313:3: N [very elderly reclusive kibbutz member] is rejected by her peers and
> compensates for it by an air of intellectual superiority and by forming friendships
> with volunteers.

The volunteers were young and energetic. Many were exotic, physically attractive,
and, because of the heat during many months of the year, wore scant clothing.
They spoke languages other than Hebrew, languages the kibbutz members were
eager to learn. Many volunteers were admired, especially if they were eager to
understand kibbutz life.

> H, a young kibbutz man, told me: "In the past, the Ulpanistim (almost always
> Jewish) would stay and marry here. Now there is no Ulpan, just volunteers (almost
> never Jewish). Some convert and stay. The volunteers used to be my social life.
> I loved to dance and I had dancing parties in my room every night. I never held an
> official job with them because I was afraid of the increasing age gap. I noticed that
> when I approached 30, girls didn't dance with me, although they did dance with T
> who is only 20. I got to know them in the orchards. I know that Americans like to

---

[5] Henry Near, *The Kibbutz Movement: A History. Volume 2: Crisis and Achievement, 1939–
1995*, p. 246 (London: Littman Library of Jewish Civilization, 1997).

work there because they want to work outside. In the past, the *sadran avodah* (work organizer) would let me choose the volunteers I wanted for the orchards. Now he gives the 'good ones' (i.e. hard workers) to the factory."

Many of the married kibbutz members "adopted" a volunteer, with a likelihood of choosing the particular volunteer with whom they worked, particularly if the volunteer had already been on the kibbutz for a few months. Many of these volunteers came to be loved by kibbutz members:

> 76:3: Some Dutch volunteers have come to Israel for a three-week vacation, including one week in the kibbutz and two weeks of traveling. P says the volunteers always come back to the kibbutz "since life here is so cheap. Not like in Europe, particularly Holland. There was a Dutch woman doctor here who worked beautifully in the dining room. She knew what to do without being told. She worked energetically." P gave the doctor P's own kibbutz apartment when P was traveling abroad, and they reciprocated. "This year she didn't come for some reason."

> 313:8: T [very elderly kibbutz member] talked about several volunteers who had worked with her, including one religious, non-Jewish American who was wonderful. T and her husband continue to write to her, exchange photographs, etc.

All volunteers are not alike, obviously, and the different needs and strengths of the various volunteers provide important challenges and opportunities for the kibbutz.

> 297:10: Today I had lunch with the S couple [very elderly]. The wife is responsible for volunteers. She told me she has a problem. A new volunteer who is deaf had come to the kibbutz, and she had broken the good feeling that had existed among the volunteers. The new volunteer claims that others are rejecting her. She can't hear anything said to her and she must read lips. Compounding her problems, she doesn't know Hebrew. The volunteer works in the communal dining room. S wants to put her in the clothing division so that R can talk with her in English. The volunteer has been in a different kibbutz before and has good memories of her experience. She might want to be transferred there. S would accept this transfer although typically she expects volunteers to be on the kibbutz for three months minimum. We talked about disabilities and how to respond to them. S's husband thinks the best approach is to treat the person as normal and not to help her at all.

> 302:2: A talked about the fact that the deaf girl has gone. S checked her room this morning to see if in fact she had taken the 7:15 bus to Jerusalem. Last night, S got the girl's passport, money and other things in order. Today, S picked up the volunteer's work clothes. She had lasted less than a week.

Some volunteers represent access to external resources (such as house exchange) and thus are valuable to kibbutz members. But many volunteers are young, without resources, and simply traveling to "find themselves." The volunteers' lifestyles can offend the kibbutz members, and the volunteers can be verbal and critical of their host environment.

> Volunteer: The old people are always yelling at us and criticizing us. One guy yells at people not to come to the communal dining hall with dirty work shirts on. He just

hates people in general. He hates volunteers, new immigrants and anyone new in the kibbutz. He thinks that this kibbutz should have only old-timers in it. When my aunt and uncle (non-Jewish European immigrants to the kibbutz) were being voted on (in the General Assembly) everyone was in favor of skipping the trial period, but that old guy said it should be done, because these people "don't know what a kibbutz is." Then someone shouted from the back of the room—'You've been here 45 years and you don't know either!'

Volunteers are in a complex position in the kibbutz community.

> G: I was really disgusted when the *mazkir* said that the last absorption hasn't gone too well. I think he was referring to my family who volunteered and then joined. Wework very hard![6]

If lifestyle problems arise, they typically relate to drug use, the women's revealing clothing, and poor work habits.

> Young person: And then there was this volunteer named Mike. He was tested (psychologically) before coming to the kibbutz and it was discovered that he uses drugs. When the *mazkir* heard about it, he said that the guy had to leave right away. They were so terrified of having a drug problem in the kibbutz. The *mazkirut* must have called the police too, because Mike and my boyfriend [a member] were frisked at the gate.[7]
>
> I am really disgusted that they had the police search a *kibbutznik* and had him put his hands up! I think the *mazkirut* in general does not understand young people. We've been asking for a clubhouse for years. I don't like the way the volunteers and the Ulpanistim are treated, like garbage and cheap labor. If you [a member] talk to a volunteer you get a bad reputation.[8] But I don't care; I spend lots of time with them. The Venezuelan group has a much easier time here[9] because they speak a little Hebrew, but primarily because they promise to send the kibbutz presents.

Then there are volunteers who are motivated to become involved and stay. This is the kibbutz dream, in most cases, because the kibbutz is an institution oriented to integrating Jews from around the world into kibbutz life and into Israeli society. It is a proselytizing community, although the proselytizing is typically low key. M is a good example.

> 87:1: When I got back to the kitchen, I was asked to help M clean chickens. M is a 21-year old American graduate of Vassar, who came on Ulpan, then became a volunteer and now would like to become a "guest" so that she can eventually become a candidate and then a member. She has been on the kibbutz since January.

---

[6] This is another indication that the measure of one's worth hinges on the quality of one's work.

[7] A fence surrounds the kibbutz and its entrance has a large metal gate next to which stands a guardhouse, somewhat similar to the entrance of a gated community in the United States.

[8] The bad reputation hinges on the suspicion that the *kibbutznik* and volunteer have a sexual liaison.

[9] This is a group of wealthy Jewish Venezuelan youth whose members have developed a formal relation between their school and this kibbutz following the liaison work of a kibbutz member in their community.

She has a kibbutz boyfriend and is living with him, so the kibbutz is not giving her a room, I think. There is no one in charge of her category of people—not S who is in charge of volunteers, nor L who is in charge of the Ulpan. So she doesn't know how to get her pair of shoes to work in the kitchen, which she wants to do.

She majored in economics and "lives, breathes economics." She thought it was pretty ridiculous to get a Ph.D. at age 24 and wanted to travel, since she hadn't yet done so extensively. So she came to Israel. This is her first trip here. She has worked in various places in the kibbutz, particularly in the communal dining room and with the children, starting as an assistant *metapelet* doing lots of cleaning in the children's house and then taking on more responsibility. She likes children and still has good relations with them, but she found the work boring.

Recently she went to Tel Aviv and walked into the Tel Aviv branch of the kibbutz factory looking for work. They took her on and she started reorganizing the office procedures, including how to create form letters to respond to requests for information, how to plan advertising campaigns. She was involved in an exhibition of the factory's products. She felt she was using some of her skills but was whisked out of there after three weeks because "volunteers aren't allowed to work down in the Tel Aviv office." She told me that "There is no such policy but since there isn't anything explicit, someone is saying it."

M generalizes from this experience to say that the kibbutz does not utilize its own people's talents well. Not just the volunteers. [J is a case of someone with nursing skills who is not engaged in nursing on the kibbutz because she is a volunteer.] M thinks things are stagnating. People just do a job; they also watch TV. She thinks one of the problems is *protektsia* at some of the kibbutz jobs.[10] Once you've got one, you don't let go of it. Family connections help. There is also the problem of "dead weight" at the factory. These are older people who have been in their jobs for a while and can't be moved because this is *not* exclusively a profit-motivated industry. The older people have managerial type jobs. The old people don't rotate their jobs; just the young ones do, she claims.

She thinks the kibbutz is very boring in the winter months but a lot could be done. For instance the dining hall is used only once per week at night (for bridge games, but actually also for *sichat kibbutz*) and there could be lots of activities such as games for children, games for adults, rummy, bingo with small prizes, etc. There was a lecture a while back by a psychologist about drug use, but she says that the kibbutz doesn't know how lucky it is with the small amount of drug use that actually exists here.

I asked her why she wants to be a member if she is so critical of the kibbutz, and she said that she likes the POTENTIAL that's here and would like to help change things, and thinks she can. However she also believes that the young people, fresh out of the army, will be hard to inspire because they accept things the way they are. She likes the rural qualities of the kibbutz; being able to walk out into the fields, see fruit growing, etc. She also thinks the values are good. The only thing she liked about Vassar was its location.

---

[10] For a full discussion of the concept of "protektsia," see Brenda Danet, *Pulling Strings: Biculturalism in Israeli Bureaucracy* (Albany: SUNY Press, 1989).

Finally, some volunteers had long-term obligations in their workplace and supervised me.

> 35:1: Arrived in the kitchen at 6:30 a.m. A young woman member told me to help J, a volunteer, to clean chickens, which looked utterly disgusting. But after I got gloves and got the hang of it, it wasn't so bad. Just take out whatever guts remain and cut off the ends of the wings, necks, etc. . . The work is surprisingly not hard. You work at whatever pace you want to, it's not competitive nor is it for profit. I'll have to learn how to slow down. The volunteer agreed that the workplace is slow and she would help me slow down.

At first I was thought of as a volunteer. If I had been a volunteer, I would have elicited many of these positive and negative feelings, although I assume I would not have been perceived as a drug-taking person who would form a sexual liaison and abscond with one of the young kibbutz men. I had a bit more prestige in the kibbutz than a lowly volunteer about whom people were ambivalent anyway. Although I knew I was perceived as "not one of them," that is, not a kibbutz member, I wanted to make sure I was also perceived as "not one of them," that is, not a volunteer. Like M, I was somewhere in between. A situational identity that arose, therefore, was to not be identified as a volunteer, which I could achieve by stressing the fact that I had a family, would stay for a year, was Jewish, and spoke Hebrew.

BEING SICK

As is true of many fieldworkers, I was sick frequently in the field. I happened not to have been entirely healthy when I came to the kibbutz, and the kind of lifestyle I led there added to my nearly constant exhaustion.

> 139:1: I allowed myself to sleep in—8 a.m.(!)

Being in another country also meant that I did not have adequate immunity to the germs in my environment. Thus, I was probably unusually vulnerable to the flu and to colds. I had so many tasks (the major ones being worker, data collector and recorder, wife, and temporary single parent) that I was chronically tired and occasionally bedridden. Perhaps being sick was a way unconsciously of removing myself from the stress of fieldwork for a while, "leaving the field" with my demanding roles, and getting some care as a human being.

> 184:3: I felt sick so went back home to sleep. Woke up at 4:00 p.m. to get Yali. Walked over to my sponsor and his wife's home to ask them to bring me food when the dining room opens up. It turns out my sponsor's wife was also ghastly ill with some sort of dysentery. My sponsor later brought me eggs, bread and yogurt. Yali behaved wonderfully. I took her back to her house at 9:30 p.m. when she was really tired, but it still took me a good hour before I got out of there. Slept through till 11 the next morning.

I probably also picked up some of the illnesses in the children's house where my daughter lived. Usually I plowed forward and tried not to miss any days of work or any planned interviews. When I did have the flu (or whatever it was), however, I had no choice; I simply had to go to bed. This was certainly not something I had planned for, nor was it something I wanted to do. Nevertheless, I became the recipient of care from my sponsor's wife (as a friend and person who felt informally responsible for me) and from the various people whose job it was to take care of members who are sick.

> 209:1: After a false good start, I felt sicker than ever this morning, and also tired, since I had worked enthusiastically last night on demographic tables, and gone to bed late, plus I couldn't fall asleep easily since I had so much on my mind.

People who are living on their own on the kibbutz and are too sick to take their meals in the communal dining hall can receive their meals from a person whose duty it is to provide such help to members. This helper of the sick (female) (*metapelet cholim*) can also ask the professional nurse to check in on the sick person and can notify friends and others if the person needs more than the *metapelet cholim* can provide. At one time or another I was the recipient of all of these services, and thus I got a glimpse into the kind of care an older frail person might receive. I experienced the guilt that many members feel when they cannot go to work and the organizational turmoil that results because the work must get done regardless. I experienced, as well, the warm welcoming greetings when one returns to the dining hall after an absence and receives concerned inquiries about one's health.

> 67:3: After coming back to work in the kitchen, having brought Yali to her children's house, I was plagued with a terrible headache. I attributed it to many things—the noise (in the kitchen I'm always saying, what?), the onions that irritated me when I sliced them, the tension in the kitchen, and the noise in the dining room, including the noise of the high school kid who always argues with T. I even said something to her about it. There was a loud argument between the switchboard operator and the Mexican volunteer about her saying 'shhh' when she was using the phone in her office, etc. I felt so tired and achy that I went off into a corner and ate my lunch alone, next to an open window. I dragged myself home, ate one of R's cakes, and went to sleep. Woke at 4. Went to pick up Yali. . . . I got home and felt incredibly sick, couldn't even leave my *cheder*.
>
> Really missed having a telephone so I could have called C to take Yali to the dining room. Yali wouldn't go alone to ask C since she was afraid of the dogs. My sponsor stopped by, but I said I would be there before dinner. I thought I would get better. Felt concerned that I couldn't take care of Yali, since I was alone and sick.
>
> M stopped by with her little boy but I didn't ask anything of her. Finally, my neighbor stopped by and Yali told her I was sick. They went for a walk in the direction that Yali was leading, but my neighbor was confused that Yali was leading her toward the dining room and not to my apartment. During that time I threw up and thus felt better. My neighbor said I should have stuck my fingers down my throat. Then my sponsor and C stopped by because C had noticed my absence from the dining room at dinnertime. I mentioned that I missed having a phone and my sponsor thought it was ridiculous for young people to have a phone. [I'm definitely going to recommend phones, and those who don't want them can do without or be last in line.] He said, 'They simply ask for help from

someone who stops by or they knock on their wall for their neighbor.' I asked C
to come with me to put Yali to bed . . .

Although it was a miserable day (I also didn't go to a meeting of the nominations committee to which I had been looking forward), it did teach me experientially about bad workplaces, being sick and cut off, and the helpfulness of friends.

Even sick in bed, I did not and could not discard my roles: I was still part of kibbutz society, still Yali's mother, and still took field notes.

> 189:1 (Shabbat, 1/19/80): My friends (an older couple) came around noon
> bearing gifts of home-baked cookies and pretzels, and homemade wine. The wife,
> too, is sick with a deep chest cold. She told me that this week she will work in the
> children's kitchen rather than at the factory since E, who usually is the children's
> cook, is on night guard duty. So I learned that for the elderly, as for others, there
> is rotation within one's current work, not only a succession of jobs. She said
> the work in the children's kitchen is easy, and what is particularly nice about
> it is that it is completely independent, with no one telling her what to do. She
> remembers how in the past when she was a *metapelet,* she would always prepare
> different porridges for the children, and everything was fresh, not like now
> where they serve them leftovers that have stood in the refrigerator. M came later
> with a cake.

On the other hand, being sick did excuse people from their voluntary activities
such as participating in political demonstrations:

> B told me about having attended a peace rally in Tel Aviv with about 20 people
> from the kibbutz. She considers most people to be apathetic, an attitude she con-
> demns. However, she recognizes the fact that "some people don't come because of
> health problems, e.g. Y can't walk well, T can't walk long distances, and W has a
> hearing aid which produces a lot of static when there's a lot of noise. He also has
> diabetes."

Being sick allowed me to understand—somewhat—how people are cared for when
sick, how the various caregivers sometimes create conflict, and how the patient
returns to everyday life.

> 190:1: R, the nurse, came to my room and said I could go out. V, the head of
> the health committee, came next, replacing L, the *metapelet holim,* saying she
> would bring me food, implying that I would be staying in. I told her what R had
> said, to which she responded, "If R said so, then . . ." which I understood to be an
> expression of offense at having her own authority undermined. I felt awkward but
> nevertheless went to the dining room. Felt like I was returning from outer space.
> Got good wishes from several people. Sat with my neighbor and Z, and we all
> talked about my illness. My neighbor said I should have told her; she would have
> helped me. She didn't know I was ill.
> 217:2: I don't know the hours of the infirmary and it's annoying.

Sickness and the kibbutz response to it were also frequent interview topics.

> Y: "Now I want to tell you, what it means when someone says, `They come when I'm
> sick.' What happens if suddenly you wake up in the morning—it happens to me.
> I usually don't have to lie in bed. I'm healthy from that standpoint, but it
> happens. I can't get up in the morning—a headache. I don't go to work. People come.

`What, you didn't come to work?' Someone from the workers in my workplace comes to see what's happened.

SR: The night watchman?

Y: No, the workers. It takes until 5:00 (i.e. help doesn't come until 5:00 a.m.). At 5:00 there's the night watchman who comes to ask me for the keys, he wants to take out the milk. So if I should need help, he'll go to the doctor,[11] to his friend. I've never been in that situation. So at 5:00 already someone comes from the kitchen, chats here for 15 minutes. At 6:00, L, the lovely woman who takes care of the sick people, comes with a newspaper, and she writes down what I need. `Do you want cereal or not?' Then the doctor comes, and I'm asking you not to tell them, but I don't like it when they come. I don't need it.

SR: But, if you ask for it, it's there.

Y: Without asking! If I don't ask them not to come, then they'll come. Once they brought me the doctor secretly. So, he looks and says, `I don't know who you are.' So I say, `The doctors before you didn't recognize me either, so don't feel bad.' That's regarding all sick people. [This was a dig at the doctor.]

Respect for the physician (in this case, not a kibbutz member) varies widely, depending on the service one has received.

A: The doctor visited me every day when I was recovering in bed. He works very hard.

My experience with the doctor, however, left a lot to be desired.

300:1: I went to doctor this morning since I was worried about the scrape on my leg. Waiting in the hall outside his office. Also waiting and sitting are D's daughter, then her grandmother, L. S comes out of the doctor's office, having received his shot. L goes in. R goes to check medications in the back room. C comes in for a letter. I asked the doctor if he was leaving. He said, `Come back next week if needed!'

Retrospectively, my notes about how I felt when I was sick may be instructive about how the elderly felt:

219:1: I slept late since I go to bed so late. The chair (or member) of the education committee came by to ask me to help out in the *beit yeladim* today, and also (!!!) to be a *shomeret laila* tonight (she must be kidding). That means no sleep at all. The reason for this is that apparently S had gotten into a crisis with the education committee about having only a volunteer helping her out, rather than an assistant *metapelet*. My working with her today would be an indication to her that the education committee is helping her somewhat. I would be a symbol. Besides, Yali is sick.

I did it. People motivate each other through guilt here. There is no other form of payment to get people to do things they don't want to do.

Being sick much of the time is not uncharacteristic of fieldworkers. In terms of understanding a community, it is simply one more way of "being in the field."

190:3: S said that he understood that being sick gave me an insight into health services. I said, `You really understand what I'm doing.' He said he wants

---

[11] The doctor on this kibbutz was a resident but not a member.

to read my report. He thinks the kibbutz can't improve much with regard to the elderly. [May be so.] He asked how what I'm doing can be of interest to others. He then gave me a little lecture on the 'problems of utopia.' He said there are no big problems on the kibbutz; but people make big ones out of little ones. Health and illness were not big problems! (Of course, he could say that, because he was a young healthy male.)

Many of the elderly kibbutz members whom I interviewed had an illness but preferred to "tough it out" rather than assume the sick role. Those who had lost their spouses to illness had a hard time coping with widowhood but seemed to get some relief when talking about their former husband or wife to me as a sympathetic researcher. Everyone else had already heard the stories.

> Me: I wanted to ask you what happened here when your wife died. How did the kibbutz deal with this matter? [He had already told me that she had been a diabetic.]
>
> H: Six years ago she had a stroke; half her brain and body, but she recovered very well from this. I took care of her in our house.
>
> Me: I'm glad to hear this.
>
> H: Everything continued very well. And then, one Saturday, she was working in our garden, watering, everything, and I looked through the window and said to her, "It is already 9:00; why don't you come in and have breakfast?" She said she would have a better appetite if she worked a bit longer. Then she came in and sat at the table and started to eat. And suddenly—she was sitting on a chair—there was a chair over here and a chair over here. Suddenly she fell like this onto the second chair. So I jumped and caught her like this and put her upright. There was food in her mouth. I took the food out and gave her something to drink. She spoke a bit, but not at all coherently. She was basically unconscious. So, I took her and placed her on the bed and ran to my daughter-in-law, who came with my son after first going straight to the doctor. And the doctor came. My son called the ambulance. She had suffered a second stroke. Her diabetes had caused a lot of arterial blockage. She had blocked arteries to the brain. And from this she got a stroke, and lost consciousness. So we took her to the hospital. She was unconscious for three days. She developed a high fever and died.

Nearly every older person who was a widow or widower wanted to tell me the story of her or his loved one's death, just as they wanted to tell me how and why they had immigrated to Palestine in the mid-1920s. These were the pivotal events as they looked back on their lives. This is what they wanted the stranger (me) to know.

> H: We were together nearly 50 years. And suddenly—suddenly—she disappears. I cannot come to terms with it. I cannot find a place for myself. She is no more, but it is good that she did not suffer a lot. She never felt anything. She was unconscious for the last three days of her life and never felt any suffering. That is very important. But she could have lived another 10 years!! She was only 73.

Although health services are provided for the sick, they can never replace the warm intimacy that arises in good relationships. In my case, although I received many services when I was ill, only when my husband returned from Jerusalem did I feel that my needs for healing were truly being met.

CHAPTER 10

Being a Neighbor, a Friend,
a Homemaker, a Hostess and a Leaver

The method of transportation for some kibbutz elderly.

By virtue of living on the kibbutz for a year, I became a neighbor, friend, and homemaker, my three concluding topics in this book. As a resident, I had a little 1 ¼ room home in a particular neighborhood in the kibbutz. Because I knew that where I lived would be important in terms of informal neighborly relations and perception by others, I asked in advance if I could live in a section where elderly people lived. I hoped that in the course of daily life, I would get to know some of these people as their neighbor. Per my request, my housing was situated in an area of older homes, where many of the elderly people's apartments clustered. The tie between old people and old housing arises because on the kibbutz new apartments usually are built for young people when they become members; and people tend to stay in the homes they live in, a concept known as "aging in place."[1] Instead of moving people out of the community, the "aging in place" concept focuses on modifying the physical aspects of the older person's living quarters and creating services that can be brought to the older person's home.

When telling me about the advantages of aging on a kibbutz, nearly all the elderly told me about their sense of security that they would "never have to leave," that they could age in place on the kibbutz. They would always be taken care of "by the kibbutz." On the other hand, if a widow or widower dies, and her or his apartment becomes available, a young person most likely will need it and will move in. Thus, homogeneous neighborhoods are difficult to sustain. In addition, when the kibbutz elderly become infirm and need nursing care, they move to a special facility within the kibbutz rather than stay in their home. They do not define this move as a violation of the "aging in place" philosophy, however. They just redefine "place" from personal home to larger kibbutz.

Because of the neighborhood in which I lived, I was able to observe the daily entrances and exits, the comings and goings of many older people. I was likely to meet older people I knew and could strike up casual conversations with them. In my structure, which was close to the center of the kibbutz, there were four one-room apartments side by side that made it relatively easy to know my neighbors. Beyond the issue of neighborly familiarity, there was also the norm of neighborly friendliness. Not knowing one's neighbors was considered wrong.

38:7: Y told me he's a neighbor of mine and introduced me to his wife.

Stepping outdoors from my room, I unobtrusively and inadvertently observed my neighbors' apartments.

60:2: Saw E going into his father's house.

However, because the people who lived in my housing area were a mixed group, it did not really constitute a section, as did other areas that had more homogeneous populations, for example, the neighborhoods of middle-aged families or newlyweds and young couples. Mine was a hodgepodge area. This heterogeneity plus the regular turnover in one of the four units diminished any strong neighborly feelings. For me, however, the heterogeneity of my little building's occupants turned out to be an advantage. It gave me the opportunity to meet a range of people I might otherwise not have met.

My neighbor on one side—the elderly (non-member) sister of an elderly member—was a permanent resident. The apartment on the other side was available on a rotating basis to people who needed temporary housing. In one case this was a member's adult child and her family who had been raised on the kibbutz, had departed for a while, and were now considering whether they wanted to be candidates for membership. At the start of my stay, a member brought her recently widowed, elderly mother from the city to live in the kibbutz and tried, unsuccessfully, to take care of her there. The mother's needs were overwhelming and required

---

[1] For details, see http://aipi.n4a.org/.

her daughter's full-time attention, which was impossible for her to offer, given her own children and grandchildren and her job.

I was able to document how the process evolved from the time of this great-grandmother's arrival until her death in the local (non-kibbutz) nursing home. When this older widow left the apartment for the nursing home, another member's mother moved in. This parent was on her annual visit from Belgium and was in good physical and mental health. During her two-month-long annual visits to her kibbutz member daughter, she worked a few hours per day in the kitchen. Shortly after her arrival, she walked into the kitchen where I was working, and I could observe how kibbutz members interacted with members' nonmember parents on their periodic visits.

> 47:5: M's mother got a warm hello from most of the people working in the kitchen. S, usually thought of as quite cold, came over to her and shook her hand vigorously. It's as if parents of members are incorporated into an overall "family of the kibbutz." Perhaps this is particularly true in M's mother's case because she always works in the kitchen and anyone willing to work in the kitchen is appreciated.

This observation led to a series of interviews with numerous parents who visited their adult children members or who had moved in permanently.

> 151:2: Talked to R. His mother will be my neighbor for a couple of months. She is religious, cooks at home, gets along well with other people, doesn't do much, doesn't work, and mostly reads.
>
> 172:4: D spoke to me about the fact that her mother-in-law will move in next door for 2 months. According to D, her mother-in-law is "very busy." She "goes to A's handicraft club, works, knits, etc." I offered to be a helpful neighbor.

Defining who one's neighbors are is a personal decision. People typically consider the people in one's building to be neighbors. Sometimes neighbors are people who live in the building backing up on one's own, especially if they share one's interests. I considered C and G my neighbors probably because I liked them a lot and they lived nearby (but not in my building). Nurses on the kibbutz who deal with the needs of elderly people rely on neighbors for communication and sometimes for care itself:

> 297:6: (Interview of a nurse) An elderly person who has a fever or heart disease needs home visits. There's no issue in getting word to the nurse about these problems. The neighbor tells the nurse, who in turn orders food, etc.
>
> 297:8: She sometimes has to deal with elderly people who want *her* to take care of them, instead of having to bother their children. Nevertheless, she does go to the son/daughter to tell them to help. Usually it's OK with the adult children, although sometimes they are not cooperative. They too want someone else to take care of their elderly parent. In that case, the nurse will tell a neighbor "to pop in and see if all is OK."

Neighbors in the kibbutz are typically defined as having some responsibility for one another, but calling on them for help when they are at home can sometimes be annoying.

> 147:6: S said that her neighbor J now has a phone connection directly to D. Because of this, J won't bother S any more.

> 182:1: Blown fuse. I asked my neighbor D to fix it since I had no idea where the fuse box was. He did it, but he was so rude! It's probably his personality, but perhaps as the only man in this group of houses, he feels put upon by us women with our little household problems.

Because most members did not have private telephones at the time of my study, information had to be obtained by "dropping in." When someone did obtain a phone or a pager, everything changed.

Neighborly relations obviously can be positive or negative. Neighbors can easily get into conflict with each other about the amount of noise they make.

> 342:9: The elderly P couple told me they get along very well with their three neighbors who are the Fs, M and L. "With the Fs less so because they came later (1934 as opposed to 1929!) from another kibbutz,[2] but with M and L (two single women in separate apartments), they get along very well. We are all very considerate of one another, and, you know, neighbors sometimes get into terrible rows, like about flushing the toilet at night. We always remember to turn the TV down so as not to disturb each other. We visit one another, too."

My own neighbor played her TV loud in the evening, which was annoying to me. But I, in turn, had to type and interview at night, which might have been annoying to her. I don't mean to imply that I was responding to her noise by making noise in retaliation but rather to say that neighbors have to take responsibility for the effect of their behavior on others, not just focus on what the other is doing.

> 9:4: Asked D if she minded if I type. She said no. I don't believe her.
> 60:6: I went up to D and told her that if my typing disturbs her she should knock on the wall. She said that when the shutters are closed and she has the air conditioner on, she can't hear it *so much*. May be I should believe her.
> 172:5: Until what hour is it acceptable to make noise, i.e. type?

I tried to block the noise she was making rather than get into a conflict with her. But I also had to deal with the noise *I* was making. Despite her telling me it was acceptable to her that I type in the middle of the night, I felt uncomfortable doing so. I was afraid to alienate her and thereby perhaps have her say things about me that would undermine my access to people on the kibbutz. Therefore I asked the *mazkirim* if they could arrange an office for me where I could go to type at night. Although they complied with my wish, I ended up never actually using my "office" because I did not want to walk around the kibbutz late at night and be alone in an office building typing. Even though I always felt safe from outside intruders because there was a night guard system in which armed kibbutz members rode around in jeeps making sure there were no break-ins or acts of terror, I simply did not like being alone in the middle of the night in an uninhabited office building. My solution to this problem was to write by hand if I thought the typing would disturb my neighbor. (Personal computers had not yet been developed.)

---

[2] Even after forty-five years, someone who did not join the kibbutz at the same time as this couple was thought of as a newcomer. Kibbutz members have a strong sense of belong to a cohort whose members entered together.

One reason why I was sensitive to this issue of noise was that my sponsor had told me about the conflict about noise that he had had with his neighbor.

> 6:1: For ten years my sponsor and his wife lived next to people who were noisy. He talked to them about it but to no avail. He then requested to move and within a year moved to his present home. He does, however, remain on good terms with that family. In fact, the other neighbor was irritated that my sponsor left since they had been close. Then the problem was—which new family should move into the place that my sponsor had vacated? Who would want to move into a home where the former occupant had left because of noise?

As time went on, I learned about other neighbors who had problems with each other because of noise or other factors.

> I said, "Would the solution to the problem [of the strength needed to tend gardens and the unkempt look where some old people lived] be to have young and old live in integrated neighborhoods [thinking that the young could take care of the gardens or pressure the workers to do so]?" She [elderly woman] said she would like to live in a mixed neighborhood, and very much enjoys the fact that H and Y live nearby with their four kids so she can see children [interesting since there are kids all over the place, but "seeing" must refer to being neighbors]. She is "attached to H because of her parents, S and B, who are good friends of [the elderly woman]. She arrived at the kibbutz as part of the same youth movement group as they did."

> H stops by to talk to me, as do her parents on the way to their house.

> "The neighbors are also content, including Y and H. But, it is sad that it is so quiet around there. The only person who doesn't like kids is Y, which is strange since he does have grandchildren. I think it's good for the old people to be around young, although I shouldn't make generalizations. After all, everyone is different. But the young don't always like it."

Another older person who discussed neighboring with me gave as an example E (a middle-aged woman), who lives next door to P (an elderly widower). E not only assists P but also recruits others to do so.

> He enjoys all the help he gets from them. Like R cleaning his place up, although E knows R is moving. "The trouble with P is that he takes ALL the nuts that fall from the trees [the pecans], whereas before he moved in, all the people who lived in that building shared the pecans." E thinks this is characteristic of old people— they hoard. She also sees this pattern with regard to their money. "They don't want to spend it on things." She knows that she has to wipe out her whole budget now because she is going to spend 10,000 pounds on a new set of curtains for the apartment. [Later at the dinner table, the treasurer told me that I might not have discovered it yet, but old people save their money and don't even buy presents for their kids. My sponsor, also at the table, said that soon there would have to be a *takanon* (policy) for inheritance.]

Old people who are neighbors help each other; it is not just the young who help their elders:

> 128:2: T was not home but rather at her neighbor's (H) who was not feeling well. Lying down on couch. By her bed were large pictures of her grandchildren.

On her shelf more pictures. But the person who was comforting her was her elderly neighbor (not the grandchildren).

When assessing where one lives on the kibbutz, more important for older people than convenience or friends is the presence of one's own children and grandchildren or at least one's family.

> H told me that he does not live in the elderly section of the kibbutz because he wants to live closer to his daughter.
>
> Z lives alone, next to F, her late husband's brother.

For the adult children, on the other hand, it is important to live among one's peers and to have playmates for one's children.

> 147:3: L (young man, *mazkir* whose parents are not kibbutz members and do not live on the kibbutz) doesn't like where he lives, although he has lived there for 6 years. No other young people around. He's last in line for new housing in the newest neighborhood. "Because of where I live, I do favors for the elderly. I take them on a stretcher in the middle of the night, if needed. But I think my children's noise bothers them and vice versa. The only advantage of living in this neighborhood is that I get a 'cake' every once in a while. And my children have yet another grandpa. I am not in favor of mixed housing. I also feel that it doesn't work the other way around. The A couple (elderly) are not in that great touch with their current neighbors, because they are the only older people among the young."

Because neighbors are expected to be friends or at least friendly, nonneighbor friendships are considered harder to maintain.

> 289:4: L (very young woman) says: I can't really get close to C (a woman her own age) since she doesn't live in my neighborhood.

Thus, the friendships that develop when people live next to each other may not survive when people move to another section of the kibbutz.

> 96:6: M said she and her husband formerly were neighbors of E whom she considers brilliant. But after the death of E's wife, whereas everyone expected her to help him, she felt he was no longer their friend because he had moved. "Now his neighbors are L and wife who are very good people."
>
> 289:4: H visits him (he is in mourning) every day, because they used to be neighbors, she told me.
>
> 289:4: A says she is terribly upset by the death of D because they used to be neighbors and D's children would come over all the time to watch TV when the old people had TVs and the young didn't. (Television sets were distributed by seniority of age groups.)

The concept of neighbor exists on the kibbutz and implies responsibilities and relationships that are particularly useful for anyone who needs care, particularly the elderly. As a neighbor, I saw a whole world of meaning and social organization open up to me.

BEING A FRIEND

Becoming and remaining a "friend" were essential for my emotional well being and for my status in the community. Communities around the world vary a great deal as to how friendship is defined—among Americans, a friend is made quickly and probably dropped quickly as well. In other societies, friends are made slowly and may last forever. Societies differ as to the numbers of friends a person should have and what the relationship should consist of. Friendships can run deep or shallow; can be firm or fragile; can be based on enjoyment only or on a deep sense of trust and commitment; can be exclusive or inclusive. I realized that as a temporary person, I could be only a superficial friend in this society. Nevertheless, my time-limited friendships that emerged in the field were sought and welcomed. As I watched my friendships develop, I tried to see what the parallels were for kibbutz members, particularly the elderly.

As a friend, I was invited to a person's home for celebrations, could meet his or her friends and relatives, and was able to join in their informal conversation. Frequently my presence led the conversation to topics in which I was interested.

> I went to R's house for her 50th birthday celebration. At the gathering, there was much joking about age, because it was her "big birthday," and because of my research topic. "Should you tell people what your age is; should other people tell what their age is? What is the meaning of each age? There are Jewish texts about this topic: 60 is old age; another age is when you can give advice." They seemed to be trying to take the sting out of getting old.

Although, as mentioned earlier in this book, I worked in six kibbutz branches, I nevertheless was not a worker in *all* the branches.[3] Therefore, if I was using "acquaintance on the job" as a means of segueing into an interview request, I had to find means for the people with whom I did *not* work. For this reason, I tried systematically to develop relationships with people who worked at other branches of the kibbutz economy. One example is a friendship I developed with a kibbutz member on the basis of our both being academics. This friendship eventually led to an invitation to my husband and me to the home of this man and his wife for a Shabbat tea to meet city friends of theirs who also were academics. At the tea, I spent as much time as I could with the (kibbutz member) wife, whom I had had a hard time getting to know in other contexts. When I got back to my room, I wrote up the conversation as if it had been an interview.

One setting in which I did not work was the metal shop. In order to get to know the people there, I hung around this workplace after the mechanic fixed my daughter's stroller.

> 289:5: In the afternoon I had gone to the metal shop in order to pick up Yali's stroller since O, the Arab worker[4] who had soldered its axle yesterday, told me at breakfast that H (an elderly man) had finished fixing it. I went to the metal shop, but H wasn't there. It turns out that A was next door in the garage. He told me he stays open till 5:00 p.m. because he takes a break in the afternoon. Anyhow, I got the stroller by going from the garage into the metal shop even though H was not there.

---

[3] I was able to work only in places that had entry-level openings at my level of experience.

[4] My field notes reflect the consciousness in the kibbutz that workers included kibbutz members (who were not labeled as such), Arabs, who were labeled as Arabs, and volunteers, also labeled. I am embarrassed now that I called this man "the Arab" rather than refer to him by name.

Later that day, after the funeral, Yali and I stopped by H's house (even though I hardly know him) to thank him for fixing the stroller. M, his wife, was sitting in the front room—reading? H was sitting in the back room—reading? I got a warm welcome and an invitation to sit down. They plied Yali with candies. Yali then played and interacted with them with no inhibitions, although I don't think she knows them. She asked for the bathroom, for toys, for permission to walk up their stairs. She played with a ball and rings they gave her.

H asked where I work and guessed correctly—in the chicken coop with S. He then said, "She says she washes 10,000 eggs a day, true?" I said "no," but perhaps I should have equivocated [am I calling S a liar?]. M said S claims she has a special movement that enables her to work fast. [Are these old kibbutz members still comparing their work efforts and accomplishments?] N said that S is addicted to talking, and many things come out. Perhaps this is another one. We began to gossip like old friends even though we hardly know one another.

In order to be someone's friend on the kibbutz, I had to understand what friendship meant to kibbutz members, particularly to the elderly whom I was interested in getting to know. In a community in which people live together and engage in exchanges all day, every day, friendship is different than in societies without much social interaction.

Esther, an elderly woman, said that she is S's friend. She likes S's company, and she empathizes with S's difficulties.

295:6: E says about S: —"She knows how to talk, she has gone through some hard times and continues to have difficulties particularly since her son is going blind because of diabetes. E sits with S sometimes and listens to her criticism, and sometimes tells her she doesn't agree."

Empathy is not always easy to express when people are in continuous contact. Despite being an outsider and a person much younger than the people I was studying, I tried not only to learn about but also to empathize with people's concerns. On the kibbutz, as in many societies, friendship provides more than empathy—it is also a wonderful source of information.

323:3: D, H, S, and Y are a friendship group of old ladies over the age of 80. S informed D that I had interviewed her. Y stops by D's house frequently and sees the other women. I mentioned to D that I live between her and Y, which she already knew. D told me that Y brought the apple cake (to T, a middle-aged woman), which T then offered me. T said that Y suffers terribly from migraine and sometimes wakes up in the middle of the night and has to do something, so she bakes a cake. T loves the old ladies. She talked to me about getting fat from the ladies' cakes, and asked why I don't gain weight. She told me about D who has always been thin. "Now she says it doesn't take much time to wash since there's not much there besides bone." This light conversation was a lot of fun.

The information can be trivial, but it keeps you "in the know" and thus part of the society. The information derived from these friendships taught me what is significant and how I should behave.

323:4: D has a wonderful relationship with Y because Y was R's (D's only daughter) *metapelet*. Y has relations with people of all ages, keeps learning and teaching, and has a strong personality. But D remembers when Y felt very cramped up, both in her sense of self and in her room, which was then small. Y then said to D that she wants to push the walls out with her elbows, a phrase that D remembers to this day.

D demonstrated that the point is not what you can do for someone but rather that you empathize with her situation. Empathy as the basis of friendship seemed particularly to be true of women.

> 342:9: K (a man) has a circle of four male friends that includes E, B, C (who is a master joke teller) and A. They are a 5-some.

These men may express empathy for one another, but primarily they share humor and have created a bond *against* other groups.

> 342:1: I visited E for a minute. He has just received a visitor from Kibbutz Beit Alpha, an old-timer (female) who comes by frequently. They discussed the book that had just come out about the European town in which he had lived. Her picture is in it. He has an article in it and is remembered. The two of them voiced some criticism that there was an "imbalance of personalities" within the kibbutz and not much participation by the members. But they agreed that this was more the case among younger people who don't remember the earliest period too well.

I tried to be generous and compassionate in my friendships, but I know that in many cases the friendships were not deep because I was a temporary person from abroad and people would not benefit in the long run from investing their emotional energy in me. The problem of inadequate friendships among kibbutz members, let alone between members and visitors (or strangers), was a frequent topic of conversation among kibbutz members. I was invited to spend the evening with a couple, and the two of them raised the topic of friendship, acceptance, and jealousy.

> 200:8: P (the wife): The person who was raised on the kibbutz always thinks that he is superior to someone who comes into the kibbutz from the outside and becomes a member. He believes, how should I say . . .?

Me: That this belongs to him.

A (The Husband): It would be good if he felt that way.

P: If you come from the outside, you always feel that you are somewhat less.

Me: Do you still feel that way?

A: No, today she feels . . .

P: I don't know, now I feel isolated from the youth, then I had that feeling with my own age group.

A: I'll tell you what she means. In our group, she was accepted.

P: What do you mean, accepted? C and I were the youngest in our group; C was a member of the movement and I was not. And that's a difference; it's not the same thing. But when I came, I saw a lot of things that I didn't want to see. They didn't see these things because they were on the inside.

Me: Yes, they had already accepted it and didn't see it.

P: They couldn't see it, and I saw all sorts of things, and I had severe criticism and an opposing viewpoint.

A: The conflict was not really with the young people or the people in our group but more with the founders.

> P: No, it's not exactly that way. The founders related to me with a lot of respect; they knew that I was a nurse and that I worked in the operating room, and I think that they . . .
>
> Me: Valued your ability?
>
> P: Yes, even valued it, but with the young people, they felt more jealousy and opposition that I worked outside, as if I had income on the side. What does it mean, income? It doesn't make a difference. The ten pounds (British currency) to go back and forth. Stupidity. Jealousy. I couldn't be part of their group.

Because I asked for work assignments that would enable me to meet people I wanted to interview, I frequently requested an interview after I got to know the person at work. In my mind, these "visit requests" were partly research activity and partly social. In the minds of the kibbutz members, on occasion, these visits were entirely social. Such misunderstandings were awkard. At least one time the conflict led me to lie.

> 327:3: The managers of the greenhouse [where I worked] invited me to their home. Their intent, which I did not know, was purely social. But I brought my tape recorder along. When she saw it, she said, "This is not a formal visit." I lied and said, "I know; I had just done some tape-recording work for S and brought it along." This reminded her that she owes S a visit, and we changed the subject to S.

In an article about fieldwork in an abortion clinic, Michelle Wolkomir and Jennifer Powers describe this conflation of friendship and role-related behavior as a betrayal. In their words, "examining how co-workers negotiated their way through difficult cases often felt like a kind of betrayal of friends—as though 'talking behind their backs'—an uncomfortable feeling that persisted throughout the project."[5] This process is actually ironic: I had been invited into the kibbutz to be a researcher, and yet in numerous cases behaving like a researcher felt like an act of betrayal. This dynamic occurs because field research depends on the researcher developing relations with people who then, in many cases, want to have the relationship be only affective and not instrumental as well.

I noticed that kibbutz members try to observe if you are friends with someone, and if so, a third party might ask you to do favors for *that* person:

> S asked if I would take care of a child whose mother I had become friendly with.

The favors one does for others, however, are not always a sign of friendship. Sometimes they simply reflect an obligation:

> 11:1: Typed the thing for R per his request.
>
> 97:1: J came into the kitchen to pick up the children's breakfasts and asked me to write the alphabet for her in English. Yesterday I had done it in capitals on the blackboard, but it turns out she wants it in script because she probably wants to correspond or understand the correspondence of others.

There was no way I would ever refuse her requests because she was the *metapelet* of my child!

---

[5] Michelle Wolkomir and Jennifer Powers, "Helping Women and Protecting the Self: The Challenge of Emotional Labor in an Abortion Clinic," *Qualitative Sociology* 30:153–169, 2007.

Sometimes requests were simply pretexts for interaction.

> M keeps on asking me Hebrew-English translations. Today's word— *responsibility*.[6]

Asking for help, even asking for help regularly, does not mean that the relationship is one of friendship:

> A's husband was constantly asking me for help in filling out order blanks for mail order photographic equipment catalogues.
>
> 213:1: B came in to my workplace asking for a ride to Jerusalem with my husband.

The exchange of favors turned out to be an important element in understanding the experience of elderly people on the kibbutz. One does not have to have a personal relationship in order to be entitled to ask because there is a long-range informal internal economy of favor trading.

Friendship, I discovered, is characterized by gift exchange and special invitations:

> 115:8: S came by to pick up the typing I had done for him. He brought me roses and told me he was going on a hike where there were beautiful flowers, which he would bring back for me. He invited me to hike there with him some time. I think he was trying to seduce me!
>
> 201:4: S stopped by to show me her letter for G and to invite Yali and me over for tea at 5.
>
> 38:1: Yesterday RA had invited me to accompany her this morning to the hospital in the nearby town so that I might see how she works as the coordinator of the health committee. Today AH stopped by to see me in the kitchen. He speaks English to me all the time. He wanted to ask me if I would help him compose an English wedding announcement. (Interesting request since this is a basic community ritual, no?)
>
> The next day at dinner, he asked me if I remembered his request for help in composing a wedding invitation. I said I'd come over to his house tonight or tomorrow. I decided to come tonight. Helped R and A with the wedding invitation. One question was whose name to put first. Should it be the groom's parents (R and A), since the wedding would be held at the kibbutz, or should it be the bride's? They said that I would receive a "special invitation."

Friendship is also characterized by taking risks for another:

> 92:4: P didn't give me a loaf of bread at first because she didn't want anyone else to see, but then when they weren't looking, she did.

Although many aspects of life were collectivized (eating in the dining hall, celebrating holidays, doing the laundry), they were still individually modified to signal that one is doing something with someone as a choice, not a routine or obligation.

---

[6] Words and translations were not simply an exchange between Hebrew and English but also about slang. During the year I was taught the following slang words, among others: *baal, cutter, klumnik, mefundreket, nostalgia, nudnik, ofi,* and *parasit.* R uses the terms *boded, bodedim*—a person or people without a spouse or child or parent on the kibbutz. The word *kamtzan* refers to a sick person who doesn't work, that is, is stingy.

It's like the behavior of children in recess versus in the classroom. In recess one can make choices of playmates; assigned classroom seating usually does not afford that opportunity.

After only a short time, people brought me books they had written, invited me to interview them, and invited me to their homes. At lunch one day with S, H, and P, I got the impression that such invitations were meaningful in the sense that people didn't invite casually and didn't invite everyone.

> S, H, and P were talking about a volunteer who was a friend. They even had her over their house!

I received invitations frequently and early on. Without these informal, yet specially defined encounters, life would have been much more difficult for me emotionally, and I would not have had access to people's private lives. The fact that kibbutz members live in close proximity and sometimes have deeply dissatisfying long-term interpersonal relationships made me attractive as a potential new friend—a breath of fresh air. As I mentioned in one of my feedback sessions to the kibbutz, my interviews with people were a success in part because people had a chance to talk to someone who had not yet heard their story. Similarly, these friendships mitigated the possible problem of overdependence on my sponsor. I was always looking for new alternative relationships.

By the time I left the kibbutz, I had accumulated a year's worth of interpersonal debts. People had agreed to be interviewed and had invited me to their homes or their places of work or committees. They had taught me history or recommended what I should read or see. They gathered information for me in the archives, broke me in at my workplaces, took care of Yali while I was working, and made me feel at home. Some of these friendships lasted for years after I left the kibbutz, but they were primarily not friendships with the elderly because in the years following my departure many of these people died.

BEING A HOMEMAKER

Because of predictable limitations in older people's physical mobility, housing conditions are even more important to the elderly than to younger people, who have fewer mobility concerns. One's home can become the entire living environment of the elderly. In preparation for my study, I read the report of the 1971 White House Conference on Aging, which asked, "What does housing mean to the elderly? Aside from his [sic] spouse, housing is probably the single most important element in the life of an older person."[7] Housing is one of the major problems of the elderly throughout the world,[8] but it is not a major source of difficulties or

---

[7] Proceedings of the 1971 White House Conference on Aging, 1973.

[8] One positive aspect of housing for the elderly in the United States is that by the time they are old, homeowners usually have paid their mortgage in full. Their house is thus a major financial asset. In the kibbutz at the time, there was no private home ownership.

dissatisfaction in this kibbutz. The satisfaction that elderly people in this kibbutz have with their housing is typical for the kibbutz movement in general.

> S invited me to his house. He showed me his apartment, of which he is proud. It was very clean and orderly and contained several shelves of books, a few plaques, etc. He said that he uses the kibbutz library a lot and therefore doesn't keep all the books in his house. Clearly his book collection conveys his sense of self as an intellectual, or at least as a reader.

The satisfaction that older kibbutz members felt toward their housing reflected, in part, their perception of what was feasible and suitable in a kibbutz. In other environments, individuals may have been satisfied with less or demanded more. People frequently included the yard outside their home as part of what they defined as their house.

> 286:1: E and H showed me their apartment. They are very satisfied with it. "It's *heimish* (cozy). Small but easy to take care of," they told me. He is particularly proud of his garden which he has planted on three sides of the house, part of it put up to prevent people from cutting across their yard. He gave me flowers and told me that this particular flower doesn't grow well for the neighbor across the way but it does for him! His garden includes *dekel,* of which he gives sprouts to T. Said I can learn a lot from her. He cross-breeds plants in his garden. E and H served me pecans from their tree.

Because the general level of satisfaction with housing in the kibbutz is high, elderly kibbutz members who do have some sort of a problem with housing are prone to much complaining. For almost all of the elderly on the kibbutz, their rooms are a source of pride and pleasure. As the saying goes, they told me, "A person's home is her/his castle." But it is more than a castle; it is the extension of personal identity and represents one's private territory where one can escape from public scrutiny. The elderly on this kibbutz see their rooms as evidence of the unexpected but appreciated rise in their standard of living from the days of "tents" and "huts" to the present "luxury." They are aware of having a lifestyle that has skyrocketed from the time when one had no privacy and even had to be the "third party" living with a couple in a tent to the present, when privacy is always available.

> 278:2: R told me that she has lived in three different places in the kibbutz—in a hut, on the hill, and in her current house. Each one was better than the one before.

The homes of the old people illustrate a contrast between the period of no private property and the present, when some homes are bursting with personal goods. Young people, however, who never endured the poverty of the early years of the kibbutz feel there is a long way to go in terms of home improvement. Their point of comparison is not the past but rather Israeli society outside the kibbutz.

> B talked about how uncomfortable her house is for anyone sleeping on the second floor, especially in the summer. She talked about air conditioning, which they don't have; and who has the fans, and what happened to the fans of the people who have died, did their children take them? And were they bought out of personal budget or given to the people by the kibbutz, etc.?

A few older people see an increased standard of living on the kibbutz as a negative development. They see the "fancy" housing currently available on the kibbutz as a symbol of "bourgeoisification" and the degradation of kibbutz values of simple living and complete sharing.

> Me: What do you worry about here in the kibbutz? Do you think there are people who do not have enough to do, as you now said? Which members do you feel have insufficient opportunities to develop themselves?
>
> T: [elderly man]: It's mostly women.
>
> Me: Who were widowed?
>
> T: Women who became limited. Women who think that their home, their living room, their furniture, their cake, are important.
>
> Me: And you think that it doesn't satisfy *them*.
>
> T: Ultimately, it can't. The possibilities for hobbies are endless. But their homes are their hobby. Shopping. I don't know anything about housework, but that's what I see. I'll give you an example. I decided I needed a table like this. So one of the members asked me, "Is the table you got made of Formica or something else?" I said, "I don't care." That's just an example. I don't want to dump them all in one category. There are some women who are interested in literature.

The conditions that Zionist pioneers like T found in Palestine were spartan in the extreme, sometimes contrasting to the comfortable conditions of their childhood homes. But these people have regained comfort in their old age as the kibbutz is able to afford more "luxuries." Homes are now equipped with air-conditioning and in some cases color television. These people are particularly proud of pointing to the contents of their rooms and saying, "Everything that is in my apartment, I received from the kibbutz!" The kibbutz was able to give them everything they wanted and more. With possessions comes the opportunity to compare, however. Some members are jealous of their neighbors who have "more" or criticize other people for being envious of what they have. "Why do some people have 'more' when there is supposed to be equality in the kibbutz; what foul dealing do their extra possessions represent?" they ask.

At the time I studied this kibbutz, housing size for kibbutz families remained relatively small, although the number of children per family was large. Although there was a bed for each child in their parent's home, the children did not have a bed*room* there. Even before the women's strike that led to having some children sleep at home and the associated need to create larger homes with more bedrooms, it was difficult for the small residences to accommodate all the needs of the family. Each time new apartments were built, they grew in size compared to the former dwellings. The question arises as to whether the size of one's home or renovated home should be linked to the number of children one has. And is there any consequence for the homes of the grandparents?

> 269:6: Saw R who inquired about my health. I mentioned that I heard she was moving, but she told me this is nothing new; it's a process that's been going on for a long time. She will move next to M and gain an extra room plus a larger living room. Her current home does not have a bedroom with a door that closes [?] and she particularly needs extra room for her grandchildren who come to sleep over.

When people age and their extended families become larger, their living quarters may feel cramped. But just when the size of a dwelling might be increased, the elderly couple or individual might need a very small place that can be handled with greater ease.

> S realizes that having her young family live in a kibbutz neighborhood with older people has its advantages and disadvantages. She acknowledges that it is particularly noisy because of the small, closed-off courtyard. She also knows that having mixed or age-segregated housing is an issue, and knows that in other kibbutzim they have created a building with 2 small and 2 larger apartments, so that when people grow older they can move into the smaller ones.
>
> "But," I said, "that probably would not work out here, since the old people want to hold on to their rights." "You understand what's going on," she said.

Because I was a resident with a little household, I, too, had to deal with some household tasks.

Taking care of daily housekeeping chores became a way of getting to know numerous people outside of a "formal research role." As it turned out, it was also a way of other people getting to know me—being householders or homemakers meant there were a lot of topics over which we could interact and form relationships.

> 9:1: I brought my dirty laundry to the central laundry. I spoke with the launderer who also makes wine. He told me that last year . . . He also complained that it was hard for members to . . .

I quickly learned that one of the most frustrating aspects of kibbutz life is that the "services" one needs are open for "business" at precisely the time when one is at work. When you get off work and want to take care of these matters, the service workers have also gotten off work. Thus, to get one's business taken care of, you have to "take off" from work, which creates problems for those with whom you work. It was also frustrating to me to recognize these problems, to devise a simple solution, and then to realize that I had not been invited to the kibbutz to criticize and "improve" everything I saw. I had to stop myself from being a "can-fix-it American" while at the same time staying in the role of "coming up with some good ideas for the elderly."

My living quarters were a rather minimal "apartment" (one and a quarter rooms with bathroom) designated for single individuals or small families. My apartment had one "lonely" rose bush in a tiny patch of lawn in front of the house and was located right behind an electric generator, at the crossroads of several paths close to the center of the kibbutz. Each of these items—the rose bush, the electric generator, and the intersection—became an object over which a conversation, and then a relationship, could develop.

> 305:4: I went back to my house and T saw me watering my rose bush(!). She gave me her sister's flower clippers and showed me how to trim the bush "scientifically."

I had no television, telephone, or oven. I did have electric outlets, a small refrigerator and gas burner, some book shelves, two adult-size single beds and one child-size bed, one table, one clothes cupboard, one small fan to ward off the stifling heat of half the year, and one kerosene heater to deal with the cold the other half. My living quarters were more austere than those of most members of the kibbutz but better than any volunteer's. When I started the project, I made do with one tiny fan. By the next spring, I found the heat so enervating that I asked for another. Being needy was functional for this project because my lack of household resources brought me into constant contact with others.

> 298:1: Walking back with R from the dining room after lunch with T and G, when S calls over to me to pick up a fan he has for me, since he remembers having said we need one. I went to his room and talked with him and M (his wife) for quite awhile. First they asked me if I had a theory about why children leave the kibbutz. . . . the perpetual question. "Why do people leave paradise?"

Housekeeping tasks allowed me to understand how members maintain some aspects of their physical living space. That knowledge, in turn, led me to question elderly members about how they managed. My problems started almost immediately.

> 5:3: I've got problems with the plumbing in my apartment, so I went to my neighbor to ask her what to do. She told me that "essentially kibbutz life is like life anywhere else. There you have to wait two months for the plumber to arrive, and here you have to wait two months." (The plumber is a member.)

Through first-hand participation I learned how elderly members deal with doing household repairs, painting, plumbing, mowing lawns, removing trash, and filling kerosene cans, for example. I also tried to make some aesthetic improvements in my home's appearance, as most kibbutz members did.

> 24:2: I said that I was asking him (in his role as coordinator of housing) if he could get me a mirror, to which he consented. And could he get my front door painted since it was so badly chipped and peeling? That was not his business, he said. Rather, he referred me to the kibbutz member in charge of painting members' houses.
>
> 60:6: I asked A if he remembered that he agreed to paint my door.

I also tried to keep what I did have in good working condition.

> 43:5: All his life M's father worked hard and people were always coming to him asking him to fix things in their house. Now he is about 75 years old. About 5 years ago people began to stop bothering him because of respect for his age. They just intuitively knew to cut back. He told me that he is now in the great position of saying—"But for you, I'll fix it!"
>
> 151:1: Tried to get the heater to work but instead it shot up flames and sent thick black smoke into my room. My wet socks, hanging on the heater, were burnt to a crisp. Have to have the heater fixed.
>
> 199:8: C said I should come to the electric workshop tomorrow morning to tell him which heater is mine. C says he "goes to" everyone because of his work.
>
> 200:5: Woke up around 6:30 a.m. since C asked me to stop by the electric shop at that time. I should have told him it was inconvenient for me. He ended up not working on it that day anyhow, since the electricians had to do outside work. Left my flashlight there, too, for repair.

205:1: Struggling with the heater again. It smoked and then broke. Morning: brought C the heater. Lunch. C told me the heater was ready.

Although the meagerness of my furnishings made life a bit uncomfortable, it also had its advantage. Because I had so little, I quickly learned about asking for and giving favors. I learned how doing this was part of the social fabric in the kibbutz, including the elderly. I learned that some people spontaneously offer help.

184:3: S overheard my interview invitation to M and told me about a TV show she had seen on 'open university' concerning gerontology, which she found interesting. She said I could come over to watch TV at her place since [she knew that] I don't have one.

197:2: I worked with a volunteer named Maria from Wales. . . . She thinks this particular kibbutz has a reputation of being 'the best' both for volunteers and members! She is 'paid well' (800 pounds/month pocket money), gets 3 air letters per week, likes her room (she shares with other volunteers), and gets along with the people on the kibbutz. She understands that you have to get along when you live so close to one another. She has already gotten cakes from Z who wants her to feel at home.

232:7: Saw where L and G live. She said I could bake a cake at her house if I want to, since I don't have an oven. There is no such thing as minding one's own business here! Everyone's business is everyone else's.

I also learned that I was dependent on other people to do their jobs and that they could define these services as favors or as their job. How they responded to my requests for these services would help shape my relations with them.

41:1: Told him that I would like my chair fixed because I have no other chair to use outside.

60:6: He said I could leave my chair outside my house since I had told him it had torn strips. He would pick it up and fix it for me.

190:1: I woke to the sound of M beating on my door to fix my toilet in response to my note, I suppose. Hope my note wasn't too strong. Don't know all the norms about how to ask for services. But I do need a bathroom!

These matters were particularly important for me to understand because responsibility for household maintenance and the activities of daily living have a major impact on older people's quality of life. As I experienced the regular housekeeping issues that were a bit difficult, I wondered how older people cope with them.

19:2: I went for my laundry sack. Hard to find! It hangs from a clothesline like all the other sacks and looks identical. Who picks them up for the elderly? Also, how can older people who are not so mobile take advantage of special opportunities that come up? Who helps them with these specific tasks?

19:2: My sponsor's wife told me that special cheese was being distributed today. I was entitled to two large chunks. But I had to stand around on a special platform that was awkward to get to behind the kitchen. I saw Z there who said she was bringing D (elderly man) his cheese.

I learned that some services (e.g., lawn mowing, laundry) were provided to all as a matter of kibbutz policy. Other chores one had to do on one's own (e.g., plant flowers in front of your house). What complicated the matter was that services provided by kibbutz policy were actually carried out by members for each other, and the relations among these members were not always good.

> 211:1: My sponsor's wife was arguing with the plumber about something she wants done. [His family had previously been the neighbors of my sponsor's family and had quarreled, so my sponsor's family moved to another building.] The plumber doesn't want to do it. Not like in the private enterprise system where she could take her business elsewhere. [There's no other plumber.] It seems that to a certain extent, service workers control members who need their services.

> 305:4: T walked back from the greenhouse with me and showed me the neglected area behind her house. The problem is that the *merakez meshek* is supposed to hire someone to cut down the 3 dead trees, but this hasn't happened yet. In the meantime, the roots are spoiling the earth and she can't plant there. Another problem she has is with communication. Since she and her husband are a couple, they don't have a phone hook-up with anyone else, but her husband is very sick and sometimes she needs help in the middle of the night. She can't turn to Q since she doesn't know her so well(!), and her other neighbor H sleeps with sleeping pills, plus locks the door. N is supposed to fix something up for her, since he works for the electric shop now, but there is no action.

As a temporary resident, I tried to live within the kibbutz budget allocated to me. I got a little experience in what that meant, but in actuality, just as I had additional private resources, so did most of the kibbutz members.

> 41:1: I went to see the head of the laundry supplies to get towels. They cost around 200 pounds each. She gave me socks. I got shoes from V, the mother of Z. There is a huge warehouse of shoes. E said there are two fashion shows a year—summer and winter. Most of the women buy from her. Now I have a pair of work shoes and my feet feel better.

> 53:3: Went to the *kupa* [bursar's office] to buy *asimonim* [phone tokens]. It turns out I get 10 subsidized (i.e. free) per month as a single person, rather than 20 as part of a couple. I can't get back ones from July and August because the bursar doesn't have that many on hand. I got my 10, and Yali promptly lost one.

I now understand why some of the elderly kibbutz members say they are so busy! These chores can take a lot of time, even if you are not old. Finally, I discovered that kibbutz members believed that having the appropriate home was the precondition for having guests.

> 315:2: I was invited by the former *mazkir* and his wife to their apartment since it is now fixed up and since he felt this was his *duty* after having taken care of my "case" last year when he was *mazkir*.

There was a great deal of "house pride" on the kibbutz, and one was expected to keep one's home in good condition and invite others in when one's home had been refurbished, just as we have housewarming parties in U.S. society.

BEING A HOSTESS

Kibbutzim are typically physically attractive rural places, with gently winding paths, lush gardens, broad vistas, and large swimming pools. It is not surprising, therefore, that people like to visit and enjoy these surroundings. For this reason as well, many kibbutzim have created guesthouses as income-generating businesses. As a temporary kibbutz resident with a small home, I did invite numerous relatives as well as friends from off the kibbutz to visit me, and many people took me up on the offer. In addition, other people whom I knew in Israel, the United States, or other countries stopped in unexpectedly.

> He said, "I was on my way back from skiing in the Golan, so I thought I'd say hello."

When these visits occurred, I had to drop everything I was doing and become a hostess on the kibbutz rather than a guest of the kibbutz. Because most of these visits occurred on the Sabbath, they were not entirely disruptive because I typically did not work on the Sabbath. As my guests and I talked, I found myself presenting the kibbutz and showing them around in stereotypical positive ways—"Look how wonderful the pool is"—as if to protect what had become my home from criticism. I spoke like a member rather than a researcher and realized how much I was beginning to identify with my new home.

Most of my guests ate at least one meal in the communal dining room or went for a walk with me around the kibbutz and thus became visible to the kibbutz members. For example, a mere seven days after I arrived, a couple came to visit unexpectedly from Holland. My neighbors wanted to know "who those nice people were" and thus got to know more about me because the story of my connection to Holland is long and complicated. One's guests are a clue to one's identity in the eyes of kibbutz members.

My next invited guest was a long-time Israeli female friend who did not live on the kibbutz and who is a social worker. Having my friend come to visit was crucial. Because I trust her, I could tell her about my doubts, mistakes, and fears. For example, I shared with her the fact that I made a serious error in the beginning of my fieldwork when I was overly concerned about being accepted. My blunder occurred when a young kibbutz member asked me if I was a psychologist because she had heard that I was interviewing people. For some reason, I said "yes," thinking perhaps that my answer was insignificant. It was so much simpler to say "yes" than to have to explain what a sociologist is. And besides, I had studied psychology along with sociology back in graduate school. But it turned out that my being a psychologist was important to this young woman, who then asked me if I could interpret her dreams for her and meet with her occasionally to discuss her problems. Taking on such a role, of course, was out of the question and actually would violate professional ethics. Instead of telling her I actually was not a psychologist, I said I could listen to her dream, but I don't have much experience in that field. I also told her I could not meet with her regularly. She seemed to accept my response and didn't bring it up again when we ran into each other throughout the year.

Strangely, I misrepresented myself at least one other time. The occasion here had to do with costumes that a group of women was making for a performance at a holiday celebration. One of the young women asked me if I could draw. Again, for a reason I do not understand, I said "yes," although actually I am unable to create any representational drawings. Having said "yes," however, I was then given a T-shirt and asked to draw the face of a cat. I did a terrible job and could only apologize for my lack of talent. In talking about these two embarrassing situations, I realized that a fieldworker needs an honest friend with whom she can share the puzzles of her own behavior. As self-reflexive as we try to be, there are still many areas of our lives that we cannot understand on our own. Together my friend and I agreed that my claim that I could do things for kibbutz members that were beyond my ability represented a level of insecurity vis-à-vis the younger age groups. With older people, I never misrepresented myself (except once when I told a couple I had come on a social visit after they commented negatively on my having brought my tape-recorder). I also drew on my friend's wisdom and concern in helping me deal with extricating myself from my sponsor's control. Although neither of us had the answer to my problems, the issues became clearer in my mind and less troubling by virtue of the fact that I was explaining them to her.

Other women have written about the need for women friends in the field, as in this example from the work of Lisa Moore, who studied Khmer and Vietnamese refugee women in Thailand:

> More than anything, I yearned for a woman friend to talk with, someone with whom I did not have to be ashamed of my fears. Until I was completely alone, I did not realize the extent to which I depended on the close confidence of others, even when acting independently. At first I considered this feeling to be subversive, antifeminist. Yet, it was when I did have the support of other women that I was the most grounded and able to work the most steadily.[9]

Subsequent guests whom I hosted were a sociologist/gerontologist and her husband from the United States and my "hippie" cousin and her husband and daughter from the United States, who insisted on sleeping outside on the little dried-up lawn in front of my house. My neighbors might have been astonished by my relatives' sleeping outdoors but did not say anything to me. Perhaps what they misinterpreted as my not having enough room in my home to host my relatives gave them ammunition in their frequent complaints about the difficulty of putting up guests, given the size of the members' homes.

Next to arrive were another sociologist from the United States and a professor of Middle East studies who is a friend of my husband. Then Israeli cousins of mine who had been members of a different kibbutz and were curious about how "my" kibbutz differed from theirs visited me. To all of these outsiders, I had become an exotic, an object of observation, just as I was observing the people of the kibbutz. My husband's relatives suddenly arrived, as did a college friend. Then came other Israeli cousins who wanted to know in detail how I go about doing my research. These conversations compelled me to constantly define what I was doing and sometimes to justify it.

> 77:5: I was about to take a shower after the horrible job of washing my floor, when D, V and their 2-year-old daughter N showed up as a total surprise. I must have looked terrible since I never got to take my shower. D had come all the way in his parents' car for a half hour meeting with his army officer. When we began

---

[9] Lisa Moore, "Among Khmer and Vietnamese Refugee Women in Thailand," in Diane Bell, Pat Caplan, and Wazir Jahan Karim (eds.), *Gendered Fields: Women, Men & Ethnography*, pp. 117–127 (New York: Routledge, 1993).

to talk about the kibbutz and the elderly, I mentioned to V how good things are for them. She asked how I go about doing the research. She thought the housing was not so good, but changed her mind somewhat when considering housing in terms of their needs. They were embarrassed to eat here because they could not pay. Brought chocolates and presents for Yali from my parents. Their daughter cried a lot, so they left after inviting us to visit them.

It became apparent to me that having guests was prestigious and represented a person's social capital, that is, outside relations that were developed for emotional and practical sustenance.

> 74:2: E told me she had 12 people over yesterday and they spoke 5 different languages. A stopped by and said "If you don't have guests on Rosh Hashanah (the Jewish New Year), you are sad."

People seem to love visiting the kibbutz. I began to understand the "train station" concept that members used when describing this constant traffic. I had an endless stream of visitors—cousins, friends, aunts and uncles, researchers, my parents. Oonagh O'Brien has discussed the significance of these visits in the field, particularly in terms of opening up new sets of relationships and changing the researcher's perceived identity.[10] Having guests was a way of being normal in the kibbutz. As the year went on, and as I got to know some people in other kibbutzim, they began to visit as well, and my sponsor would take me to visit yet others. After visits, kibbutz members whom I knew wanted to know who these people were. Their questions were, of course, additional ways of figuring out who I was.

In retrospect, I realize that I rarely carried out the role of internal hostess, that is, inviting kibbutz members and others to my little home as they did me. The reason is that there was no place to "entertain" in my apartment, no place even to put an extra chair. Instead I was the hostess of outsiders who simply chose to visit me—chair or no chair.

BEING A LEAVER

For one year I lived within the kibbutz world, speaking to people, raising my daughter, being cared for when I was sick, and doing my best as a worker. From the beginning, it was known that my stay was temporary. Because of my personality, I knew in advance that I would become attached to some people. I was not sure if they would become attached to me. And I certainly was unclear about how to break off all of these relations and leave the field. The more uncertain I was, the more I began to consider staying or at least planning to return. I toyed with going native, as many researchers report doing. My ambivalence was reinforced by the "don't leave" messages I was getting.

> 307:3: R [middle-aged man] said he didn't want me to leave; he likes looking at me [I don't think he meant more than he likes knowing that I'm around].

---

[10] Oonagh O'Brien, "Sisters, Parents, Neighbours, Friends: Reflections on Fieldwork in North Catalonia (France)," in Diane Bell, Pat Caplan, and Wazir Jahan Karim (eds.), *Gendered Fields: Women, Men and Ethnography*, pp. 234–247 (New York: Routledge, 1993).

I joked and said he probably just wants to know when my room would be freed up. [He is in charge of room allocation.]

342:10: K [old man] said he wouldn't let me leave the kibbutz. "You will be coming back to continue the study or whatever." He and his wife invited me to spend another evening with them. I said, "If I have time," trying not to raise expectations.

334:1: Saw M [young mother] at pool. She doesn't ask me when I'm leaving "so it won't happen." She didn't realize I was going to the States . . . She is a very committed kibbutznik, but she would like to "get away from it all, go abroad, spend a couple of months abroad with friends." She is under terrible pressure from her 'family.' I don't know what she meant, but I decided not to get into it. I can't!

Some people brought up the topic of more work we needed to do together, perhaps so that my departure would be delayed.

342:1: I visited Z [very old man] for a few minutes. We agreed to meet on Tuesday to go over names. He said the funniest thing, "If God gives me a few more years to live and another *mikre* [case] like you comes along with requests for help in research, I won't get involved. It's too much work." This seemed to me like affection.

342:1: I said he looked good despite all the trouble I put him through. But he said he feels only "so-so" and pointed to the wrinkles on his face. "I don't like being old, talking about old people, or knowing that you're thinking about it all the time."

People began to explain to me how they understood who I was. Some of it was flattering, but much of it caused me inner turmoil.

313:7: People have discussions with you because you are objective and won't tell anyone. [Told to me by high school girl.]

313:8: T [old lady] said I know everyone and I probably know them better than she does. I probably know all the gossip, like I knew that Y had been through a lot. However, I tried to defend myself against being seen as a gossip-seeker. And I also tried to not appear as if I was treating the kibbutz as an object [which in a sense I am]. This in response to L saying she wanted to come see me tonight. She wants me to help her with a problem. How am I going to straighten all of this out?

334:1: How to leave a community? How to leave a kibbutz? This is particularly difficult since its ideology is missionary. It wants to get people to come and to stay. If not me, then who? I'm a perfect candidate for membership. H called young people [disguised for me, I'm sure] 'snobs' for leaving.

334:1: E [middle-aged man] said he "pressed my button" when he asked me if it was difficult to leave. But then he brought up what I consider to be very naive notions of how relations 'on the outside' were meaningless. "You see someone at work, you say hello, that's all there is. Here relations are deeper since we live together, work, celebrate holidays, eat, play, etc."

334:1: I am feeling frustrated that I didn't have time to interview everyone, that I didn't have time to write more and communicate more. But the more people I got to know, and got to know well, the more difficult it is to break off these relationships.

Then there were the self-deprecators who downplayed their significance to me.

> 334:2: S said 'You'll miss the pool.'
>
> 334:1: People keep on telling me I'll quickly forget them. I don't know what to do with my expression of loss. They are wrong.

There were people who tried to make me feel guilty.

> 307:3: H said that "Yali will have a hard time leaving. I should take that into consideration in making my decision." What decision?

One of the most interesting phenomena that occurred as I was leaving is similar to what psychologists sometimes report happens in therapy—during the last few minutes before the session ends, the patient/client states what is truly bothering her or him. About one week before I left, the following occurred at lunch.

> 335:3: Lunch with R [elderly lady] today. She started out by saying she heard I was leaving, and then tried to convince me that I should live here. "Why would anyone who is Jewish want to live under a non-Jewish government?"
>
> She talked about what it was like in the little town where she grew up, "away from Jews." There were 8 children in her family, a maid whom her parents supported even when she couldn't work and was old, etc. R described herself as a good student in grade school. She spoke Polish perfectly so that the teacher told her mother that she does not even look/talk/act like a Jew, which was "a knife in my mother's back." Her parents were "religious, but not extreme." She got involved in the youth movement, which "changed everything in her life." She was planning to leave for Palestine, but then an incident happened, which she repeated about 50 times to me in succession right then and there.[11] [When I got back to the room, I consulted my book on mental health and aging and believe this is a symptom of

---

[11] On a Friday night, she and her father were sitting, reading next to the table on which the Sabbath candles were burning when her brothers and sisters left for their activities. Her mother was lying down in the bedroom. All of a sudden R heard a strange faint noise (*milmul*) and went to see what her mother was doing. She saw her mother's mouth "puffed out" as if she had fallen asleep with a candy in it. R tried to open her mouth to get it out. The mother was unconscious and had had a stroke, which left her right side completely paralyzed. R watched over her mother while the father went to summon a doctor. From that moment on, R did not leave her mother's side for three years! She didn't participate any longer in the youth movement, didn't plan on going to Palestine, and so forth.

A nurse (or doctor's wife) came to show R how to take care of her mother. She says she must have loved her mother and been attached to her, although beforehand she didn't realize how deep this feeling was. She didn't decide anything, just responded instinctively. She was involved in the most intimate care of her mother—feeding, bathing, and bodily needs. For six weeks (or so) her mother was unconscious. Then she was conscious and directed things from her bed. She had attacks and finally died of one such attack in R's arms.

R moved into her parents' bedroom and described to me countless times how she separated her parents' bed and put a folding cot next to her mother's bed and slept next to her. Even when R was in the deepest sleep she would wake up four or five times in the night when her mother so much as moved, in order to help her. She told me countless times that a sister of her mother's came, and her mother said to her that when R is with her she doesn't even feel as if her side is paralyzed because R helps her so well. (They became one person.)

psychosis—preserveration.] [I have put the incident she described in the attached footnote.]

Afterward I saw R pacing the floor of the dining room between where we had formerly sat and the door. It seemed to me she was lost and confused, although it is possible that I am mistaken and that she was truly looking for someone. Shortly thereafter, A, who had observed my interaction, stopped me to ask if the people with whom I speak at such great lengths really have something to say or are they just schmoozing. She can't understand it. "And why do they talk to you, and not to each other?" she asked. It seems that people's response to me is as much a puzzle to them as it is to me. This whole mysterious incident reinforced the importance of understanding the specificity of these elderly people—many came to this country leaving their parents behind and never saw their parents again because they were murdered during the Holocaust. The whole concept of "leaving" was a sorrowful underpinning of this kibbutz community. It is possible that every leaving in the present reevoked the tragic departures of the past.

My last days were filled with personal visits to say goodbye.

> 342:1: Visited Gi's place.
> 342:2: 3:00 Went to see Y at her invitation.
> 342:2: I later went to M to say goodbye . . . He wishes me luck. His son, S said
> I should say goodbye to him as well and come over, but I don't have time.
> 334:2: People want multiple goodbyes.
> Y. It's impossible that you're leaving.

As my stay was coming to an end, I also noticed some testiness toward me on the part of kibbutz members. People may have been confused by the fact that they had been open with me, and now I was turning my back on them. Perhaps they thought I was simply exploiting them after all.

> 307:2: H [an elderly man with whom I had become quite friendly] told me that he used to love dogs and have quite a few of them, and now he has none because he doesn't have the right conditions to take care of them. I asked him "why?" and he said, "What, do you need another page for your book?" I was hurt, although he was right. I can't separate my questioning self from whatever other self I might have. Do I come across this way all the time? Is it insincere?

I saved the worst for last.

> 335: An awful send-off from my sponsor. He mocked me for the [excessive] hours I had spent with the old people. "What will they do when you go? Luckily

---

After the mother's death, R went to an aunt in a distant city in order to get away. The aunt had a rich family. R didn't like it there too much. She stayed six months. Then she returned to her father, who convinced her to get reinvolved in the youth movement. Then she left for Palestine. This whole series of events surprised her even more because she had always been repulsed by sickness and has a hard time to this day caring for the sick.

R was totally locked into this memory and in her countless retellings of it and didn't seem to realize she was repeating herself. She told it each time as if I was hearing it from her for the first time. To me the whole thing felt like heavy Freudian material. The sexuality of the parents, the union with the mother, the cutting off from her society and plans, and this at the age of eighteen to twenty-one, the repulsion/attraction of sickness, bodies, and so forth.

there's a social worker coming." My sponsor "explained" why people were willing to talk to me. "When you sit with people, you just listen and don't dispute what they are saying. Therefore they want to sit with you. These people are not your friends. They are exploiting your naiveté."

In the end, neither my sponsor nor I had changed—he continued to want to undermine me, and I continued to do my work, even recording what he had said.

But why is she locked into this now? Has she always been this way? Does her husband know what's going on with her? To whom has she told this story? Why have we never spoken before? Should I mention her behavior to anyone? Do others already know?

CHAPTER 11

Theoretical Conclusions

The old age club learning about innovations in the kibbutz dairy.

The framework I have offered suggests that three types of selves exist in the field—those that one brings (personal characteristics), those that are specific to being a researcher (research related), and those that arise in the specific field setting (situational). I don't believe that it is as important to specify that a particular self belongs in one type or another as much as it is important to recognize that the various types exist. Each type can be fleshed out and given exact content in each fieldwork project. Together these specifics flesh out the idea that the key fieldwork tool is the self. I also found it interesting that when I specified these selves, I also understood the significance of who I was *not* in the field. For example, in this study of aging, I, myself, was not an elderly woman. This fact probably affected what I understood and how people related to me.

The notion of multiple selves is one way of operationalizing the popular theory of "intersectionality," which is properly driving feminist theory away from essentialism and ethnocentrism to a much more nuanced and broader understanding of social structure. Intersectionality is an ambitious theory that attempts to integrate multiple systems of social stratification (in the language of intersectionality, the word *oppression* is preferred) simultaneously.[1] Developed by feminist thinkers, intersectionality holds that we cannot discuss gender in isolation but rather must integrate it with race, age, and other social systems.

In my study of the multiple selves of the researcher in the field, I do not focus on oppression as the theory of intersectionality does. Rather, taking a more neutral approach, I argue that in understanding any person in society, we have to consider race/ethnicity, gender, religion, nationality, sexual orientation, class, disability, and many other features. It is not only society that is organized in this way but also the person herself. I recommend that we understand the self in the field not as an accumulation but rather as an intersection of selves. Certainly a researcher is not only a researcher.

A second, related implication of *Observing the Observer* concerns standpoint theory, developed by Sandra Harding and others, as a corrective to male-based social research that assumes objectivity is possible. Although standpoint theory attempts to create an alternative by constructing effective knowledge from the insights of women's experience, it implies that being a woman is the master status, the place from which knowledge arises.[2] In this book, the status of being a woman was certainly significant, but it was not the exclusive place from which I viewed the world. Although standpoint theorists recognize that any position is partial, this book provides a way of seeing how multiplicity functions in a research endeavor.

A third methodological conclusion I draw from this study of selves in the field concerns the notion of power in the interview process. One of the initial criticisms that feminist methodologists raised in our critique of social science procedures was that power was an unrecognized or underrecognized element in the relation between the researcher and the researched.[3] Power manifested itself in many ways that might include the higher education, material resources, sophisticated

---

[1] Patricia Hill Collins, "Gender, Black Feminism, and Black Political Economy," *Annals of the American Academy of Political and Social Science* 568:41–53, 2000, "Learning from the Outsider Within: The Sociological Significance of Black Feminist Thought," *Social Problems* 33(6):S14–S32, 1986, and "The Tie That Binds: Race, Gender, and US Violence," *Ethnic and Racial Studies* 21(5):,1998; pp. 917–938. S. A. Mann and L. R. Kelley, "Standing at the Crossroads of Modernist Thought: Collins, Smith, and the New Feminist Epistemologies," *Gender & Society* 11(4):391–408, 1997; S. A. Mann and D. J. Huffman, "The Decentering of Second Wave Feminism and the Rise of the Third Wave," *Science and Society* 69(1):56–91, 2005; and George Ritzer, *Contemporary Sociological Theory and Its Classical Roots: The Basics* (Boston: McGraw-Hill, 2007).

[2] Dorothy Smith, *The Everyday World as Problematic: A Feminist Sociology* (Boston: Northeastern University Press, 1987); Nancy Hartsock, *The Feminist Standpoint Revisited* (Boulder, CO: Westview Press, 1999); Sandra Harding, *Whose Science? Whose Knowledge?: Thinking from Women's Lives* (Ithaca, NY: Cornell University Press, 1991); and Carole R. McCann and Seung-Kyung Kim (eds.), *Feminist Theory Reader: Local and Global Perspectives* (New York: Routledge, 2003).

[3] For a discussion of this topic, see Shulamit Reinharz, *Feminist Methods in Social Research* (New York: Oxford University Press, 1992).

language, and mobility of the researcher vis-à-vis the subject of study. The researcher has more knowledge of what is happening in the process of obtaining data than the subject does, even with informed consent. The researcher usually has no obligation to take the subject's opinion into account when publishing the findings and thus has the ability to frame the public's understanding of the subject's life. Feminist methodologists have been concerned that the quality of this relationship has an unrecognized and perverse impact on our understanding of the world.

As a consequence of my study of aging on the kibbutz, I believe the problem of *power* in research needs to be more nuanced. As sociologists and anthropologists have noted for years, we sometimes study "up," sometimes "down," and probably sometimes "sideways." Anthropologist Laura Nader is credited as having issued one of the first calls to anthropologists to "study the colonizers rather than the colonized, the culture of power rather than the culture of the powerless, the culture of affluence rather than the culture of poverty."[4] Of course, this is more difficult for the researcher because powerful people have a greater ability to control access to them than do the less powerful. Had social researchers developed a strong tradition of studying up, clearly our methodological discussions would not have been so concerned with our excessive power in the research relation. Nevertheless, I am not suggesting that we should abandon "studying down." In fact, the feminist insight about the power relations related to gender requires that we hear the voices of the relatively powerless in order to understand social reality because the powerful have had a much greater role in defining that reality.

I am suggesting, however, that "power" is not always the relevant defining concept in the interview relation. To be concerned about whether my study consisted of studying up, down, or sideways (i.e., a study of my peers) would not be useful. Rather, I think we need new concepts. Relistening to the taped interviews I conducted, I suggest that *holistic interviewing* may be a useful term, meaning that the interviewer is interested in the whole person, not in pieces of data that she or he can provide. Without being melodramatic, one could contrast the "I-Thou" underpinning of holistic interviewing with the "I-it" of data-driven interviewing.[5]

Another concept might be the "teacher-student" relation. Throughout my study, I thought of myself as a student of the kibbutz, a student of the individuals I met and interacted with, and particularly a student during my interviews. I asked my interviewees to teach me about their lives. I asked them to clarify ideas that I didn't understand and to correct me when I reiterated their ideas, particularly if I got them wrong. Perhaps if I had been a kibbutz member myself, I would have had less of a "please teach me" approach, but I am not sure it would have made much of a difference. Rather, I believe that the "please teach me" approach is the very essence

---

[4] Her article, "Up the Anthropologist—Perspectives Gained from Studying Up," in Dell H. Hymes (ed.), *Reinventing Anthropology*, pp. 284–311 (New York: Pantheon Books, 1972), is discussed in Orin Starn, "Rethinking the Politics of Anthropology: The Case of the Andes," *Current Anthropology* 35(1):13–18, 1994.

[5] Martin Buber, *I and Thou* (New York: Touchstone, 1923/1996).

of any researcher's attitude in this type of research. The "please teach me" approach requires humility on the part of the researcher and time on the part of the person being studied. It does not demand that the researcher suspend critical thinking, suspicion, hypotheses, and any other intellectual tools.

Finally, *Observing the Observer* introduces the concept of time as a possibly useful additional tool for understanding the field setting. If we think of research as having before, during, and after phases, the only segment that is clear is "during." Theoretically, we can label all of the researcher's experience and training as the "before." It is during that phase that all the hypotheses are formulated, all the life experiences become integrated into the researcher's self, and the researcher develops research skills (e.g., interviewing, taking field notes, etc.). In the "during" phase, the researcher is immersed in the site, collecting data, writing, and photographing. And then we enter the poorly defined "after" phase. When does it begin? And when does it end? From which "time standpoint" does the researcher say, "This is what it means"? When do you write the study? In my case, I have chosen a variety of "time standpoints," including this one that is nearly thirty years after the "during" phase ended. I don't believe this is a better or worse choice than any other, as long as it does not claim to represent what the kibbutz is today. In fact, the hindsight of time has enabled me to see things more clearly than was possible at the time.[6] And it keeps on changing. That is the standpoint of time.

---

[6] See Amia Lieblich, "Kibbutz 2008: A Way, a Place or a Home?," in Michal Palgi and Shulamit Reinharz (eds.) *One Hundred Years of Kibbutz Life* (in process).

EPILOGUE

In the years since I studied aging on the kibbutz, I have engaged in numerous related projects. Wanting to make the history of this unusual society clear to people who were unfamiliar with it, when I returned to the United States I tried to determine who was responsible for the first kibbutz. I was astonished to discover that it was a woman. I probably noticed her role rather than just accept standard histories because I had started teaching women's studies courses at the University of Michigan. *The Plough Woman: Memoirs of the Pioneer Women of Palestine*[1] showed me the key role of Manya Wilbushewitz Shohat in defining the ideology and structure of the kibbutz in 1907–1908, which she called the "collective." My excitement at this "discovery" was so great that I dedicated several years to research about Manya.[2]

Since then I have watched from afar as the kibbutz I studied, and kibbutzim in general have changed. I have also returned to Emek a few times to visit. During these years, the kibbutz as a national institution has undergone enormous transformations, particularly with regard to economics and the degree to which people live a collective lifestyle. A large group of kibbutzim have become "privatized."

---

[1] Edited by Rachel Katznelson Shazar, translated by Maurice Samuel (New York: Herzl Press, 1975); revised edition edited and annotated by Mark A. Raider and Miriam B. Raider-Roth (Hanover, NH: Brandeis University Press, 2002).

[2] See Shulamit Reinharz, "Toward a Model of Female Political Action: The Case of Manya Shohat, Founder of the First Kibbutz," *Women's Studies International Forum* 7(4):275–287, 1984; Shulamit Reinharz, "Manya Wilbushewitz-Shohat and the Winding Road to Sejera," in Deborah Bernstein (ed.), *Pioneers and Homemakers in Pre-state Israel*, pp. 95–118, 1992 (Albany: SUNY Press), reprinted in Esther Fuchs (ed.), *Israeli Women's Studies: A Reader* (New Brunswick, NJ: Rutgers University Press, 2005); Shulamit Reinharz, "Our (Forgotten) Foremother: Manya Shohat (1880–1961)," *Lilith*, Fall 1995, pp. 28–33; Shulamit Reinharz, "Manya Wilbushewitz Shohat," in Margaret R. Higgonet (ed.), *Lines of Fire: Women Writers of World War I* (New York: Penguin, 1999); M. Golani and J. Reinharz, *Manya Wilbushewitz Shohat: A Critical Collection of Her Writings* (Jerusalem: Yad Ben Zvi, 2005) (Hebrew); and Shulamt Reinharz, "Finding Our/My History: The Case of Manya Wilbushewitz Shohat," in Judit Gazsi, Andrea Peto, and Zsuzsanna Torony (eds.), *Gender, Memory, and Judaism*, pp. 119–122 (Budapest: Balassi Kiado, 2007).

Nevertheless, kibbutzim continue to require the strategies and means to meet the needs of their elderly. Not all of these means are financial. Rather, one need is to find people who will listen to the stories of the elderly. I predict that finding such people will be increasingly difficult because the individuals who now take care of the infirm elderly on kibbutz are "foreign workers," particularly gentle Philippine women who are not Jewish and do not speak much Hebrew. Perhaps in this regard my sponsor was right: "When you (Shula) sit with people, you just listen and don't dispute what they are saying. Therefore they want to sit with you."

After leaving the kibbutz and returning to the United States, I maintained a lively correspondence with several members, which then dwindled to the occasional holiday card and then ended for all but one or two people. Individuals sent me invitations and newsletters, and gradually these also stopped arriving. On my few return trips to this kibbutz, I was both saddened and pleased. The sad aspect related to all the people who had died. Because of my previous practice of always taking field notes to record my conversations and observations, I found myself taking notes on these visits as well, even though they took place years after I left the field.

> Sunday October 4, 1987. G told me that ES had died, that TW had moved to a different kibbutz neighborhood to be closer to his son and then moved to Beit Something, which seems to be the sick rooms on the kibbutz, and then had died. That Y is not feeling well and has recently gotten into an argument with two women who work in the kitchen, one of whom is D, over which pot to use. This argument was published as two letters in the kibbutz publication. G said that S had died. [G knew how much all of these people meant to me.]
>
> But [two other people] were doing fine. She told me that H has been dragging up stories about his wife, and wanted to see the protocols of the time about decision that were made "against" her, and someone went and *changed* the protocols [so he would have peace of mind].
>
> G said that YM had started to work in the archives and was straightening things out. That E and K still worked there. That Z was OK.
>
> She thinks RY was responsible for throwing out [the two people I mentioned in my discussion of work], and that the husband was a fabulous worker, and that people respected the wife in the social work school.
>
> There is still a lot of tension about trips abroad, G told me. For the past three years there have been *no* kibbutz-sponsored trips. People go only for business. G's husband does not want to ask for permission to travel abroad because he believes it is childish to do so. But D, the current (co-)*mazkir* (along with NA) was so furious at him for *not* asking, that she called him half an hour before the trip and told him not to go. D had been informed by the *sadran avodah* that G's husband was taking the trip.
>
> R recently put on a fabulous show of "Winnie the Pooh" to celebrate the birthday of the kibbutz. There were two performances and his son wrote the music. T reads to H since his eyesight is no longer so good. G said people remember me and the work I did because it was so unusual to have one-on-one interviewing.
>
> There are now some guest apartments. One adult daughter came from abroad and stayed in one of the apartments for seven months with her three children. G told me that she was annoyed that articles about her own son always defined him as the son of her husband, his father, and not the son of his

mother— herself! In the same way, G told me, L is annoyed that her children are referred to as the children of [another famous person on the kibbutz].

SA seems to be doing well. But after MY died, Z lost the will to live and died. TY is alive.

My friend says people still remember the work she did as coordinator of the old age committee. She thinks it was very helpful to her to have someone to talk to at the time—me. She also thinks having phones has changed everything on the kibbutz because you can so easily call someone. She calls several older people to wish them a good year. She says there is a *chuka* [similar to a constitution] for the kibbutz, but the rules constantly change. I have a feeling that it is becoming more and more of a bureaucratic place. She says there are now two hairdressers. She says that my sponsor *arranged a fabulous trip for himself* this year, to the States, Prague, Oslo, and Kiev.

I returned another time with my two daughters and introduced them to kibbutz members. They commented to me that there are not enough children on the kibbutz. I was given a tour of the old age facility designed to provide nursing care and of the old age recreation center. I returned another time and was shown the new archive where the interviews I had taped had been transcribed (with the individual members' permission) and entered into a large cabinet of tapes and transcripts. I was shown the bookshelf on which my interim and final report to the kibbutz rested.

And I returned another time—in March 2007—and found extraordinary changes. The kibbutz dining room—the former hub of the community—was no longer in use by the kibbutz but was rented out to the public. Various small buildings on the kibbutz had been converted into businesses owned by nonkibbutz individuals. While I was being shown around the museum, replete with the film about the history of the area and taken to the sophisticated archive, a set of cars drove up decorated with ribbons and flowers indicating a wedding. The young bride and groom got out of one of the cars with a photographer. As they had their picture taken in front of various old buildings, I asked the museum director what was going on. She told me that the kibbutz had become a favorite place—a kind of backdrop—a picturesque site—to have wedding pictures taken. It had become scenery. Across the street from the kibbutz but on kibbutz property, where an agricultural field had once provided the setting for young Polish Jews to show how hard they could work, new houses had been sold to people who wanted to live in a picturesque setting without the demands of kibbutz life. Together the kibbutz and the peripheral neighborhood were creating a new social structure with new pioneers who may later define a new form of aging. Recently, in fall 2009, as I was completing this book, I emailed G to tell her that I had finished and to ask her to obtain permission for me to use a few photographs. At the same time that she emailed back to tell me I had permission from everyone depicted in the photos, she also told me that my sponsor had died. Even though much of this book deals with the problematic relation with a fieldwork sponsor, his death seems to represent the true end of this project. I will remain both frustrated by him and grateful to him for giving me access to this kibbutz and to my opportunity to study its elderly in context.

The kibbutz as a wedding backdrop.

BIBLIOGRAPHY

Adler, Patricia A. *Wheeling and Dealing: Ethnography of an Upper-level Drug Dealing and Smuggling Community*. New York: Columbia University Press, 1993.

Adler, Patricia A., and Adler, Peter. *Membership Roles in Field Research, Qualitative Research Methods Series 6, A Sage University Paper*. Newbury, CA: Sage, 1987.

"Aging in Kibbutz Society." In *Gerontologia 1* Ramat-Gan: Israel Gerontological Society, 1975.

Back, Les. "Gendered Participation: Masculinity and Fieldwork in a South London Adolescent Community." In *Gendered Fields: Women, Men & Ethnography*, edited by Diane Bell, Pat Caplan, and Wazir Jahan Karim. New York: Routledge, 1993.

Barkai, Nurit. "To Re-construct the Community: Lesbians on a Kibbutz." In *Sappho in the Holy Land: Lesbian Existence and Dilemmas in Contemporary Israel*, edited by Chava Frankfort-Nachmias and Erella Shadmi. Albany, NY: SUNY Press, 2005.

Bateson, Mary Catherine. *With a Daughter's Eye: A Memoir of Margaret Mead and Gregory Bateson*. New York: William Morrow, 1984.

Bernstein, Deborah S. *Pioneers and Homemakers: Jewish Women in Pre-State Israel* Albany, NY: SUNY Press, 1992.

Bettelheim, Bruno. *The Children of the Dream: Communal Child-rearing and American Education*. New York: Macmillan, 1969.

Bijaoui, Sylvie and Avrahami, Eli, "Co-optation and Change: The Women's Sections of the Kibbutz," in Michal Palgi and Shulamit Reinharz (eds.), *One Hundred Years of Kibbutz Life: The Arts, Work and Reinvention* (in process).

Blumberg, Rae Lesser. "As You Sow, So Shall You Reap: Updating a Structural Analysis of Sexual Stratification in the Kibbutz." *Gender & Society* 1, 1987.

Brandow, Selma Koss. "Illusion of Equality: Kibbutz Women and the Ideology of the 'New Jew.'" *International Journal of Women's Studies* 2, 1979.

Brinkley, Joel. "Kibbutzim, Israel's Utopias, Develop a Flaw: Debt." *The New York Times*, March 5, 1989.

Brown, Karen McCarthy. "Writing about 'the Other.'" *The Chronicle of Higher Education*, April 15, 1992.

Buber, Martin. *I and Thou*. New York: Touchstone, 1923/1996.

Buechler, Hans C. "The Social Position of an Ethnographer in the Field." In *Stress and Response in Fieldwork*, edited by Frances Henry and Satish Saberwal. New York: Holt, Rinehart and Winston, 1969.

Caplan, Pat. "Learning Gender: Fieldwork in a Tanzanian Coastal Village, 1965–85." In *Gendered Fields: Women, Men & Ethnography*, edited by Diane Bell, Pat Caplan, and Wazir Jahan Karim. New York: Routledge, 1993.

"Change on the Kibbutz." *Time Magazine*, November 6, 1972.

Clifford, James, and Marcus, George E., eds. *Writing Culture: The Poetics and Politics of Ethnography*. Berkeley and Los Angeles: University of California Press, 1986.

Coffey, Amanda. *The Ethnographic Self: Fieldwork and the Representation of Identity*. Beverly Hills, CA: Sage, 1999.

Cohen, Mitchell, ed. *Class Struggle and the Jewish Nation: Selected Essays in Marxist Zionism*. New Brunswick, NJ: Transaction Books, 1984.

Collins, Patricia Hill. "Learning from the Outsider Within: The Sociological Significance of Black Feminist Thought." *Social Problems* 33, 1986.

———. "The Tie That Binds: Race, Gender, and US Violence." *Ethnic and Racial Studies* 21, 1998.

———. "Gender, Black Feminism, and Black Political Economy." *Annals of the American Academy of Political and Social Science* 568, 2000.

Couser, G. Thomas. "Disability and (Auto)Ethnography." *Journal of Contemporary Ethnography* 34, April 2005.

Criden, Yosef, and Gelb, Saadia. *The Kibbutz Experience: Dialogue in Kfar Blum*. New York: Herzl Press, 1974.

Cumming, Elaine, and Henry, William E. *Growing Old: The Process of Disengagement*. New York: Basic Books, 1961.

Danet, Brenda. *Pulling Strings: Biculturalism in Israeli Bureaucracy*. Albany: SUNY Press, 1989.

Davidman, Lynn. *Tradition in a Rootless World: Women Turn to Orthodox Judaism*. Berkeley and Los Angeles: University of California Press, 1991.

de Tocqueville, Alexis. *Democracy in America*. New York: Vintage, 1954.

Deacon, Desley. *Elsie Clews Parsons: Inventing Modern Life*. Chicago: University of Chicago Press, 1997.

Easterday, Lois, Papdemas, Diana, Schorr, Laura, and Valentine, Catherine. "The Making of a Female Researcher: Role Problems in Fieldwork." *Urban Life* 6, 1977.

Fishman, Aryei. "The Religious Kibbutz: A Note on the Theories of Marx, Sombart and Weber on Judaism and Economic Success." *Sociological Analysis* 50, 1989.

Fleuhr-Lobban, Carolyn, and Lobban, R. C. "Families, Gender and Methodology in the Sudan." In *Self, Sex and Gender in Cross-cultural Fieldwork*, edited by T. I. Whitehead and M. E. Conaway. Urbana: University of Illinois Press, 1986.

Flyvbjerg, Bent. "Five Misunderstandings about Case-Study Research." *Qualitative Inquiry* 12, 2006.

Foigel-Bijaoui, Sylvie. "From Revolution to Motherhood: The Case of Women in the Kibbutz, 1910–1948." In *Pioneers and Homemakers: Jewish Women in Pre-state Israel*, edited by Deborah Bernstein. Albany: SUNY Press, 1992.

Geertz, Clifford. "Thick Description: Toward an Interpretive Theory of Culture." In *The Interpretation of Cultures: Selected Essays*. New York: Basic Books, 1973.

Gerson, Menachem. *Family, Women, and Socialization in the Kibbutz*. Lexington, MA: Lexington Books, 1978.

Glaser, Barney, and Strauss, Anselm. *The Discovery of Grounded Theory: Strategies for Qualitative Research*. Chicago: Aldine, 1967.

Gleser, Maya Narash. "Kibbutz Women as Office-Holders and Their Social Status." *Kibbutz Studies 31*. Efal, Israel: Yad Tabenkin, 1990.

Gluckman, Max. "Gossip and Scandal." *Current Anthropology* 4, 1963.

Goffman, Erving. *The Presentation of Self in Everyday Life*. New York: Anchor Books, 1959.

Golan, Shmuel. *Collective Education in the Kibbutz*. Merchavia, Israel: Education Department of the Kibbutz–Artzi Hashomer Hatzair, 1961.

Golde, Peggy. *Women in the Field: Anthropological Experiences*. Chicago: Aldine, 1970.

Goldscheider, Calvin. *Israel's Changing Society: Population, Ethnicity and Development*. Boulder, CO: Westview Press, 1996.

Halperin, Liora R. "Is It Really Fate? The 'Women's Question' on the Kibbutz in the Midst of the 1936 Arab Revolt." Unpublished manuscript, 2003.

Hancock, Black Hawk. "Learning How to Make Life Swing." *Qualitative Sociology* 30, 2007.

Harding, Sandra. *Whose Science? Whose Knowledge?: Thinking from Women's Lives*. Ithaca, NY: Cornell University Press, 1991.

Hartsock, Nancy. *The Feminist Standpoint Revisited*. Long Grove, IL: Westview Press, 1999.

Hill, Michael R. "The Methodological Framework of Harriet Martineau's Feminist Analyses of American Society." American Studies Association, November 2, 1990.

Hill, Michael R., and Hoecker-Drysdale, Susan, eds. *Harriet Martineau: Theoretical & Methodological Perspectives*. New York: Routledge, 2001.

Holmes, Monica B., Holmes, Douglas, and Bergman, Simon. "The Israeli Kibbutz as a System of Care for the Elderly." *Community Research Applications, Inc.*, March 1983.

Horigan, Francis. *Psychiatric Abstracts Series No. 9, The Israeli Kibbutz: Psychiatric, Psychological and Social Studies with Emphasis on Family Life and Family Structure: A Survey of the Literature*. Washington, DC: U.S. Department of Health, Education, and Welfare.

Horowitz, Ruth. "Getting In." In *In the Field*, edited by Carolyn D. Smith and William Kornblum. New York: Praeger, 1989.

Howell, Jayne. "Turning Out Good Ethnography, or Talking Out of Turn?" *Journal of Contemporary Ethnography*, 2004.

Hunt, Jennifer C. *Psychoanalytic Aspects of Fieldwork, Qualitative Research Methods Series 18, A Sage University Paper*. Newbury Park, CA: Sage, 1989.

"Ideology, Myth, and Reality: Sex Equality in Israel." *Sex Roles* 6, 1980.

Joseph, Suad. "Relationality and Ethnographic Subjectivity: Key Informants and the Construction of Personhood in Fieldwork." In *Feminist Dilemmas in Fieldwork*, edited by Diane L. Wolf. Boulder, CO: Westview Press, 1996.

Junker, Buford H. *Field Work: An Introduction to the Social Sciences.* Chicago: University of Chicago Press, 1960.

Kafkafi, Eyal. "The Psycho-intellectual Aspect of Gender Inequality in Israel's Labor Movement." *Israel Studies* 4, 1999.

Kahn, Susan Martha. *Reproducing Jews: A Cultural Account of Assisted Conception in Israel.* Durham, NC: Duke University Press, 2000.

Kamm, Henry. "Even in the Kibbutz, Socialism Is Under Challenge." *New York Times International,* September 10, 1991.

Kanter, Rosabeth Moss. *Commitment and Community: Communes and Utopias in Sociological Perspective.* Cambridge, MA: Harvard University Press, 1972.

——. *Evolve!: Succeeding in the Digital Culture of Tomorrow.* Boston: Harvard Business School Press, 2001.

Kelsky, Karen. *Women on the Verge: Japanese Women, Western Dreams.* Durham, NC: Duke University Press, 2001.

Kershner, Isabel. "The Kibbutz Sheds Socialism and Gains Popularity." *New York Times,* August 27, 2007.

"Kibbutz Movement Facing Lean Times." *New York Times,* December 3, 1989.

Lavi, Zvi, ed. *Kibbutz Members Study Kibbutz Children.* New York: Greenwood Press, 1990.

Leggett, Karby. "Pay-as-You-Go Kibbutzim." *Wall Street Journal,* May 26, 2005.

Lengermann, Patricia Madoo, and Niebrugge, Gillian, eds. *The Women Founders: Sociology and Social Theory, 1830–1930: A Text/Reader.* Long Grove, IL: Waveland Press, 1998/2007.

Lieblich, Amia. *Kibbutz Makom: Report from an Israeli Kibbutz.* New York: Random House, 1981.

Lombardi, John R., and Stack, Carol B. "Economically Cooperating Units in an Urban Black Community." In *Anthropology and the Public Interest: Fieldwork and Theory,* edited by Peggy Sanday. New York: Academic Press, 1976.

Manderson, Lenore. "Taboo: Sex, Identity and Erotic Subjectivity in Anthropological Fieldwork." *Oceania* 67, 1997.

Mann, S. A., and Huffman, D. J. "The Decentering of Second Wave Feminism and the Rise of the Third Wave." *Science and Society* 69, 1995.

Mann, S. A., and Kelley, L. R. "Standing at the Crossroads of Modernist Thought: Collins, Smith, and the New Feminist Epistemologies." *Gender & Society* 11, 1997.

Marcus, George E., and Fisher, Michel M. J. *Anthropology as Cultural Critique: An Experimental Moment in the Human Sciences.* Chicago: University of Chicago Press, 1986.

Martineau, Harriet. *How to Observe Morals and Manners.* New Brunswick, NJ: Transaction Books, 1838/1989.

——. *Society in America.* Garden City, NY: Anchor Books, 1961.

Mayer, Tamar. "From Zero to Hero: Masculinity in Jewish Nationalism." In *Israeli Women's Studies,* edited by Esther Fuchs. New Brunswick, NJ: Rutgers University Press, 2005.

McCann, Carole R., and Kim, Seung-Kyung, eds. *Feminist Theory Reader: Local and Global Perspectives.* New York: Routledge, 2003.

Mead, Margaret. *Blackberry Winter: My Earlier Years*. New York: Pocket Books, 1972.

Melman, Yossi. "Struggling to Survive, Kibbutzim Lose Identity." *Los Angeles Times*, January 6, 1991.

Merton, Robert K., Fiske, Marjorie, and Kendall, Patricia L. *The Focused Interview*. New York: Free Press, 1956/1990.

Metzler, Ken. *Creative Interviewing*. Englewood Cliffs, NJ: Prentice Hall, 1977/1989.

Mills, C. Wright. *The Sociological Imagination*. New York: Oxford University Press, 1959/2000.

Mirovsky, Arik. "The Kibbutz Movement—Round Two." *Haaretz Weekly*, March 28, 2008.

Mishler, Elliot G. *Research Interviewing: Context and Narrative*. Cambridge, MA: Harvard University Press, 1986.

Moore, Lisa. "Among Khmer and Vietnamese Refugee Women in Thailand." In *Gendered Fields: Women, Men & Ethnography*, edited by Diane Bell, Pat Caplan, and Wazir Jahan Karim. New York: Routledge, 1993.

Morales, Edmundo. "Researching Peasants and Drug Producers." In *In the Field*, edited by Carolyn D. Smith and William Kornblum. New York: Praeger, 1989.

Myerhoff, Barbara. *Number Our Days*. New York: Touchstone Books, 1978.

Near, Henry. *The Kibbutz Movement: A History: Crisis and Achievement, 1939–1995*. London: Littman Library of Jewish Civilization, 1997.

O'Brien, Oonagh. "Sisters, Parents, Neighbours, Friends: Reflections on Fieldwork in North Catalonia (France)." In *Gendered Fields: Women, Men & Ethnography*, edited by Diane Bell, Pat Caplan, and Wazir Jahan Karim. New York: Routledge, 1993.

Palgi, Michal. "Gender Equality in the Kibbutz—From Ideology to Reality." In *Jewish Feminism in Israel: Some Contemporary Perspectives*, edited by Kalpana Misra and Melanie S. Rich. Hanover, NH: University Press of New England, 2003.

Palgi, Michal, Blasi, Joseph Raphael, Rosner, Menachem, and Safir, Marilyn, eds. *Sexual Equality: The Israeli Kibbutz Tests the Theories* (Kibbutz Studies Book Series). Norwood, PA: Norwood Editions, 1983.

Powdermaker, Hortense. *Stranger and Friend: The Way of an Anthropologist*. New York: W. W. Norton, 1966.

Rabin, A. I., and Hazan, Bertha. *Collective Education in the Kibbutz*. New York: Springer, 1973.

Raider, Mark A., and Raider-Roth, Miriam B. *The Plough Woman: Memoirs of the Pioneer Women of Palestine*. Hanover, NH: Brandeis University Press, 2002.

Reinharz, J., Reinharz, S., and Golani, M. *Manya Wilbushewitz Shohat: A Critical Collection of Her Writings*. Jerusalem: Yad Ben Zvi, 2005.

Reinharz, Shulamit. *On Becoming a Social Scientist: From Survey Research and Participation to Experiential Analysis*. San Francisco: Jossey-Bass, 1979.

——. "The Elderly Population in Kibbutz: Problems and Suggestions." Manuscript, 1980.

——. "Aging on a Kibbutz: Some Ideas for American Community Psychology." *Division of Community Psychology Newsletter*, Summer 1981.

——. "Toward a Model of Female Political Action: The Case of Manya Shohat, Founder of the First Kibbutz." *Women's Studies International Forum* 7, 1984.

——. *Feminist Methods in Social Research.* New York: Oxford University Press, 1992.

——. "Manya Wilbushewitz-Shohat and the Winding Road to Sejera." In *Pioneers and Homemakers: Jewish Women in Pre-State Israel.* ed. Deborah S. Bernstein, Albany, NY: SUNY Press, 1992.

——. "Our (Forgotten) Foremother: Manya Shohat (1880–1961)." *Lilith,* Fall 1995.

——. "Manya Wilbushewitz Shohat." In *Lines of Fire: Women Writers of World War I,* edited by Margaret R. Higgonet. New York: Plume, 1999.

——. "Finding Our/My History: The Case of Manya Wilbushewitz Shohat." In *Gender, Memory, and Judaism,* edited by Judit Gazsi, Andrea Peto, and Zsuzsanna Torony. Budapest: Balassi Kiado, 2007.

"Relief for the Elderly." *Jerusalem Post,* July 17, 1980.

Richardson, Laurel. "The Collective Story: Postmodernism and the Writing of Sociology." *Sociological Focus.* 21, no. 3 (1988): pp. 199–208.

Ritzer, George. *Contemporary Sociological Theory and Its Classical Roots: The Basics.* Boston: McGraw-Hill, 2007.

Rose, Dan. *Living the Ethnographic Life, Qualitative Research Methods Series 23, A Sage University Paper.* Newbury, CA: Sage, 1990.

Rosenfeld, Eva. "The American Social Scientist in Israel: A Case Study in Role Conflict." *American Journal of Orthopsychiatry,* volume 28, July 1958, pp 563-571.

Scheper-Hughes, Nancy. *Death without Weeping: The Violence of Everyday Life in Brazil.* Berkeley and Los Angeles: University of California Press, 1992.

Schrijvers, Joke. "Motherhood Experienced and Conceptualized." In *Gendered Fields: Women, Men & Ethnography,* edited by Diane Bell, Pat Caplan, and Wazir Jahan Karim. New York: Routledge, 1993.

Schwartz, Richard. "Some Problems of Research in Israeli Settlements." *American Journal of Orthopsychiatry* 28, 1958.

Sered, Susan. *What Makes Women Sick? Maternity, Modesty and Militarism in Israeli Society.* Hanover, NH: University Press of New England, 2000.

Shapira, Anita. *Land and Power: The Zionist Resort to Force, 1881–1948.* Stanford, CA: Stanford University Press, 1992.

Singer, Andre, dir. *Strangers Abroad* [motion picture]. Birmingham, England: Central Independent Television, 1985.

Skeggs, Beverly. "Theorizing, Ethics and Representation in Feminist Ethnography." In *Feminist Cultural Theory: Process and Production,* edited by Beverly Skeggs. New York: Manchester University Press, 1995.

Smith, Dorothy. *The Everyday World as Problematic: A Feminist Sociology.* Boston: Northeastern University Press, 1987.

Snarey, John. "Becoming a Kibbutz Founder: An Ethnographic Study of the First All-American Kibbutz in Israel." *Jewish Social Studies* 46, 1984.

Spiro, Melford. *Kibbutz: Venture in Utopia.* New York: Schocken, 1956.

——. *Children of the Kibbutz: A Study in Child Training and Personality.* Cambridge, MA: Harvard University Press, 1958.

——. *Gender and Culture: Kibbutz Women Revisited.* Durham, NC: Duke University Press, 1979.

Srinivas, M. N. *The Remembered Village.* Berkeley and Los Angeles: University of California Press, 1976.

Stack, Carol B. *All Our Kin: Strategies for Survival in a Black Community*. New York: Harper & Row, 1972.

——. "Writing Ethnography: Feminist Critical Practice." In *Feminist Dilemmas in Fieldwork*, edited by Diane L. Wolf. Boulder, CO: Westview Press, 1996.

Starn, Orin. "Rethinking the Politics of Anthropology: The Case of the Andes." *Current Anthropology* 35, 1994.

Steinberg, Jessica. "In Soy Food, Kibbutzim Find Manna for a Modern Age." *New York Times,* April 20, 2004.

Tal, Ran, dir. *Children of the Sun* [motion picture]. 2007. Loma Films, Tel Aviv.

Talmon, Yonina. *Family and Community in the Kibbutz*. Cambridge, MA: Harvard University Press, 1972.

Tiger, Lionel, and Shepher, Joseph. *Women in the Kibbutz*. New York: Harcourt Brace, 1975.

Timmermans, Stefan. "Cui Bono? Institutional Review Boards and Ethnographic Research." *Studies in Symbolic Interaction: A Research Annual*, N. Denzin, Ed., Vol. 19, pp. 155–173.

"Up the Anthropologist—Perspectives Gained from Studying Up." In *Reinventing Anthropology*, edited by Dell H. Hymes. New York: Pantheon Books, 1972.

"Utopias for the Elderly: Kibbutzim, Social Planning and Historical Communes." In *Communal Life: An International Perspective,* edited by Yaacov Oved, Idit Pazm, and Yosef Gorni. New Brunswick, NJ: Transaction, 1987.

Van Hollen, Cecilia. *Birth on the Threshold: Childbirth and Modernity in South India*. Berkeley and Los Angeles: University of California Press, 2003.

Van Maanen, John. *Tales of the Field: On Writing Ethnography*. Chicago: University of Chicago Press, 1988.

Van Maanen, John, Manning, Peter, and Miller, Marc, eds. "Editors' Introduction." In *Psychoanalytic Aspects of Fieldwork* (Qualitative Research Methods Series #18), Jennifer C. Hunt. 1989. Newbury Park, CA: Sage Publications.

Warren, Carol A. B. *Gender Issues in Field Research, Qualitative Research Methods Series 9, A Sage University Paper*. Newbury Park, CA: Sage, 1988.

——. "Gender and Fieldwork Relations." In *Contemporary Field Research: Perspectives and Formulations*, edited by Robert M. Emerson. Prospect Heights, IL: Waveland Press, 2001.

Weingarten, Murray. *Life in a Kibbutz*. New York: Reconstructionist Press, 1955.

"Who Am I? The Need for a Variety of Selves in the Field." In *Reflexivity and Voice,* edited by Rosanna Hertz. Thousand Oaks, CA: Sage, 1997.

Whyte, William Foote. *Learning from the Field: A Guide from Experience*. Beverly Hills, CA: Sage, 1984.

——. *Street Corner Society: The Social Structure of an Italian Slum,* fourth ed. Chicago: University of Chicago Press, 1993.

Wiseman, Jacqueline P. *Stations of the Lost: The Treatment of Skid Row Alcoholics*. Chicago: University of Chicago Press, 1970/1979.

Wolf, Diane L., ed. *Feminist Dilemmas in Fieldwork*. Boulder, CO: Westview Press, 1996.

Wolkomir, Michelle, and Powers, Jennifer. "Helping Women and Protecting the Self: The Challenge of Emotional Labor in an Abortion Clinic." *Qualitative Sociology* 30, 2007.

Women's Realities, Women's Choices (Hunter College Women's Studies Collective). New York: Oxford University Press, 2005.

Yassour, Avraham, ed. *Kibbutz Members Analyze the Kibbutz.* Cambridge, MA: Institute for Cooperative Community, 1977.

Yuval-Davis, Nira. "Bearers of the Collective: Women and Religious Legislation in Israel." In *Israeli Women's Studies,* edited by Esther Fuchs. New Brunswick, NJ: Rutgers University Press, 2005.

INDEX